GORMAN, Robert A. The dual vision: Alfred Schutz and the myth of phenomenological social science. Routledge & Kegan Paul, 1977. 234p (International library of sociology) bibl index 77-352273. 8.75 ISBN 0-7100-8450-1

Perhaps the most significant occurrence in sociological theory in the past decade has been the attention given to the long overlooked work of Alfred Schutz. More than any other individual, Schutz is responsible for a growing interest in phenomenological sociology. This is the first book-length criticism of Schutz's work. Gorman has carefully studied appropriate sources in phenomenology. He argues that Schutz's attempted synthesis of phenomenological subjectivity and naturalistic science is "logically indefensible" and fails to satisfy the requirements of either perspective. Gorman goes on to suggest his own alternative phenomenological method, which, he contends, is more consistent than that offered by Schutz. Although this book is short, it covers a great deal of ground and necessitates a familiarity with a large body of phenomenological literature. It is likely to create worthwhile debate among phenomenologists in sociology, and deserves a place in graduate school libraries. Readers of the book will benefit from recent and radically different interpretations of Schutz provided in Maurice Natanson's *Phenomenology, role, and reason* (1974) and Rodman Webb's *The presence of the past* (1976).

The dual vision

International Library of Sociology

Founded by Karl Mannheim

Editor: John Rex, University of Warwick

Arbor Scientiae

Arbor Vitae

A catalogue of the books available in the **International Library of Sociology** and other series of Social Science books published by Routledge & Kegan Paul will be found at the end of this volume.

The dual vision

Alfred Schutz and the myth of phenomenological social science

Robert A. Gorman
Assistant Professor in Political and Social Science,
Hampton Institute, Virginia

[redacted]

Routledge & Kegan Paul
London, Henley and Boston

[redacted]

First published in 1977
by Routledge & Kegan Paul Ltd
39 Shore Street,
London WC1E 7DD,
Broadway House,
Newtown Road,
Henley-on-Thames,
Oxon RG9 1EN and
[redacted]
9 Park Street,
Boston, Mass. 02108, USA
Manuscript set by Computacomp
Printed and bound in Great Britain by
Morrison & Gibb Ltd

ISBN 0 7100 8450 1

[redacted]

Contents

Introduction

The contemporary study of society is fired by our quest for scientific truth. The very spirit of our age is tangible evidence of the fruits of science: by superimposing intellect on natural forces and processes we mobilize our energies for creating a mechanized civilization oriented towards the needs and desires of omnipotent humanity. Worldly phenomena are isolated, studied, and explained; and, through this procedure, brought under the effective control of inquisitive intellect. The same, it is hoped, can be accomplished in our attempts at understanding and harnessing forces underlying social interaction. Social scientists superimpose the scientific framework on a reality that is thoroughly soaked in human experience, always assuming their efforts will eventually initiate a stage of cultural development allowing us to mold society in response to expressed desires. Social science, like natural science, strives to intellectually decipher an unrestrained, directionless, domineering environment, choreographing the future to the rhythm of operational human goals.

However, this similarity in intention is not paralleled by similar results. While our ability to explain natural phenomena has grown dramatically, social scientists find themselves without any universally valid generalizations to facilitate explanation, prediction, and control. The fruits of social science do not yet justify the intense effort. Although natural catastrophes are explained in terms of pre- and post-dictive laws, and at least partially controlled through our vast technological capabilities, social catastrophes and crises seem immune to either scientific explanation or human manipulation. As our body of natural scientific knowledge and technological skills increases, we are confronted by a simultaneous growth in social conflict, tension, and violence - none adequately accounted for by methods and procedures which accomplished so much in the non-human natural world. We seem helpless in the face of social unrest that cries out for attention and remedy.

The traditional response from the scientific community is the belief and contention that more research - more time - will yield social knowledge comparable in significance to the facts of natural science. But not everyone accepts this rationale. A group of social scientists has recently emerged contending basic structural changes are needed in scientific technique. The inadequacies of contemporary social science indicate far more than merely a need for new research and more patience: social science, as it is and has been practiced is qualitatively deficient, incapable - in principle - of adequately explaining society. In particular, it fails to recognize and take into consideration the foundational, irreducible nature of social actors, inherently free agents who define for themselves the world they perceive and act in. Social science is doomed to failure unless it evolves a revised method appropriate to this phenomenological understanding of knowledge and reality. It is not that the effort to scientifically explain society is misconceived; only the method must be altered to suit the actual quality of human interaction.

The phenomenological reformulation of social scientific method is the dominant theme of this book. This unfolds in a heuristic critique of the single most important and influential figure in the movement to phenomenologically re-define, or 'humanize,' social science: Alfred Schutz. My inclination to concentrate on Schutz in explaining phenomenological social science as a whole is invited by the lack of critical scholarly attention he has heretofore attracted. Fellow phenomenologists have treated Schutz with an aura of admiration and subservience which, though deserved in respect to the seriousness and scholarship of his work, is not justified by its actual quality. This contention will be defended and pointed towards an indictment of the whole effort at phenomenologically re-defining scientific method. An analysis such as this seems particularly appropriate and timely in view of the actual evolution of methodological theory and the increasingly important role Schutz occupies. The book rigorously describes Schutz's phenomenological method and attempts to situate it within an unfolding historical and analytical context. It maintains, briefly, that Schutz endeavors to solve the fundamental predicament of contemporary social science: reconciling sentient, meaning-endowing social actors to an empirical scientific method stressing generalization. The difficulties Schutz and other phenomenologists encounter are due their desire to achieve an artificial union of subjectivity and objectivity (i.e. their 'dual vision'), and their refusal to accept the radical implications of a subjective epistemology.

The text's format is systematic and purposeful. Chapter 1 describes, in historical perspective, the methodological problems confronting phenomenological social scientists. It focuses primarily on the relevant writings of Max Weber and Edmund Husserl, because these are the two most direct influences on Schutz's intellectual development, and because phenomenological methodology is based on the theoretical groundwork undertaken in Weberian social science and Husserlian philosophy. Chapter 2 describes Schutz's own contributions to this historical dialogue. His philosophical anthropology and sociological method are presented in detail, though specific arguments irrelevant to the text's overall intentions are purposely slighted. Chapter 3 critically analyzes Schutz's system from logical and empirical points of view. It offers a case study of the oldest approach to social science - decision-making theory - attempting to operationalize Schutz's theoretical scientific method. The analytical critique is confirmed by the peculiar, dis-heartening evolution of decision-making theory, and the almost surrealistic form of social data collection known as ethnomethodology. Chapter 4 broadens our outlook by examining what philosophers mean when they speak of 'science.' My purpose here is to illustrate how the inadequacies of Schutz's system are due to the impossible burden he shoulders: the search for an empirical social science based on phenomenological principles is misconceived from the beginning, and the relevant work done in the field - in addition to Schutz's - only proves this point. The final chapter offers an alternative phenomenological method, and, in particular, details ideological implications of a consistent phenomenological approach to social inquiry. Phenomenology, I contend, is 'radical' both as an epistemological critique and a philosophical rationale for social commitment and action.

One final word: though the argument is directed at illustrating the overwhelming difficulties involved in scientifically studying subjectively meaningful social action, it is not so pretentious that it denies the massive body of data and theory already established or hypothesized in the social sciences. I am seeking to place social science in a perspective; drawing the limits of what we can expect of it and what it can hope to produce. I fully accept Weber's assertion:

> To affirm the value of science is a presupposition for teaching in a university. I personally in my very work answer in the affirmative, and I also do so from precisely the standpoint that hates intellectualism as the worst devil, as youth does today, or usually only fancies it does. In that case the word holds for these youths: 'Mind you, the devil is old; grow old to understand him.' This does not mean age in the sense of the birth certificate. It means that if one wishes to settle with this devil, one must not take to flight before him as so many like to do nowadays. First of all, one has to see the devil's ways to the end in order to realize his power and his limitations.

1 Phenomenology and methodology of social science: the origins

The problem of reconciling individuality with a rigorous scientific method, the prime motivation for all of Schutz's published writings, has been an issue of scholarly concern since the mid-nineteenth century, especially among the German philosophers and sociologists who preceded Schutz and shaped his intellectual development. Schutz's particular contribution to this dialogue is basically eclectic, assimilating important ideas of a number of these German scholars. His ability to abstract the central theses of relevant arguments and place them into an explicit intellectual framework developed primarily by Husserl gives his theory its character of being a magnified residue of a debate that was becoming increasingly ambiguous. Schutz's eclectic approach, in other words, serves not only to crystallize the issues, but also throws into sharp relief the speculative intellectualizing that surrounds an issue of great practical importance.

1 MAX WEBER'S METHODOLOGY IN ITS HISTORICAL CONTEXT

In their historical context, Schutz's writings are determined efforts at mediating the irreconcilable positions of the neo-Kantians and positivists, both active in German scholarship in the years preceding World War I, and the romantic, intuition-oriented reaction epitomized by the so-called Baden School, consisting of Dilthey, Windelband, and Rickert.(1) At issue in this debate is the applicability of scientific method, as described in the natural sciences, to the study of society, in particular to our understanding those individual actions constituting the substance of human history. The positivists contend social phenomena are analogous to things of nature in that both are studied according to a method outlined by physicists while uncovering natural laws governing the movement of inert matter. Natural science serves as a rubric within which social behavior is treated as a species of natural phenomena, amenable to a similar type of causal analysis. Responding to this argument, Wilhelm Dilthey develops his own ideas on the nature of social science, ideas which, filtered through the words of Windelband, Rickert, and Weber, exert a profound influence on Alfred Schutz's social science.(2)

Dilthey contends there is a basic difference between studying nature ('Naturwissenschaften') and studying society ('Geistewissenschaften') because of the inherently different subject matter each discipline deals with.(3) With natural science, we uncover the kingdom of nature: objective, inanimate, existing entirely apart from humanity. Studying society, on the other hand, consists of investigating the kingdom of human mind, where all cultural phenomena are mental products of a human consciousness that is subjective and totally immersed in emotion and intellect. Social reality is distinct from natural reality, and the primordial differences between the two necessitate a different method of study for each. Whereas inanimate, material bodies are investigated in the hope of uncovering natural laws governing their movement, there are no causal, mechanistic, measurement-oriented models of cultural or historical behavior because the human spirit is not bridled by natural forces. There are no independent natural variables determining the cultural products of free human spirit.

Since human behavior is always value-imbued, the positivist's emphasis on evolving a value-free, 'objective' social scientific method is of little or no use in our search for valid social knowledge. In its stead, Dilthey insists that reliable cultural and historical knowledge is gained only by identifying and isolating common ideas, feelings, and goals of a particular historical period. These metaphysical forms constitute the spirit of an age ('Zeitgeist'), and determine social actions of spiritual creatures living and acting in their presence. Historians must orient themselves towards searching for, and discovering, these spiritual threads that unite a people to their culture and their historical era. Dilthey's transcendent social ideas constitute the essence of social history, the broad spiritual categories that make each separate social act subjectively meaningful and fulfilling.

A distinctive requisite of all cultural disciplines, for Dilthey, is that the observer, as a human being studying other human beings, has access to the inner world of others' experiences. By 're-living,' or imaginatively reconstructing, the other's experience in terms of our own, and identifying the two by a vaguely described type of analogical inference, we achieve a 'sympathetic understanding' ('Verstehen') of a particular actor and culture. Ultimately, Dilthey hopes to understand cultural phenomena 'from within' by empathetically reconstructing that spiritual form which prescribes the meaning each act has for the actor. It is clearly impossible to accomplish this task within the logic of natural scientific method. The study of nature is therefore absolutely distinct from the study of society, and the latter is 'objective' in a spiritual sense totally alien to natural science.

Dilthey's ideas fix the course of all future investigations into the methodology of social science. At one pole stands the positivist viewpoint, identifying society as one element of nature, and declaring natural scientific method suitable to its study and explanation. At the other pole is the intuitionist perspective of Dilthey, in which society is a product of unique subjective intentions of spiritual actors, explainable only by an abstract process of creative understanding not permitted by natural scientific method. To the former, social actors are conceived as entities reacting to external stimuli just as inanimate phenomena do; the latter proclaims individuality to be essentially spiritual and creative. Here are two organic interpretations of human nature and the methods of social inquiry. The character of ensuing methodological controversy will be shaped by representatives of one or another of these views trying to 'include' or synthesize the other approach in their own.

The first such attempts are performed by Dilthey's contemporaries, Wilhelm Windelband(4) and Heinrich Rickert.(5) Whereas Dilthey concludes reality is fragmented into spiritual phenomena, expressed in culture, and natural phenomena of the inanimate world, Windelband and Rickert postulate instead that reality is indivisible and always the same. Such a conclusion appears to support the positivist thesis. In fact, Windelband and Rickert are not prepared to admit this, siding instead with Dilthey in declaring natural science inadequate for explaining culture and history. They reconcile their seemingly opposing positions by stating that differences between methods of social and natural inquiry are based on logic rather than abstract metaphysical speculations concerning the dichotomy of reality. Cultural acts take place within the same reality as natural phenomena, but, because of their particular character, logically require an alternative explanatory method. In other words, the quality of subject matter determines, for observers, what type of explanation will suffice.

There are, for Windelband and Rickert, two methods of investigation: that which explains phenomena by laying down broad covering laws of universal applicability; and the opposing method of explaining unique phenomena according to characteristics which make the phenomena unique in the first place. The former method, which Windelband terms 'nomothetic' and Rickert 'generalizing,' uncovers the general laws of natural science. It is applicable only when studying the general, repeatable regularities that concern physical and natural scientists. In contrast, the latter method, which Windelband calls 'ideographic' and Rickert 'individualizing,' focuses on describing unique events in their concreteness and individuality. It is a feature of historical inquiry that we, as observers, find significant primarily those unique historical events or particular cultural phenomena somehow relevant to our own interests, and consider such events and phenomena important in themselves. In submerging them under generalizing laws we lose the distinctive qualities that make these phenomena important for us as objects of study. It is therefore imperative that subject matter of history and culture should not be confused with that of natural science. By distinguishing the two, it becomes logically necessary to utilize different explanatory methods to preserve the integrity of both. 'Thus, a distinction is made between the natural sciences which seek to establish general laws, and the cultural sciences which isolate individual phenomena in order to trace their unique development.'(6)

These ideas of Windelband and Rickert are first steps in the attempt to transcend the positivist-intuitionist debate. The ambiguity surrounding Dilthey's metaphysics is rejected, as is the positivists' efforts at equating cultural behavior and natural phenomena. Yet the new position is still incomplete and unclear. Dilthey bases his method on the objectivity of metaphysical 'Zeitgeisten.' Studying history and society is no less scientific than studying nature, but it is clearly a different kind of science: founded on spiritual rather than empirical criteria of objectivity. Windelband and Rickert are not abandoning Dilthey's desire to establish a new 'cultural science,' but they are rejecting his criteria of valid, objective, knowledge. If studying society implies dealing with the unique and particular, in what sense is this study 'objective' if we ignore Dilthey's concern for universal spiritual forms guiding particular human occurrences? The only alternative is admitting the absolute uniqueness of each social act, and the total lack of criteria for establishing a cultural science, or even studying culture objectively. With no underlying criteria of objective historical knowledge to build on, anything - including an observer's speculative or 'unreasonable' assertion - qualifies as valid knowledge. If the regression to metaphysics is admitted, how do we logically contend there is only one aspect to reality without assuming the empirically unverifiable premise that natural phenomena are also manifestations of spiritual forms? If this assumption is made, then the 'objectivity' of nomothetic, or generalizing, explanations is based on spiritual criteria - but this is definitely not what Windelband and Rickert mean when they contend these types of explanations are valuable only to physical and natural scientists. In brief, Windelband and Rickert have failed to explain how we can scientifically explain aspects of cultural behavior apart from either the metaphysical assumptions of Dilthey or the positivists' demand for criteria of objectivity based on empirically confirmed regularities of nature. Their attempts to avoid both metaphysics and empirically verified causal explanation has left them with nothing at all. Schutz recognizes the dilemma, and for this reason devotes much of his early career to constructively criticizing the ideas of Max Weber. For it is Max Weber who first directly confronts these issues.

The influence of Windelband and Rickert is obvious even in a brief perusal of Weber's early ideas.(7) He accepts the logical separation of natural and cultural sciences Windelband and Rickert prescribe, but rejects their contention these sciences are classified by different methods. Instead, Weber feels every science can and does use both (i.e. nomothetic or generalizing, and ideographic or individualizing) methods, the choice at any time depending on the discipline's research goals. This is so, Weber claims, because there is no significant difference between subject matters of the natural and social sciences. Uniqueness and historicity are manifest in nature as well as humanity, while general covering laws can explain human behavior and natural phenomena. In practical terms, this means sociology has recourse to generalizing method in its empirical research, and biology or astronomy occasionally studies unique aspects of particular phenomena. Social reality is much more complex and inexhaustible than either Windelband or Rickert suspected. Their facile separation of social and natural science is not justified, given this complex nature of reality, nor is their insistence on two distinct, isolated methods related to two distinct subject matters. For Weber, there is nothing in the nature of reality that requires our abandoning one explicit scientific logic of inquiry for all types of social and natural investigation.

How, then, does Weber distinguish his position from that of the positivists? In effect, he does not reject the theories of Windelband and Rickert as much as he re-evaluates their significance. The latter's two methods, while inappropriate to the actual nature of reality, do abstract two different types of behavior patterns from the complex whole. In this sense, both methods depart from reality for conceptual purposes, and neither is in any epistemological sense 'higher' than the other. However, this does not mean they are not useful. On the contrary, our interest in the social world focuses on exactly those aspects of it that are unique, qualitative, and individual, while our interest in the natural world focuses on more abstract phenomena, those exhibiting quantifiable empirical regularities. Weber assigns a new vitality to the methods of Windelband and Rickert: though each is utilized to study either natural or social phenomena, neither implies the existence in the world of qualitatively different subject matters requiring alternative methods of explanation. We adopt one or the other method because we ask different questions and want to know different things about natural and social phenomena.

Weber's concept of 'value-relevance' ('Wertbeziehung') illustrates his approach to this complex issue.(8) Whereas in the natural sciences we investigate abstract concepts which are quantitatively measured, in the study of human affairs what we define as significant - objects deemed worthy of study - is constituted by values we implicitly or explicitly accept. The former is objective, the latter necessarily value-oriented and subjective. What we choose to study in society, and why we study it, are selected from the infinite flux of historical happenings within which we find ourselves, and determined by relevant socially conditioned values. The needs of people, expressed in the values of their society, largely determine what is considered relevant or significant knowledge in the social sciences. Put simply: the contrast between social and natural science occurs because in the social sciences alone are humans both the subject and object of inquiry. Knowledge of society is therefore self-knowledge. We are more intimately concerned with our own motives, customs and values, however, than with physical objects of natural science, and will consequently utilize these social characteristics in defining what social phenomena we find worthy of explanation. Ultimately, in studying society we hope to clarify the meaning our own conduct - inseparable from these motives, customs and values - has for ourselves. For this reason the self-defined uniqueness and individuality of concrete cultural and historical phenomena are more important to us than the general laws uncovered by a method more appropriate to natural scientific inquiry.

Before continuing, we must emphasize how Weber has succeeded in separating his own view from that of the positivists. If, as Weber's methodology implies, it is at least theoretically possible to study society nomothetically, why not concentrate only on that social knowledge which is scientifically validated according to the norms of natural science, and consider all other knowledge speculative? His answer: by utilizing natural scientific method to study society we neglect precisely those issues important from a social point of view, concentrating instead on the regular, mechanistic-type behavior we regularly perform in our daily lives but rarely think or care about. This is an important point, one we shall return to in our critique of Schutz's method. Weber feels that natural scientific method, when transplanted to the study of human behavior, will produce knowledge which is epistemologically valid, but largely irrelevant, explaining generalizable, unimportant (at least from our own subjective perspectives), mundane activities.

We have thus far examined Weber's critique of intuitionist and positivist approaches to methodology. It is not yet apparent how Weber proposes to study unique, particular behavior scientifically. How, in other words, will Weber traverse the gap separating Dilthey from the positivists without sacrificing invaluable elements of both arguments? Weber's response lies in his general sociological method, constructed primarily in his massive, unfinished, 'Economy and Society.'(9)

The concept of 'Verstehen,' or 'interpretative understanding,' is the key to understanding how Weber proposes to explain an event in terms of its uniqueness rather than in terms of a general law, without sacrificing the explanation's scientific validity.(10) This process, as Weber means it, permits social observers a way of investigating phenomena that does not distort what is actually occurring to the people involved. Its goal is to recreate the meaning observed actors experience at the moment of action. Weber thus makes it clear that, in scientifically studying society, we direct ourselves towards social actors and, in particular, the meaning observed social acts had for them.(11) 'Verstehen,' as a means of understanding social behavior, is the link between Weber's early views concerning the value of positivist and intuitionist approaches to methodology and his own sociological method. The concept of 'Wertbeziehung' detailed the subjective origins of any meaningful social science. 'Verstehen' extends this thesis by describing a method that clarifies how values of social actors are made the focal point of social investigation. Since the essence of social reality lies in the interaction of individuals, all valid social analysis refers back to individual behavior, and this behavior is shaped by the subjectively intended meaning of the agent. Action is defined 'by virtue of the subjective meaning attached to it by the acting individual (or individuals),'(12) while 'the term "social behavior" . . . is reserved for activities whose intent is related by the individuals involved to the conduct of others and is oriented accordingly.'(13) The basic attribute of a social act is its subjectively meaningful relatedness to the actions of others. Those attempting to scientifically explain society must be certain their 'object of cognition is the subjective meaning-complex of action.'(14)

Implications of Weber's 'Verstehen' thesis appear, for some, to suggest social science aims at uncovering psychological causes of behavior, determinants that are subjective and not necessarily related to empirical fact. This viewpoint is often held by psychology-oriented methodologists who contend Weber's use of terms such as 'reliving' ('Nacherleben') and 'empathy' ('Einfuhlung') in relation to the operation of

'Verstehen' involves investigating an actor's 'inner' psychological states. The profundity of Weber's theory, however, is most explicit in his ingenious contributions to the positivist-intuitionist debate, his developing a method giving equal consideration to the subjective uniqueness of human action and the necessity of understanding such behavior 'scientifically,' as this term is interpreted by natural scientists. Had Weber actually implied that such vague procedures as 'reliving' or 'empathy' were the only ways to validate social scientific knowledge he would, of course, have been unable to accommodate the rigid norms of empirical method. This theory would be only a modification of Dilthey's ideas, in which objectivity, if it is to be present at all, would have to be found in transcendent metaphysical forms. Weber understood this well enough. While admitting 'Verstehen' is facilitated by an empathetic reliving of social acts, this procedure is also admittedly limited: 'To be able to put one's self in the place of the actor is important for clearness of understanding but not an absolute pre-condition for meaningful interpretation.'(15) 'Verstehen,' interpretative understanding, is a useful tool in our efforts at understanding subjective attitudes, but does not suffice as scientific explanation. Weber's overriding goal remains putting 'Verstehen' to use in creating an objective, intersubjectively verifiable method of social research that is not caught in a web of spiritual ambiguity.(16) Interpretative understanding is only a partial means of grasping the subjective meaning of social acts, one that must be substantiated by statistical data. Interpretation is valid only when accompanied by supporting empirical evidence.

Weber's next task is to explain how authentic social knowledge, value-related in origin and subject matter, and concerned with subjective meaning-complexes of social action, can be integrated into an objective framework that will permit our accumulating scientifically valid historical and social empirical data. This difficult problem is underlined by Weber's contention that all wordly phenomena, no matter how unique or particular, are products of antecedent, causally-related conditions. What appears in the world has to appear in just that way, and only empirical evidence reveals the necessity behind observed reality. The process of validating social knowledge takes place within objective, empirically confirmable relationships which scientifically explain social acts by uncovering their causes.

Weber did not mean by 'causality' the reduction of all social acts to an inclusive causal law. This is the procedure of natural science, it differs in crucial ways from that used in studying society. To causally understand human interaction we abstract from the complex whole of social reality limited and unique antecedents and consequences related to observed phenomena. The whole of social reality is too complex for developing inclusive causal laws of behavior, but particular social phenomena can be causally explained by referring to select surrounding conditions. The causal relationships uncovered are only an infinitesimal part of a complex social whole. Today it is perhaps more correct to speak of probability than causality in describing this aspect of Weber's social science. Since only a limited number of antecedents and consequences are isolated in any one case, we are discovering, at best, only a single cause among many possible existent ones. Our predictive power is reduced to the level of probability because there always remains the possibility other, perhaps significant, causal events lie unnoticed in the maelstrom of surrounding events. When the probability of correct prediction derived from discovering an antecedent cause appears high, Weber refers to this as 'adequate causation'; if it is low, 'accidental causation.' There is no mention of the 'necessary' causation of the natural sciences.(17) Though Weber's writings are replete with references to empirical probabilities of prediction, we cannot assume he totally capitulates to positivism on this issue.(18) By altering the definition of causation and stressing the uniqueness of social behavior, Weber apparently rules out the possibility of a universally valid system of scientific theory for the social sciences.(19)

When studying history, perceptive historians select relevant antecedent conditions by imaginatively negating particular events to determine, by means of comparative analysis of analogous cases, their significance in the total act's unfolding.(20) For the more general study of society, Weber has to create a method for recognizing relevant antecedent phenomena which would, simultaneously, reflect subjective meaning-complexes experienced by actors. Explanations of social behavior are both causally adequate, in revealing particular causes that in all probability always have the same consequences, and meaningfully adequate, revealing the experienced subjective meaning accompanying the action.(21) Conscientious social scientists apprehend the social world without eliminating the subjective integrity of meaning-endowing actors. To fulfill these necessary criteria of objectivity, Weber creates the 'ideal type':(22)

> An ideal type is formed by the one-sided accentuation of one or more points of view and by the synthesis of a great many diffuse, discrete, more or less present and occasionally absent concrete individual phenomena, which are arranged according to those one-sidedly emphasized viewpoints into a unified analytical construct. In its conceptual purity, this mental construct cannot be found empirically anywhere in reality.

The ideal type superimposes on actual social behavior one objectively possible course of action. It is an extreme rationalization, giving an explicit, recognizable meaning to elements of our experience not ordinarily so clearly understood. Theoretically, this 'meaning' may originally be what observers feel actors subjectively perceive, or the observers' own subjective perceptions of events. Either extreme is allowable in the Weberian system, as well as constructing different ideal types for the same phenomena, provided we follow with rigorous empirical research. The various 'causes' uncovered by applying different ideal type constructs are all equally valid because of the complex, infinite nature of social reality. Ideally typical stereotypes eliminate the tight, logical constructions of natural scientific method from impinging on a social world not encouraging such analysis. They are used to compare our own ideas with reality, and, by observing differences between the two, arriving at new, more inclusive ideas based on actual empirically confirmed causes.

Here is the kernel of Weber's unique contribution to the methodology of social science. First, with the positivists, Weber agrees there is no valid knowledge apart from empirical evidence. Holistic concepts, when applied to the study of nation or economy, are metaphysical because they go beyond the limits of empirical verification. They are, for this reason, unscientific and of no value to social science. In their place we provide a variety of ideal constructs, limited in scope only by our interests and beliefs, whose scientific value is determined by the fruitfulness of empirical studies relating each construct to the real world. Second, these ideal constructs are also alternatives to a scientism which ignores the subjectivity implicit in all social interaction. When applied to specific social events or situations, they should aim at revealing actors' subjectively meaningful experiences. In so-doing, these ideal types are the pivotal concept in Weber's social science: they attempt to reconcile the essentially subjective nature of social behavior with the scientific need for empirical verification of all knowledge.

Yet how, when constructing ideal types for studying social behavior, are observers sure they have attached the same meaning to an act the agent, either consciously or sub-consciously, has? Weber responds by dividing all social behavior into four ideal types: rational goal-oriented ('zweckrationell') conduct; rational value-oriented ('wertrationell') conduct; affectual ('affektuell') conduct; and traditionalist ('traditionell') conduct.(23) Weber's interpretative sociology explains behavior of the first type, for rational goal-oriented behavior is the ideal type of social conduct most susceptible to rational proof. It alone permits social scientists to evaluate empirical data according to preconceived rational criteria implicitly accepted by both observer and actor. This makes it easier to see how empirical facts deviate from the ideal, and what irrational or accidental factors cause this deviation.(24) The investigative procedure is rather simple.(25) Observers discover whether selected empirical acts in fact lead to results consistent with the agent's subjective (rational) intentions. They do this by creating an ideal construct indicating a typical rational desired goal, and the adequate typical rational means for achieving the proposed goal. By empirically comparing observed actions with the ideal construct, observers can judge whether social actors made the right assumptions as to their expectations of the conduct of others, how the goal could have been more efficiently achieved, and what unforeseen factors may have influenced the outcome. In this procedure, certain causal factors, relevant to the ideal type, are isolated. Since there is no single ideal type for any instance of rational behavior, observers construct as many as they wish in order to reveal different causally related antecedents of the selected action.

2 SCHUTZ'S CRITIQUE OF WEBER

Weber's methodology has had a profound influence on all contemporary efforts at defining the limitations and implications of social scientific explanation. In considering Alfred Schutz, however, this influence is even more direct than in any other single case. Schutz's ideas are motivated by Weber's in both a positive and negative sense. Of the three main elements in Weber's methodology - the concept of value-relevance, the process of 'Verstehen,' and the use of ideal types to link empirical fact with subjective meaning - Schutz agrees, at least in principle, that all are valuable and necessary tools for building a theoretical bridge connecting science and subjectivity. He accepts Weber's insistence on the inherently subjective quality of human behavior, and the need for social science to take this subjectivity into account. Consequently, he agrees that a scientific method ignoring this human perspective while accumulating data is distorting the behavior it pretends to faithfully explain. He also adopts Weber's belief that only empirically verifiable facts are reliable and worthy of the label 'scientific knowledge.' Finally, Schutz agrees empirically validated ideal types are the only means we have for effectively satisfying logical requirements of science while remaining true to the actual quality of social reality. In brief, Schutz accepts all the major ideas of Weber's methodology, from the belief that scientific understanding of meaningful behavior is in fact possible to the particular methods Weber develops to scientifically catch the human element of social behavior.

Schutz is so impressed with the quality of Weber's approach to social science that his own writings are intended more to perfect than supplant it. This notion of perfecting is a key to understanding Weber's influence on Schutz: he contends, in effect, Weber does not remain true to his original principles and therefore does not realize the promise of his ideas. Weber is correct in pursuing all his major goals, but the vagueness of crucial parts of his analysis prevents him from achieving the desired synthesis. In particular, Schutz feels Weber's almost obsessive concern for avoiding the ambiguities of empirically non-verifiable psychological thinking has rendered his social theory more ambiguous than it might have been. An adequate explanation of social action does imply understanding the meaning this action has for the actor, but what does Weber mean by the word 'meaning'? This is definitely not a trivial question, for 'meaning,' whatever Weber implies, is the cornerstone of interpretative social science. Weber's prime goal is to scientifically explain human action, 'all human behavior when and in so far as the acting individual attaches a subjective meaning to it.'(26) The method he proposes requires our creating ideal constructs that are clues to actual subjective motivations of involved actors, the 'complex of subjective meaning which seems to the actor himself or to the observer an adequate ground for the conduct in question.'(27) Unless we know what 'meaning' refers to we can never be certain how Weber interprets terms such as 'action' and 'motivation,' and the process of 'Verstehen' is too vague to be operationalized. Concomitantly, if all these terms are ambiguously defined, there is no explicit criteria for recognizing their empirical expressions in the social world. Empirically verified data, based on idealized constructs, can indeed be collected by eager social scientists; but how are we sure it is subjectively meaningful data, empirical expressions of actual subjective attitudes? Weber chooses to scientifically investigate social action, subjectively meaningful behavior which takes the behavior of others into account. Does a knee-jerk in response to a doctor's stimulus constitute such an action? Apparently not because it is not subjectively meaningful - or is it? How are we sure if we don't know what 'subjective meaning' means? This example is self-evident, but the same problem is faced when considering common behavior patterns such as mailing a letter, going to church, voting, or responding to a command. How does this social behavior become subject matter for Weberian social scientists without a more explicit definition of 'meaning'? We can, in our present confusion, never be sure whether or not social behavior is subjectively meaningful.

If we are unsure about which empirical phenomena are subjectively meaningful, we are even less certain how to construct the idealized models necessary for guiding our empirical investigation. Such constructs must, in an extreme or utopian sense, reflect the meaning a typical actor will experience under specified typical conditions. But, lacking an explicit definition of 'meaning,' model builders must fall back on a groundless, intuition-like mental process. When completed, the constructs may reflect meanings most people experience in a given situation, but they may not. Why, for example, is rational, goal-oriented behavior, that category Weber calls most amenable to scientific analysis, necessarily meaningful behavior? There is no effort to prove it is so, and, lacking such proof, we can as easily assume it is not meaningful. In this case, rational behavior, based on criteria Weber does explicitly develop, qualifies primarily as subject matter for the natural sciences. Such meaningless behavior is better analyzed by an approach stressing the discovery of inclusive, objective, causal formulas not affected by subjective variables. There is, in other words, no epistemological basis either for Weber's division of social action into four ideal typical categories, or for believing his sociological method is best suited to understand rational action.

Weber's relevant comments primarily clarify the problem, rather than provide answers. He criticizes various ways of understanding the word 'meaning.'(28) Disciplines such as jurisprudence, logic, ethics and aesthetics deal only with 'true' or 'valid' meanings not empirically verifiable. Empirical disciplines, the only ones qualified to be called 'scientific,' must avoid 'a priori' premises, focusing instead on the meaning acts and relationships have for those actively engaged in their pursuit. The fact remains, however, Weber eliminates various interpretations of 'meaning' without himself filling the obvious void.(29)

In a broader sense, Weber attempts to travel the gap between subjectivity and science without ever developing any clear idea what subjectivity is. To adequately define 'subjective meaning' we must investigate the nature of subjectivity. What an individual perceives as meaningful, and therefore what the term 'meaning' expresses, varies if we interpret subjectivity as the product of Freudian-like instincts, biological or environmental determinants, or the free, spontaneous actions of an unhindered actor. Although Weber probably identified more with this last possibility than any other, he was too empirical-minded to deal at length with the relevant philosophical issues. One consequence is the paradoxical quality of Weber's conclusions concerning related but even more abstract notions such as 'freedom' and 'alienation.'(30) More important is the effect of this failure on his methodology: with no philosophical groundwork to build on, Weber's concepts of 'value-relevance,' 'Verstehen,' and especially the ideal type constructs, all become carriers of a non-existent notion of subjectivity. As such, they lose their clarity and scientific value. Whereas, in theory, Weber's ideal constructs are capable of performing the dual functions of preserving the subjective integrity of each actor and satisfying the empirical requirements of scientific method, in reality the cards are stacked from the beginning. By neglecting to deal with various philosophical problems related to the nature of subjectivity and meaning, it is easy enough to manufacture a reconciliation. Unfortunately, it is one of words only, philosophically vague and empirically inadequate; it solves the apparent contradiction by ignoring it. Weber, in attempting to intellectually transcend the extremes of subjectivism and scientism has, instead, ignored one and distorted the other.

Alfred Schutz devotes his first published work, 'The Phenomenology of the Social World,'(31) to correcting these inadequacies in Weber's methodology. Schutz contends all these issues can be confronted only by adding to interpretative sociology a thorough philosophical analysis of subjectivity and the meanings of terms like 'meaning,' 'action,' 'motivation,' and 'understanding.' Weber's own failure to undertake this task adversely affects his methodology, rendering it, in the end, unsatisfactory. Schutz, in search of philosophical moorings, turns to Edmund Husserl for guidance.

3 EDMUND HUSSERL'S PHENOMENOLOGY

Edmund Husserl originated the philosophical movement known as phenomenology.(32) This philosophy, distinct from all previous philosophical systems, aims at coming to terms with the world by accurately describing all its aspects as they appear in the subject's consciousness. It refuses to unquestioningly accept the validity of any conceptual scheme, rationalistic or otherwise, and similarly questions the empirical findings of all the positive sciences. Consequently, it is a philosophy which doubts the truthfulness of all socially accepted knowledge until it is absolutely confirmed by a method emphasizing the consciousness of perceiving observers. To facilitate our grasping Husserlian phenomenology as related to Schutz's criticism of Weber, without getting mired in the intricacies of Husserl's arguments themselves, I will concentrate primarily on outlining the chronological development of Husserl's thought exhibited in his own important works.(33) Husserl's ideas concerning the nature of science will be carefully discussed in chapter 4, leaving the remainder of this one for a perusal of the major philosophical principles of Husserlian phenomenology.

Edmund Husserl received a PhD in 1881, with a thesis in mathematics dealing with the calculus of variations. In 1886, after hearing lectures given by Franz Brentano, he decided to abandon mathematics for a career in philosophy. Husserl considered himself an advocate of a philosophical movement known as psychologism, which considered psychology the basis of all human interpretations of valid knowledge. This view is expressed in his first book, 'Philosophie der Arithmetik' (1891), which defends an argument favoring psychology as the epistemological background of mathematical concepts. Within ten years, however, Husserl realized that his search for certainty, his hope of uncovering a pure, absolute knowledge to be used in creating a revolutionary new philosophical system, could not be satisfied by an approach limiting itself to investigating vagueries of subjective psychological meaning. It was not long before Husserl officially repudiated his early position and set out to uncover a foundational philosophy which would guarantee the truthfulness of psychological statements.(34)

Though Husserl was well-read in post-Renaissance western philosophy, and was profoundly influenced by the seminal work relating to the nature of consciousness done by Descartes, Hume, Kant, and William James,(35) his approach to philosophy was affected most directly and profoundly by Franz Brentano. Not himself what Husserl would later term a phenomenologist, Brentano's writings nevertheless serve as building blocks for Husserl's attempt to reach beyond psychologism to a broader theory of objective knowledge. Many aspects of Brentano's work influence Husserl, ranging from his criticisms of traditional concepts of empiricism and description of essential structures of empirical matter, to his investigating the interrelationship of time and consciousness. All these topics are avidly pursued in Husserl's own later version of phenomenology,(36) but none influenced him as much as did Brentano's concept of intentionality.(37) The idea of intentionality is created by Brentano to distinguish between mental or psychological activities (such as thinking, desiring, hating, etc.) and physical phenomena. It is the unique attribute of the former class of activities to 'intend' its object, in the sense of focusing consciousness on it and thereby bringing it to the attention of the subject. Psychology, which studies these intending acts, is ultimately concerned with describing the nature of consciousness, a topic distinguishing it from natural science. Though Brentano still locates objective knowledge outside the mind, his concept of intentionality started Husserl thinking about the structure of consciousness and the relationship between consciousness and objectivity.

Husserl's consideration of this concept is important, probably decisive, to his development as a philosopher.(38) His early writings on logic, inchoate efforts at developing a core concept of a more general phenomenology, are devoted to philosophically elucidating intentionality.(39) In these studies Husserl expresses the dual goals of closely analyzing the intentional structure of consciousness and describing objects as they present themselves to consciousness. Pure description means, for Husserl, describing 'the things themselves,' and these are conceived as objects of consciousness. The intentionality of consciousness thus becomes a fundamental postulate of Husserlian phenomenology. All perceptual acts, where a subject becomes conscious of something, have a directional character, implying the active 'movement' of consciousness beyond itself to include (i.e. 'intend') an object within its sphere. The intentional object, what Husserl calls the noema, is merely a correlate of the act of intending, or noesis. Objects of consciousness are objects intended in the noetic processes of perception, including thinking, remembering, willing, imagining, desiring, etc. They do not exist 'in themselves,' or apart from our perceptions, as the natural sciences imply, for if phenomena are not intentional objects we are not aware of them and they don't exist. Consciousness is the substructure or root of all knowledge.(40) Correlatively, 'the fundamental principle of phenomenological method requires that one's conscious processes, as themselves given in reflective perception, be acknowledged as genuine data.'(41)

Our perceptions, therefore, consist of intended objects, and subjective awareness is the unity of noesis and noema. But there are modifications of our perceptions, how things 'appear,' which change the meaning intended objects have for us. These originate either in the noetic process of perception, or in the noema itself. Of the former, our different attitudes or moods, as well as the different memories we have of previous similar experiences, will both affect the meaning intended objects have for us. While the latter, the noema, may point to other non-perceived elements of itself (the 'inner horizon'), or to larger non-perceived elements of the environment it is located in (the 'outer horizon'). All these non-perceived (but apperceived) spatial and temporal elements of an experience alter the subjective meaning we attach to it. Over time, if these spatial and temporal anticipations are fulfilled in subsequent perceptions, a unification occurs in which particular perceptions, rather than just succeeding one another, organize into a coherent and sustained process. The thing perceived unfolds in an increasing determinateness constituted by the fulfillment of anticipations. This, in turn, constitutes a horizon of typicality, determining, to a degree, how an object pre-predicatively presents itself to us. Everything we perceive appears as one of a special kind, and is controlled by the category of phenomena, included within the horizon of typicality, it entails. The horizons of typicality are reflected in society's pre-predicative values and customs, which impose their meaning on phenomena and are continually in flux, always influenced by new, intentional acts of perception.(42) Though critical of various aspects of this theory of typicality,(43) Schutz draws heavily from it in constructing a method of scientifically explaining social behavior. Husserl, more than Weber does in his own concept of the ideal type, offers cogent insights into the precise quality of typical social behavior patterns.

In sum, the character of perceived objects, for social actors, is directly related to the intentional acts they are part of, which are not primordially initiated but derived from accepted social meaning patterns, expressed in typical values and customs. Each of our experiences is generally more complex than it first appears, consisting of many intentional acts, each of a different type. If we desire to sift through these complex experiences and uncover the sphere where things appear to us primordially, we must reconstruct the original lived experiences in which a phenomenon originally appears as itself. Husserl calls this investigative method 'intentional analysis.' Its goal is to systematically break down a complex experience into its component intentional acts, and arrive at its meaning as constituted in our actual lived experiences, isolated from social forces. Natural science, as Husserl sees it, accepts the derivative world of meaning shaped by social values and customs, neglecting to study reality as it is primordially given in experience.

Intentional analysis, revealing the primary lived experiences structuring subjective meaning, can be interpreted as one expression of a simplistic solipsism which interprets all knowledge as subjectively relative. Husserl's search for absolute knowledge requires he advance some kind of criteria by which our many subjective processes of perception will coalesce at a level of experienced reality that is also objective, or intersubjectively verifiable. Since objects are always intended by consciousness, describing their universality is possible only by means of an intellectual intuition revealing their non-empirical essences. Husserl's early thought never offers an explicit method for achieving this, or criteria of evidence adequate for validating essences. The ambiguity was a consequence, in a sense, of his desire to refute psychologism: in concentrating primarily on the noema, Husserl shows objects exist only as correlates of consciousness, and their analysis cannot be initiated by a psychology adhering to epistemological premises native to natural science. A subjective constitution of essences, necessary for his theory to advance beyond solipsism, is not accomplished through a logical analysis of consciously intended objects. Only in the ego, or subject, can Husserl eventually find the proper means for uncovering essential aspects of these objects. The turning point in this endeavor coincides with the publication of 'Ideas' in 1913, when Husserl introduces the 'phenomenological reduction,' based on the 'epoché,' as an irrefutable path to pure and absolute consciousness. Since the world, and all knowledge we have of it, is constituted by our conscious perceptions, Husserl here uncovers a method leading to pure and absolute knowledge.

Husserl transcends subjectivism by carefully removing from our perceptive processes all subjective elements that might hinder pure description. Instituting what he calls an 'epoché,' or bracketing, of the world, Husserl systematically suspends belief in the world, worldly objects, and statements concerning knowledge of the world. Within the 'epoché' are all practical and theoretical statements of scientific knowledge, including those confirmed by empirical evidence. Observers, existing in the real world when instituting the 'epoché,' also suspend belief in their own mundane existences.(44) The 'epoché' thus eliminates any personal position or attitude relating to factual existence. In this sense it differs from Cartesian doubt, which, by explicitly denying the existence of the world and the self, actually defends a certain point of view in regard to reality. Once the 'epoché' is realized it operates for the whole duration of our descriptive analysis, preventing impure empirical facts from intruding. The entire process of suspending belief in the world and in one's self expresses what Husserl means by 'phenomenological reduction.' As it is actualized, the natural, common-sense world we live and act in is 'reduced,' or purified, into one totally devoid of subjective or empirical assumptions.

The phenomenological reduction reveals consciousness as existing alone within the brackets. From a position of absolute doubt, observers uncover, as a 'phenomenological residue,' one element existing independent of all others: consciousness. It, therefore, is fundamental or primary to the world of objects, an irreducible component of any conceivable epistemology. Husserl terms the mechanism of consciousness that is undraped of mundane disguise, the residue of the phenomenological reduction, 'pure' consciousness.(45) He concludes, 'consciousness itself has a being of its own which in its absolute uniqueness of nature remains unaffected by the phenomenological disconnexion.' Here, at last, is a root concept directly pointing us to a new theory of objectivity and a new philosophical method. In consciousness Husserl finds 'a region of Being which is in principle unique, and can become in fact the field of a new science - the science of Phenomenology.'(46)

The phenomenological reduction confirms Husserl's earlier analysis of the intentionality of consciousness.(47) If the one irreducible component of life is identified as pure consciousness, then it is relatively easy to reconstruct the process of perception. Take, as an example, the desk I am writing on. In the natural, or common-sense, attitude I perceive this desk and I unquestioningly accept its existence. However, when I perform the phenomenological reduction, in which belief in the desk and its physical existence is carefully bracketed, I must nevertheless concede that my perception of this desk is without any doubt part of the phenomenological residue. Since pure consciousness alone is unaffected by the phenomenological reduction, and my perception of the desk is present in pure consciousness, I can validly conclude consciousness itself has intended the perceived object. When I consciously perceive an object, my consciousness intends this object and includes it within its sphere of awareness. All perceptions are, in this sense, intentional. Again, since consciousness alone is 'pure,' the irreducible foundation of my knowledge of the world, and I perceive the desk through the intentionality of consciousness, I do not have to - there is no reason to - assume this desk exists as a physical object in the outer world, independent of my perception of it. When I phenomenologically investigate my perception of this desk I realize that 'desk' in fact means 'desk as I perceive it,' or 'desk as it appears to me.' Because consciousness is the basis of all conceivable knowledge I can have of this desk, its truth or reality is expressed only in consciousness, with no way to verify whether or not it has a material equivalent in the bracketed outer world.

Though in earlier writings Husserl's emphasis on pure description precluded the possibility of an ego existing behind acts of consciousness, in 'Ideas' he realizes a transcendental foundation for all consciously intended knowledge is necessary to insure the universality of his philosophy. He constitutes this transcendental factor by performing a second reduction on pure consciousness, the residue of the original phenomenological reduction. By means of this second 'transcendental phenomenological reduction'(48) Husserl discovers the pure or transcendental ego which pervades all acts and objects of consciousness, giving sense and validity to the world, and constituting the world's meaning.(49) The transcendental ego connects the subjectivity of perception to the objectivity of a universally accepted epistemology. It is like an anonymous consciousness, manifest in all those performing the transcendental phenomenological reduction but belonging to no-one in particular because of its universality. In our experiences as transcendental egos we constitute absolute, apodictic knowledge; it is the universal constitutive force of all our experiences and all possible knowledge because it is the essence of consciousness, that part remaining as the transcendental phenomenological residue. By means of the reduction, Husserl has successively purified consciousness of its contingent subjectivity, and uncovered apodicticity, the core of all consciousness and knowledge.

This concept of the transcendental ego must be handled with care, for, technically, Husserl did not mean to acknowledge those mysterious, otherworldly connotations generally associated with transcendentalism. The transcendental phenomenological reduction is called 'transcendental' because it uncovers the pure ego for which the world has meaning, an ego transcending the meaningful world by constituting the meaning this world has in the subject's consciousness. Strictly - though perhaps not practically - speaking, it is not conceivable apart from our perceptions of the world. This procedure is, therefore, 'phenomenological' in its focusing on this world (and no other) and viewing it as a phenomenon 'reduced' or filtered back to primordial meaning-giving experience. Herbert Spiegelberg indirectly compares the transcendental ego to reflections on a smooth surface:(50) these reflections can only occur in relation to viewers, and are therefore partially dependent on them. Yet the reflections are also independent because the actual constitutive elements exist prior to, and in no direct way depend upon, the viewers. So, too, the transcendental ego exists independent of empirical subjects, yet in no way is understandable apart from them. Although this pure ego is the fountain of universality, reliable knowledge is expressable only through the consciousness of thinking subjects, whose subjectivity has been purified by the transcendental phenomenological reduction.

In one sense Husserl's treatment of the transcendental phenomenological reduction conflicts with his earlier concern for a consciousness which merely intends objects of its attention, objects already 'there' to be perceived. If the transcendental ego actively constitutes objective knowledge, how can it also passively intend an object somehow independent of its constituting ability? In 'Ideas,' Husserl is ambiguous about the intentionality of consciousness, claiming it is both passive or receptive, as well as active or constituting. The problem is worked out in his next two works, 'Formal and Transcendental Logic' (1929)(51) and the 'Cartesian Meditations' (1931). Husserl finally tailors his concept of intentionality to snugly fit the implications of the transcendental phenomenological reduction. Consciousness no longer simply receives objects into its sphere, but by means of the transcendental ego, actively constitutes them. With the transcendental ego the source of absolute knowledge, by actively constituting perceived objects it guarantees the true being of objects is expressed in their appearance. Similarly, because the transcendental ego is accessible to anyone willing to perform the necessary phenomenological reductions, it is possible for all to consciously intuit the essentials of perceived objects.

In these middle years, most of Husserl's efforts go into reconciling his idea of the transcendental ego as the sole constituting force of all knowledge with the obvious mundane reality of a world co-populated by many transcendental subjects. Husserl's problem originates in his own criteria that nothing is known with certainty unless it is constituted, as an object of cognition, by the transcendental ego. In order to present a realistic theory of intersubjectivity he has to show how the Other, who is constituted as an object by my transcendental ego, can be constituted as a subject, capable of constituting his own objects. The logical difficulties in this endeavor are obvious, proving too great for even Husserl's piercing intellect. The essentials of his argument, provided in the 'Cartesian Meditations,'(52) are inadequate to the stated purpose of proving the existence of the Other without already assuming it.(53)

Although a framework for the philosophy of subjectivity demanded by Schutz is now present, there remains outstanding a vital aspect of Husserl's thought, one profoundly affecting Schutz's own ideas. This appendage to his basic phenomenology is created by Husserl in the years of turmoil and unrest following 1930. Caught in the midst of confusing political and social events, and forced to flee Germany because of his 'non-Aryan' ancestry, Husserl is determined to unearth the root philosophical causes of this rampant irrationality. Though convinced his philosophy, as it was, contained elements of reason and rationality Europe was thirsting for, it was also apparent people of influence even within his own country had failed to recognize the value of his teachings. Inflexible in his belief, Husserl felt a new beginning, a dramatic restatement for all to hear, was necessary if his transcendental phenomenology was to exercise the practical influence proper to its philosophical quality. Accordingly, he begins his venture, in 1935, with a series of carefully planned lectures directed at the moral lassitude of European civilization. These have since been termed the 'Krisis' lectures.(54) Their concern with the 'Lebenswelt,' or life-world, of contemporary Europe represents the last great theme of Husserl's lifetime effort to revolutionize philosophy.

Husserl begins these lectures by claiming that current events in Europe, and the sickness of the European mind, both indicate a systematic betrayal of an idea which has historically characterized western civilization: the ideal of a universal knowledge based on reason. This ideal refers not to a restricted body of knowledge, but to a concept of reason which provides a foundation for rationalizing experience and co-ordinating the diverse labors of scholars in respect to common goals and shared tasks to be performed - in brief, a bond uniting humans to each other and the universe. Husserl traces the history of this idea from ancient Greece to the present.(55) Crucial to his argument is the pivotal quality of Galileo's thought. Galileo is seen as the inaugurator of modern science, primarily because he located objectivity in the world of natural phenomena, totally isolated from the independent world of thinking minds. In so doing, Galileo originated the objectivistic thesis which unalterably severed human beings from any meaningful connection with their surrounding natural environments, destroying both the teleological world-view of the Greeks and the inclusive Christian universe of the middle ages.(56) This new idea is now propelling the elaborate technicalization and mechanization of our western society, and is also a prime instigator of the moral decay gripping European civilization, isolating individuals in a state of helpless submission to amoral, technological behavior-patterns.(57) Descartes and Kant recognized this tragic duality of existence, but neither had the philosophical resources to unite human beings with their world. Contemporary philosophy must offer us universal knowledge that can restore to reason its traditional transcendental character. Anything less will forfeit humanity to the uncontrollable, inhuman forces even now surging everywhere. For Husserl, transcendental phenomenology has the intellectual and spiritual profundity necessary to rescue us from this tragic fate.

For philosophy to achieve this goal, it must begin by turning itself towards the pre-reflective, pre-given fabric of social life we normally function in. This pre-predicative world, the 'Lebenswelt,'(58) is the presupposition underlying all our lives and activities, compelling us to unquestioningly accept the world we find ourselves in. All things and beings we orient ourselves towards are rarely perceived in themselves, but are predictably defined as part of the world we live in, just as we also belong in that world. The world is always there as a pre-given, implicitly 'announcing itself' in all our dealings. Since this inarticulate awareness of the world is the basis for all our mundane functions, the world itself, the 'Lebenswelt,' is the unformulated premise or presupposition of all our activities and knowledge.(59)

The 'Lebenswelt' is an intersubjective world because we implicitly assume the existence and similar experiences of interacting individuals. It therefore has an historico-cultural connotation: the 'idea' of the world we pre-reflectively experience in our everyday lives is a product of the culture and times we live in. The 'Renaissance world,' for example, includes those everyday experiences usual to people who lived at this time in history, combined with the unquestioned world-view readily available to them. This type of mundane consideration of the world is native to the cultural sciences, which deal only with particular empirical examples of human communities. As a method of scientific investigation, it is not Husserl's prime concern.

The cultural sciences are not alone in their intimate relationship to the 'Lebenswelt,' although this fact has been obscured. Modern science, at least since Galileo, has idealized nature and treated it with idealized concepts obfuscating the role subjectivity plays in constituting knowledge. In the minds of contemporary people, the 'Lebenswelt' has been superceded by these idealized concepts created by natural scientists. In fact, the concepts of science, logic, and mathematics, occur within, and are justified and validated in the evidences of, the 'Lebenswelt.' All theoretical truth, contrary to the idealized version of science prevalent today, is founded upon such evidences. 'Objective science . . . asks questions only on the ground of this world's existing in advance through pre-scientific life. Like all "praxis," objective science presupposes the being of this world . . .'(60) In other words, all the products and theories of natural science presuppose those non-reflective acts of consciousness through which the 'Lebenswelt' appears as pre-given and prior to scientific activity. Scientific knowledge is therefore relative, unknowingly built on the foundation of the 'Lebenswelt.' To clarify the real meaning of 'objectivity' we must turn our conscious awareness towards the 'Lebenswelt' and uncover the vital role pre-reflective consciousness plays in our constituting what we believe is 'science.' This discovery will substantiate the view that 'objective' laws of nature have their roots in the unquestioned world of everyday life; only the popularly accepted but entirely unfounded claim to 'objectivity' cloaks their actual status as cultural facts pertaining to the 'Lebenswelt.'(61) The 'Lebenswelt,' not the world of natural science, is therefore the most universal of themes to investigate.

Since 'objective science,' in the Galilean (modern) sense, is the super-structure built on the foundational 'Lebenswelt,' in developing a science of the 'Lebenswelt' we bracket out objective science; we perform an 'epoché' on objective science to consciously reach out towards the actual phenomenon we are searching for, the 'Lebenswelt.' Husserl presents two possible methods of scientifically explaining this elusive subject matter. The first entails an ontological description of specific, empirical 'Lebenswelten,' deriving invariant structures essential to them from idealized concepts constituted through the phenomenological reductions.(62) This method enables us to study essential aspects of our pre-reflective conscious lives.(63) Husserl, reflecting the trend of his life's work, rejects this in favor of a more general program of phenomenology. He feels our scientific understanding of the 'Lebenswelt' is accelerated by removing ourselves from our naive attitudes, our unquestioning acceptance of the life-world and everything in it. Consequently, we include within the brackets of our reduction not only objective science, but also the 'Lebenswelt' itself. By suspending our belief in the 'Lebenswelt' we are no longer actively engaged in its activities. Being detached, disinterested observers, we are now able to analyze the stream of conscious life as it continually flows by, perceiving features of the 'Lebenswelt' as pure phenomena appearing in the mind exactly as experienced. The purified phenomena now appear as correlates of our conscious acts. Since it is through consciousness that being emerges, we are now able to describe the true, objective features of the 'Lebenswelt.' If we simultaneously bracket consciousness itself, and, by performing the transcendental phenomenological reduction grasp the transcendental ego, we constitute absolute essences of the phenomena we are studying. Essential, transcendent features of all 'Lebenswelten,' including the empirical one we experience, are understood scientifically only by our attaining the transcendental ego and constituting them apodictically.(64)

Recapitulating, Husserl, in the 'Krisis' lectures, points out the primary significance of our pre-reflective, pre-given forms of conscious behavior in understanding both the world we live in and the 'objective' sciences, theoretical and empirical, pretending to describe this world. He describes two possible methods of scientifically investigating this pre-reflective life-world. The first includes an ontological analysis of our own particular 'Lebenswelt,' focusing on our pre-reflective attitudes and oriented towards revealing the essential nature of our own conscious beings in the 'Lebenswelt.' The second, that method favored by Husserl, involves a process of transcendental phenomenological analysis more in tune with his past inclinations, bracketing the 'Lebenswelt' itself, and stressing a broader constitution of essences by the transcendental ego. Husserl's philosophical program, in either case, is transcendental phenomenological, in that observers can, by successive purifications of their subjectivity, arrive at a synthesis of objective and subjective levels of reality. There is an important similarity between the two paths Husserl offers for guiding our scientific investigations of the 'Lebenswelt.' He bases the ontological method on the premise there is a 'universal,' or 'essential,' mode of existence transcending all subjective experiences within an empirical 'Lebenswelt,' but also manifest in each particular one. Similarly, he bases his more general phenomenological analysis on the premise there are universal, essential modes of existence for all empirical phenomena we experience, and by analyzing these essences 'Lebenswelten' in general, and all valid knowledge, are scientifically reconstructed. Always Husserl maintains the belief that structures of a particular life-world and within all possible life-worlds do exist, and are uncovered by one or another of his analytical methods - both of which are based on the universal constituting powers of the transcendental ego. It is in this sense, stressing the universality and objectivity of the transcendentally constituted results, that Husserl refers to his 'science' of the 'Lebenswelt.'(65)

This fact is obscured by writers who pretend to see in Husserl's last writings the germ of a non-transcendental existential viewpoint, in which the 'Lebenswelt' emerges as a correlative, inseparable, constitutive structure of consciousness, the 'bottom-line' which defines the meaning and knowledge we experience.(66) Consciousness, in this view, is inseparable from the 'Lebenswelt.' This interpretation, in addition to being non-defendable by a careful reading of the 'Krisis' lectures, annihilates the continuity and consistency of Husserl's life-work. If the 'Lebenswelt' is the primary constitutive structure of individual consciousness, what role does the transcendental ego - pure, absolute consciousness - play? If, on the other hand, the transcendental ego is, in fact, transcendent, then it must be the sole constitutive structure of all knowledge, including knowledge of the 'Lebenswelt'; if it isn't, then we must ignore most of Husserl's writings, including parts of the 'Krisis' lectures where the transcendental ego is assumed or discussed. Since Husserl never repudiated his writings, choosing instead to further refine his concept of transcendence in each succeeding effort, we can only assume in these lectures Husserl utilizes his analysis of the 'Lebenswelt' as a propadeutic to a transcendental phenomenology of consciousness.(67) Husserl's transcendental phenomenology differs in key respects from existential philosophy. An attempt to bridge the gap through Husserl's writings alone is doomed to failure.(68)

Alfred Schutz understands these problems well enough, yet he too fails in attempting to 'de-transcendentalize' Husserl's philosophy. Schutz's own thought owes much to Husserl's writings on the 'Lebenswelt.' He accepts Husserl's definition of the nature and importance of the pre-reflective, pre-given life-world of everyday existence, and devotes most of his professional life trying to achieve Husserl's goal of scientifically understanding it. This granted, which of Husserl's two prescribed methods did Schutz choose: an ontology of our conscious experiences - filtered through the reductions and purified by the transcendental ego - of a

'Lebenswelt,' or a more general phenomenological investigation into the essences of all empirical phenomena? The surprising answer is that Schutz chose neither. He attempts to scientifically investigate the 'Lebenswelt,' but does not use either of the methods Husserl describes as necessary to the task.

How, then, does he accomplish this scientific analysis? This will be our topic in the following chapter. Here it is important to note that Schutz, at least provisionally, accepts all of Husserl's major ideas we have described except one: he doubts the value of Husserl's second, the transcendental phenomenological reduction in facilitating our discovery of scientific knowledge. In particular, he is skeptical of the role the transcendental ego is given, and questions whether or not there really are such things as apodictic essences constituted by this pure ego. Even now we see the germ of a logical problem Schutz will have to solve if he is to be successful: by abandoning the transcendental ego and its correlative absolute knowledge, and simultaneously accepting Husserl's belief in the supremacy of individual, subjective consciousness in formulating the meaning each person experiences, Schutz has apparently eliminated the only element in Husserl's scheme that is in any way 'objective.' In effect, Schutz is attempting to found a 'science' of the 'Lebenswelt' on a conceptual system lacking objectively (universally) valid criteria. This is a dubious project, at best, and one that may prove too big for him. Whereas Weber is justifiably criticized for neglecting to provide a developed concept of subjectivity, in embracing only part of Husserl, Schutz may have abandoned the universal criteria of valid knowledge equally necessary for the task of successfully bridging the gap between Dilthey and the positivists.

SUMMARY AND CONCLUSIONS

The preceding pages have briefly described the intellectual environment surrounding Schutz and the theoretical origins of the relationship between phenomenology and the methodology of social science. A summary of the principle ideas will serve as a concise introduction to the next chapter.

1 Schutz's work originates in the methodological debate, primarily among German scholars, concerning the nature of social science. His ideas, like those of Rickert, Windelband and Weber before him, are efforts at building bridges between those who insist upon the unique, even

spiritual, quality of human behavior, and those believing it is only by subsuming behavior under inclusive, empirically-confirmed laws that valid social knowledge is possible. Schutz's intended goal is to preserve the integrity of unique subjects without sacrificing the exactness and clarity of empirical scientific explanation.

2 Schutz accepts Weber's insistence on the primacy of empirical scientific method. Knowledge must be empirically validated before it is accepted as scientific, and the social sciences must remain, in this sense, value-free.

3 Schutz similarly accepts, though only in general terms, the three main concepts of Weber's methodology: value-relevance, 'Verstehen,' and the ideal type. Social knowledge must, as Weber claims, be interpretative in understanding subjective attitudes. The unit of social analysis is the individual, and each defines his or her own situation before acting. Scientific knowledge, to accurately describe what has, in fact, occurred in society, must reveal the subjective meaning complexes a social act has for involved actors. A most useful tool for this task is the ideal type concept. Only by empirically comparing an extreme rationalization of behavior to what actually takes place, and measuring the gap separating the two, can we hope to approach a scientific explanation of social action.

4 However, Weber has not provided us with exact criteria for understanding what subjectivity means, and what terms such as 'meaning,' and 'action' really connote. Without an explicit theory of subjectivity we cannot be sure what Weber means by value-relevance and 'Verstehen,' and we have no criteria for constructing useful, subjectively meaningful, ideal types. Weber's analysis, though correct in its broad aims, lacks clarity. It needs additional philosophical groundwork for developing an explicit definition of subjectivity. Only then can Weber's general principles become both intelligible and empirically useful.

5 Schutz feels Edmund Husserl provides this needed philosophy. Husserl claims the ultimate source of meaning and understanding is found in consciousness, and action is broadly understood as the end product of a conscious process of perceiving and defining our situations as we experience them. The basic quality of consciousness is its intentional character: perception implies the inclusion, or 'intending,' of objects within the sphere of awareness. Knowledge is a function of consciousness; while absolute knowledge is constituted by a pure or transcendental ego, the final residue of a series of

phenomenological reductions. The synthesis of objectivity and subjectivity occurs only through this methodical purification of consciousness. Weber's notion of typicality is also expanded by Husserl. What we perceive now is intimately connected with temporal and spatial perceptions previously constituted in our consciousness. Each newly perceived object is therefore categorized according to conditions independent of the present: it is represented as a species of some practical sort or type already pre-formed in consciousness and based on these previous perceptions. New perceptions take their place within the scope of this typicality, and are partially determined by it. Using these principles of Husserlian phenomenology, Schutz hopes to clarify and strengthen Weber's sociological method.

6 Schutz is particularly impressed with Husserl's later description of the 'Lebenswelt,' that pre-reflective world of everyday existence in which meanings and values are unquestioningly accepted. Husserl feels by 'scientifically' understanding the 'Lebenswelt,' consciously constituting knowledge related to it through a transcendental phenomenological reduction, we also understand the essence of social reality. Schutz believes he can best accomplish Weber's goal of interpretatively understanding meaningful behavior by utilizing most of Husserl's phenomenology in the service of scientifically investigating the 'Lebenswelt.' However, Husserl's 'science' is founded on the merging of objectivity and subjectivity in the transcendental ego, while it is precisely this transcendental element in Husserl that Schutz will reject.

We now know who Schutz is speaking to, and what language he speaks in. Our next task is to describe exactly what he says.

2 Phenomenological social science

The corpus of Alfred Schutz's methodological writings is directed at creating a scientific method which does not subjugate a meaning-endowing actor to objective, impersonal laws. Given the nature of this task, it is surprising that the list of Schutz's published writings is so small. It consists, in fact, of only one completed full-length book and numerous articles which have been compiled into a three-volume anthology.(1) This relative paucity of published writings is partly due to the extreme care and meticulousness Schutz exhibits in writing and re-writing each work, and partly the result of a Jekyll-Hyde type of life in which days are spent pursuing money and success in the business world, leaving only nights to teach and write. It is imperative, in examining Schutz's methodology, that we bear in mind the intellectual context within which he writes, especially his perception of Weber's sacrifice of subjectivity, the unintended result of Weber's avoiding relevant philosophical issues, to the rigors of scientific method. Schutz's primary goal, in all his writings, is to utilize Husserl's phenomenology as a means of correcting this failure. In this chapter we shall describe Schutz's own efforts and see if his expanded notion of subjectivity is reasonably incorporated into a valid scientific method.

1 THE SOCIAL STRUCTURE OF INDIVIDUALITY

Husserl's description of the 'Lebenswelt,' that pre-reflective, non-questioning existence of individuals in the common-sense world, serves as Schutz's point of departure. Husserl used this concept to facilitate our ascent into the realm of the transcendental ego, where universally valid knowledge is constituted. Schutz, on the other hand, feels that the 'Lebenswelt' itself, in particular the 'natural attitude' characterizing our unquestioning acceptance of social values in the 'Lebenswelt,' should be made the primary focus of attention. Instead of leaving the empirical world in search of abstract absolutes, Schutz proposes to work from within it in hope of uncovering scientific knowledge related to our everyday activities. 'The common-sense world,' 'the world of daily life,' and 'the everyday world' are some of the expressions Schutz uses to describe the world experienced by men and women within that state of consciousness described by Husserl as the natural attitude. Schutz intends to pursue a phenomenological analysis within the framework of this mode of consciousness. His efforts are therefore directed at the mundane, non-transcendental sphere of social life characterized by our everyday existence.

Schutz is careful to emphasize the exact form our consciousness takes within the common-sense world. As Husserl previously stressed, the existence of our world, and its quality, are pre-given and unquestioningly accepted. This unthinking acceptance manifests itself in three fundamental assumptions characterizing the natural attitude.(2) We assume, first, the constancy of the structure of the world, never doubting that it is, and will remain, what it appears to be. Next, we assume the constancy of the validity of our experience of the world. The ultimate criteria of reality, within the natural attitude, is my experience of it, and, within the limits of this attitude, this experience will remain constant - almost predictable. Finally, we assume the constancy of our ability to act upon and within the world. This world is the scene of both our normal actions and the environment posing resistance to these actions. It is the arena of social action, where individuals come to terms with others and themselves through their various relationships. Since action will depend on the structure of the world and my experience of it, and these are constant and valid, we can assume our purposeful behavior will almost always have intended results. These three assumptions constitute implicit facts of the common-sense world. To verify them, the essential conditions necessary for there to be a common-sense world must be described. This is accomplished only by a phenomenological analysis focusing on the empirical life-world and the mode of consciousness native to it. It is the philosopher's task, as Schutz conceives it, to delve underneath the pre-reflective attitude in order to analytically reconstruct the common-sense world.

Even at this early point, a certain inconsistency in Schutz's thinking surfaces. His explicit goal is to remain within the world of the natural attitude and phenomenologically describe consciousness. However, as Gurwitsch has pointed out, 'the very rise of philosophical problems and their formulation in radical terms motivates the phenomenological reduction and, hence, the abandonment of the natural attitude.'(3) Schutz is attempting to apply the results of phenomenological analysis to a sphere where the reflective attitude itself is forbidden. It is questionable, and in a later chapter worthy of some discussion, whether or not this is philosophically justifiable. Schutz is ambiguous on this and similar problems: at crucial points in his argument he has a tendency to assume the validity of certain vacuous or ill-defined ideas upon which the logical consistency of his overall theory depends. These assumptions are apparently not based on observable evidence, phenomenological or otherwise, and seem unwarranted. In this particular case, after observing that 'In ordinary social life we are no longer concerned with the constituting phenomena as these are studied within the sphere of the phenomenological reduction,'(4) Schutz implies that knowledge gained through the reductions is applicable to behavior in the natural attitude. Without explicitly defending the thesis, Schutz accepts the results of an extraordinarily reflective procedure of constituting knowledge, and applies them to the common-sense world, where social action is non-thinking behavior resulting from pre-reflective processes. He then proceeds with his phenomenological analysis of the common-sense world.

Individuals define for themselves the reality of the world they encounter in the natural attitude. This conclusion necessarily follows Schutz's acceptance of a phenomenological epistemology. We are all born and raised separately, assimilating the values of our own surroundings. Accordingly, depending on the particular motives, beliefs, desires, aspirations, etc., we have learned, we will experience the world differently and act in the world from a different point of view. Each unique environment, or, as Schutz terms it, each 'biographical situation,' positions individuals in the common-sense world and defines that world for them. 'The' world, when filtered through my biographical situation, becomes 'my' world.

The most important component of our biographical situations is the knowledge we use in interpreting experiential events. This knowledge of ours, called the 'stock of knowledge at hand,' constitutes the unique pattern or scheme by which we assimilate new events and experiences in an orderly, systematic way.(5) At any moment our stocks of knowledge at hand consist of typifications of the common-sense world. By adopting this Husserlian concept of typicality, Schutz identifies the common-sense world, as perceived by actors, as one of familiarity and personal involvement based on their stocks of knowledge at hand. The world is organized by rules of typicality: principles, founded in our unquestioned past experiences, allow us to anticipate the meaning we will experience in our perceptions of familiar objects, things, and people. In other words, 'the outer world is not experienced as an arrangement of individual unique objects, dispersed in space and time, but as "mountains," "trees," "animals," "fellow-men."'(6) We observe a particular animal and immediately categorize it as a 'dog' because the creature exhibits the features and behavior we recognize as adhering to dogs, i.e. resembling our past experiences of those characteristics we have come to believe all dogs exhibit. Similarly, we perceive all other aspects of the common-sense world in typical ways, including social roles and relationships such as parents, soldiers, friends, enemies, etc. The process of accumulating these typifications begins in childhood and lasts throughout life. Problematic situations of concrete existence are perceived and formulated according to our stocks of knowledge at hand. Any action we take to alter or rectify these situations is grounded in the typically apprehended experiences we have accumulated through our lifetimes. Even if our stocks of knowledge at hand prove to be inadequate, the improvising and innovating which follows similarly proceeds along typically possible lines.(7)

Reality, for both Husserl and Schutz, does not exist in some abstract realm awaiting discovery by inquiring observers. It is, rather, embedded in the conscious perception of the world each individual experiences, the result not of passive discovery but of an active, disciplined process of subjective constitution. We are unique in alone constituting real objects and events, and giving meaning to the world. This is a basic principle of Husserlian phenomenology, and the one Schutz adopts to remedy Weber's incomplete social science. Here, Schutz contends our basic mode of living in and understanding the common-sense world depends upon our categorizing, or typifying, these admittedly unique beings. We learn to deal with people and objects by subsuming them under broad generalizations and replacing their unique subjectivity with impersonal descriptions and expectations. Our knowledge of the world is a function of subjective perception, yet, in this case, by objectifying those we come in contact with we seemingly deny the universality of even this statement and fall, instead, into a solipsistic dilemma. If I perceive people as objects, and if knowledge of the world is constituted through my perceptions, then reality is a function of what I perceive; it is totally personal and relative, certainly not generalizable. Knowledge, in this sense, is personal rather than subjective.

Schutz's response to this dilemma is pivotal to the rest of his argument and deserves to be repeated: (8)

> all typification consists in the equalization of traits relevant to the particular purpose at hand for the sake of which the type has been formed, and in disregarding those individual differences of the typified objects that are irrelevant to such purpose. There is no such thing as a type pure and simple. All types are relational terms carrying . . . a subscript referring to the purpose for the sake of which the type has been formed. And this purpose is nothing but the theoretical or practical problem which, as a consequence of our situationally determined interest, has emerged as questionable from the unquestioned background of the world just taken for granted. Our actual interest, however, is the outcome of our actual biographical situation within our environment as defined by us.

Typification is a means for coming to terms with the world, and does not actually describe its real or essential qualities. Types do not exist in themselves, 'pure and simple,' but are relative concepts expressing particular motives and interests of unique individuals who define their environments and give meaning to the world. They are formed as a consequence of certain problems preoccupying an actor at a particular time, and vary with the subject matter of the problems. Each type is created with reference to a subjectively relevant problem, and helps to organize relevant information into meaningful channels in order to solve it. A series of types of new or unique objects is created by emphasizing common characteristics of these objects relevant to the problem at hand, and each separate problem requires a separate and distinct kind of typification. Since the system of problem-relevances depends on subjective definitions of the environment, the same object or person can be relevant or irrelevant, typified or untypified, typical or atypical in relation to the different unique interests of the onlookers. Thus, behavior appearing 'strange' to bewildered parents may seem normal or 'typical' to a child-psychologist, depending upon their respective definitions of the situation. 'The field of everyday experience is at any particular moment structured into various domains of relevances, and it is precisely the prevailing system of relevances that determines what has to be assumed as being typically equal (homogeneous) and what as being typically different (heterogeneous).'(9)

Schutz is determined to avoid Weber's mistake of paying only lipservice to subjectivity. People create types in the common-sense world according to their own subjectively meaningful criteria, based on their worldly perceptions and definitions. The notion of problem-relevance means to uphold the dignity of meaning-endowing subjects, even in the face of all those regularities of behavior characterizing the common-sense world. Husserl's phenomenology has served its intended purpose of providing a philosophical basis for this idea of subjectivity.

However, Schutz is primarily a social scientist, and it is becoming progressively more apparent that in supplying the missing link of subjectivity into Weber's scheme he is making it increasingly difficult to reconcile this scheme to the equally necessary element of empirically verified scientific explanation. If meaning and knowledge are actually constituted subjectively, there is little reason to develop broad generalities and apply them empirically when studying society. Indeed, there are no criteria for developing these generalities in the first place, since, to be valid, they would have to reflect each individual interpretation of the world, and these would not necessarily coincide to each other or to any one common generalization. Schutz cannot fall back on Weber or Husserl. He now confronts the core problem of the social sciences: whether or not they are reconcilable to a study of free, meaning-endowing actors.

Obviously, the concept of typification has to be modified. Schutz does this by declaring the existence, in the world of everyday life, of a socially approved system of typifications which form the way of life for an in-group by constituting a system of relevances everyone takes for granted. All typifications comprising our stocks of knowledge at hand, though expressed individually according to particular biographical situations, are generated out of a common social structure. We interpret the common-sense world subjectively, based on our stocks of knowledge at hand and, indirectly, the typifications comprising this knowledge. These typifications are now defined as existing independent of each individual as a product of society everyone accepts and takes for granted. Knowledge is necessary for us to meaningfully interpret the world. But this knowledge, 'as to its content and the particular forms of typification under which it is organized, is socially derived, and this in socially approved terms.'(10)

This socially approved knowledge consists of formulas, or 'social recipes,' intended to allow members of a group to define their situations in the reality of everyday life in a typical manner. These recipes constitute the cultural pattern of the group they are related to, and serve several important functions.(11)

1 They determine which facts and events must be treated as equal for the purpose of solving in a typical manner, typical problems which might emerge in typical ways.

2 They transform unique actions into typical functions of typical social roles, originating in typical motives aimed at bringing about typical ends. In other words, the knowledge we have of our positions and roles in society is socially derived. We are expected to act in certain typical ways depending on our situations. By learning the behavior expected in each situation, we act in typical, socially approved ways and expect correspondingly typical, socially approved responses.

3 They serve as a scheme of interpretation and orientation, and as a means of discourse for members of an in-group. Because we expect typical responses to our typical behavior, we can act and expect to get results.

4 They assure the success of such interaction by standardizing and institutionalizing typifications in the form of social controls such as mores, morals, laws, rules and rituals. What is known in common, or 'objectively' known, by all who experience one system of relevances is the universally shared way of life prescribed in the social recipes, including its values, habits and in-group rules for 'good' behavior.

Social recipes are therefore the most important element in our defining a situation. In crossing a crowded city street, for example, we immediately, almost automatically, see the ready-made recipe which is appropriate and realize we must cross only when the light turns green. The same is true for every other possible situation we experience in the common-sense world: we define it according to the relevant social recipe and act in the corresponding, socially-approved manner. Although these recipes may not always remain meaningful,(12) as long as they are unquestioningly accepted as parts of the common-sense world they remain the most significant elements in our subjective definitions of this world.(13)

Our stocks of knowledge at hand, consisting primarily of socially derived knowledge, may originate in any of a number of ways, ranging from our eye-witness experiences to our depending on the opinions of a second or third observer.(14) It is not necessary to experience knowledge first-hand for it to be accepted as socially approved and valid. However, the most important factor determining the quality of our stocks of knowledge at hand, and therefore the one most influencing our personal definitions of a situation, is our membership in voluntary and involuntary social groups.(15) We will consider relevant only those social recipes corresponding to our economic and social classes, including jobs, associations, clubs and any other organizations we participate in. Our perceptions of the world will depend on the socially approved, typical behavior patterns a person in our position is expected to live up to. It will resemble the perception of any other person occupying a similar position and accepting as typically relevant a similar set of social recipes. Our self-identities in society consist of those self-typifications reflecting the typical, socially approved behavior any person occupying our position is typically expected to exhibit. These self-typifications 'are arranged in a particular private order of domains of relevances that is, of course, continuously in flux.'(16) Our freedom, then, is defined by our ability to choose the part of our personalities we will participate in each group membership with, and how we will privately order the various groups to which we belong.

This, inchoately, is how Schutz chooses, without violating either, to synthesize subjectivity and science. We are all unique actors, each a product of a biographically determined situation belonging to only one person. Meaning and knowledge, factors determining how we define our situations, are constituted subjectively through our perceiving and experiencing the world. Our perceptions, however, depend upon the type of knowledge we bring to bear in meaningfully organizing the constant experiential bombardment of people, objects, and events. This knowledge, in turn, consists of socially derived and approved recipes prescribing the type of behavior expected from us in each typical situation we experience. The nature of the recipes we find relevant depends largely on the particular social and economic groups we belong to, each group prescribing typical behavior expected in typical situations. In brief, we define the common-sense world as unique subjects who think in typically familiar patterns and act in typically familiar ways. With these principles in hand, Schutz turns to the more detailed analysis of social action which must necessarily precede his formulating a useful sociological method.

2 THE INTERSUBJECTIVE COMMON-SENSE WORLD

He begins by returning to the individual actor and explicating basic phenomenological principles. Perhaps the most fundamental of these describes the primary grounding of being in subjective space and time: we define our spatial environments according to where we stand; we define temporality according to our concept of now. Terms such as 'behind,' 'in front of,' 'on the side of,' 'now' and 'later' all are defined in terms of our own positions in space and time. As with our biographical situations and our stocks of knowledge at hand, we define our spatial and temporal worlds according to our uniquely structured subjectivities.

This spatial and temporal structure of our everyday worlds is categorized into two elements.(17) There is, first, the world within our actual reach, what Schutz terms 'the working world,' corresponding to our concept of 'now,' or the present. Within this zone is the 'manipulatory sphere,' which is open to modification by movements of our bodies or artificial extensions of our bodies (e.g. tools and instruments). This is the portion of the outer world we act on. The make-up of both the working world and the manipulatory sphere change as we move our bodies. Second, there is the world within our potential reach, including that potentially restorable world of our pasts and the potentially attainable world of our futures. Both these worlds are real because we consciously experience them in relation to our actual positions in time and space, but in neither do we actively pursue a goal.

Schutz utilizes this phenomenological description of space and time for constituting intersubjectivity in the common-sense world. He is unsatisfied with Husserl's inadequate solution to the problem of phenomenologically constituting the Other.(18) The problem of intersubjectivity does not, as Husserl assumed, exist between transcendental egos, but exists as an issue only in the mundane world of our everyday lives. Within this common-sense world, intersubjectivity is taken for granted as an unquestioned assumption. Philosophers phenomenologically describe the natural attitude in order to understand how and why the Other exists. If they prove the existence of an alter ego within this mundane world, then this proof cannot be impugned by metaphysical or ontological assumptions.

This effort begins by focusing on the subject's spatial perspectives.(19) The position of our own bodies constitutes the 'here,' the body of fellow man constitutes 'there.' If we move 'there,' the body of fellow man still constitutes a 'there' for us, although it is a 'here' for him. Even though we can never stand in his 'here,' we attribute to him a reciprocity of perspectives because we perceive the objects and events of the world in the same manner from his 'there' as from our 'here.' This reciprocity of perspectives is taken for granted in the common-sense world. It means that objects and events of experience are intersubjectively available and appear about the same to all normal people. This argument depends on Husserl's complex concept of 'appresentation,' which, briefly, 'pairs' or 'couples' an existing perceived object with another similar object implied by the original, but never itself actually appearing. In this case, the Other's body appresents a conscious ego, just as we perceive our bodies and egos as inseparable.(20) In describing the interchangeability of 'here' and 'there' between egos, the reciprocity of perspectives emerges as a necessary condition for a shared, intersubjective world.

Only when we turn to our temporal perspectives does this proof of intersubjectivity become sufficiently clear.(21) Our reciprocity of perspectives implies that in the common-sense world we recognize individual bodies as differing from inanimate objects because they are fellow people, alter egos. We understand a human body has within it an ego possessing a world of cognitive awareness much like ours. Though in general we know more about ourselves than about the alter ego, there is a sense in which our knowledge of him surpasses our self-knowledge. When we reflect on ourselves, we perceive only past acts, for the act of reflecting implies looking at that part of ourselves that 'has been' already, and is now looked at from a distance. The present is inaccessible to the reflective attitude. But, on the contrary, our knowledge of the Other is accomplished within the immediate present by grasping his subjectivity in our present streams of consciousness. The alter ego is, consequently, defined as 'that subjective stream of thought which can be experienced in its vivid present.' We share with our fellow humans the same present, 'in a word: we grow old together.'(22) Our grasping the simultaneity of the Other, and his grasping our actually occurring streams of consciousness, makes possible our being in the world together. This common sharing of the present constitutes 'the general thesis of the alter ego's existence.' We can now see that the stream of thought that is not ours, but which we experience in its present, is structually similar to our own. The Other acts and thinks as we do, and his stream of thought shows the same through and through connectedness as ours. Furthermore, he experiences our presents in the same way we experience his. Yet, since we can never experience the consciousness of the Other in the same completeness as he experiences it, our understanding of his existence is only discontinuously given to us, and never achieves the fullness present in his own subjective consciousness.

Now that Schutz has phenomenologically explained the existence of an intersubjective common-sense world, he sets out to detail the broad range of alter egos present in society.(23) There are, generally speaking, four kinds of persons comprising the society we live in: first, there are our 'predecessors,' who lived before us and who we know only through what we read; next, our 'contemporaries,' alive now and with whom we share a temporal reality; 'consociates' are a special kind of contemporary with whom we share both a temporal and spatial reality; and, finally, there are our 'successors,' who live after we die and remain forever anonymous to us. These four kinds or types of our fellow humans - predecessors, contemporaries, consociates, and successors - comprise all the possible subjects we can experience in the common-sense world. Of these, our consociates exist as the most personally meaningful because they alone are directly related to our constituting the 'reciprocity of perspectives' and the 'general thesis of the alter ego's existence.' Only with consociates do we share the same space and time and live in what Schutz calls a 'face-to-face' situation. By so-doing, we grasp the unique, simultaneous aspects of our alter ego as he expresses them in his acts.

To have a face-to-face situation, we must be aware of the Other's existence and pay attention to him. This awareness, a 'Thou-orientation,' is the form by which an alter ego is pre-predicatively experienced in temporal and spatial immediacy. If the Other adopts a similar awareness of us, then there results a 'pure we-relationship,' in which we all experience, to an incomplete degree, the subjective meaning each of us gives to events now occurring. This we-relation is therefore possible only in the on-going experiences of a face-to-face situation. If we stop to analyze or reflect, we negate its spontaneity and no longer participate in a we-relationship. The we-relationship is a formal concept determining the quality of social relationships in face-to-face situations. Since it consists of types of acts ranging from sexual intercourse to casual conversation, it obviously is characterized by varying degrees of intensity, intimacy and interest, depending on circumstances. What does remain constant is the peculiar way we perceive the person with whom we are dealing. In confronting any other object or person in the common-sense world we bring a pre-constituted stock of knowledge at hand, containing within it a network of typifications based on previous experiences. Only in a we-relationship do we witness the Other's spontaneous actions and understand the meaning he assigns them. By experiencing his spontaneous, meaningful present, we do not have to depend entirely on our stocks of knowledge at hand to understand and calculate what he will do. Instead, we treat the Other as a unique subject, acting in a subjectively meaningful manner, in particular, non-generalizable circumstances.(24)

As we move further away from the direct experience of a we-relationship there are less personally experienced characteristics of the Other to guide our apprehension. In their place, we utilize course-of-action types prescribing typical, expected behavior, from typical actors, in typical circumstances. Only in the pure we-relationship do we understand the individual uniqueness of our fellow-person in his or her own biographical situation. As we turn from this relationship, as we begin dealing with those not in direct contact with us, we use this impersonal typification system. These course-of-action constructs become increasingly anonymous, i.e. increasingly impersonal and general, as we orient our behavior away from direct, personal contacts. Thus, the typical behavior we expect from the mailman is more impersonal and anonymous than the typical behavior expected from the school crossing guard, because we are usually more personally acquainted with the latter. But both these course-of-action types are more anonymous than the typical behavior we expect our friends to exhibit when we meet accidentally in a restaurant. As interaction becomes increasingly de-personalized and anonymous, the constructs assume a more important role in determining how we perceive the world and orient our actions in it. Since typifications are socially-engineered, we can all assume everyone in the common-sense world will perceive this world identically and act predictably in it.

We characterize social behavior of our predecessors, comtemporaries, and successors only by using ideal, course-of-action types. This is so primarily because the vast majority of our social relationships are not subsumed under the pure we-relationship we maintain with consociates. The only way to pass from direct to indirect social experience, while maintaining our abilities to meaningfully interact with the Other, is to generalize our knowledge of him through our adopting socially approved ideal course-of-action types describing the typical behavior expected in typical situations. These ideal constructs deal with personal or characterological types, functional types, or typifying schemes for highly anonymous social collectivities such as 'the state,' or 'the economy.' Each typification may involve other typifications; the more sub-strata of typifying schemes, the more anonymous is the ideal type. What is particularly important, however, is our recognizing that ideal types describe only certain attributes of a fellow human being, and do not take into consideration subjective modifications of these attributes occurring within the on-going experiences of a concrete and unique individual. 'Hence, the . . . ideal type merely refers to, but is never identical with, a concrete Other or a plurality of Others.'(25) Though we expect the mailman to deliver and pick up our mail in a typical manner, we cannot pretend that in this ideal type we have caught the uniqueness of the individual who, in fact, is our mailman. Social relationships between contemporaries depend on mutual acceptance of a scheme of typifications and expectations relative to each actor as a personal ideal type. The more standardized, or institutionalized, a typifying scheme, the better is the chance that the typifying scheme we ascribe to our partners is shared by them. Only in the pure we-relation do we deal with our partners as meaning-endowing subjects functioning in their own biographical situations. All other social interaction in the common-sense world depends on ideal typification.

'Social structure is the sum total of these typifications and of the recurrent patterns of interaction established by means of them. As such, social structure is an essential element of the reality of everyday life.'(26)

Schutz's argument thus far can be summarized in an hypothesis: in the common-sense world, free, meaning-endowing subjects interact with each other primarily by adopting socially engineered and approved formulas which typically categorize both the world and behavior expected from themselves and others within the world. He has utilized this hypothesis to explain phenomena such as culture, intersubjectivity, and social behavior. As yet, however, he has only assumed the hypothesis itself is true. In particular, Schutz has to show us why, even within the unquestioning existence of the natural attitude, these socially prescribed formulas are necessarily subjectively meaningful. If we do, as Schutz contends, experience the world as unique subjects, why must we unquestioningly accept as meaningful only those impersonal typifications others, apparently, accept? Schutz has offered no convincing rationale for our studying social action in a general, scientific manner. He turns to an analysis of the individual actor in his search for an answer.

3 INDIVIDUAL ACTION IN SOCIETY

Weber, according to Schutz's critique, had failed to adequately define what he meant by subjectively meaningful action. Schutz, on the other hand, is careful to explicitly define each of his terms. Action, defined as spontaneous human conduct self-consciously projected by an actor and oriented towards the future, is distinguished from the Act, the accomplished action.(27) This is projected as the goal of the action and is, in fact, brought into being by the action. Action would be abstract and pointless if we had not already fantasized or projected a proposed goal to be its result. When acting 'what is visible to the mind is the completed act, not the on-going process that constitutes it. It is the Act . . . that is projected, not the action.'(28) Consequently, action is distinguished from other behavior in that it alone is 'the execution of a projected Act.' The subjective meaning of an action is its corresponding projected Act; 'meaning' and 'action' are inseparable.(29)

All action requires an actor to project an act as already completed, for only if the fulfillment of the anticipated future act is assumed can the proper means of achieving it be found. The 'project' is the act as it is anticipated as already accomplished. Even though, when acting, we think of a future state of affairs, the project itself 'bears the temporal character of pastness.'(30) Since acts are simultaneously viewed as past and future, Schutz declares they originate in the future perfect tense ('modo futuri exacti'). All human acts must be thought of in these terms, and hence all acts are consciously conceived in the future perfect tense. Working is action in the outer world, based on a project and characterized by the intention of bringing about a certain state of affairs by means of bodily movement.(31) Deciding on the quality of this work is a complex and totally subjective process.

All choosing between projects is preceded by doubt: about which elements of the world to be considered relevant, which projects to accept as ours, and how best to achieve our goals. The world at first appears as an infinite series of open possibilities. Our unique biographical situations limit these to a series of possibilities relevant to our subjective interests, what Schutz calls our 'problematic possibilities.' We must decide which of these problematic possibilities, and their corresponding projects, to adopt, considering each one at a time. Each succeeding consideration corresponds to a succeeding temporal state of consciousness, indicating that while we decide what to do we are simultaneously growing older and constantly adding new experiences to our stocks of knowledge at hand. We are never the 'same' persons in considering each of our alternative problematic possibilities. Every time we re-consider an old project, that project differs from what it was, our perception of it being modified by intervening time and experience. Problematic possibilities factually co-exist in 'outer time'; but actual alternative possibilities constantly change through their being considered successively in 'inner time' ('durée'). We choose our projects in this inner time by selecting the project capable of bringing about that state of affairs considered by us, at the subjective moment of choice, as best. The resulting decision synthetically unites all the problematic alternatives into the actual act.(32) This whole process of decision is one in which(33)

> the ego . . . lives and develops by its very hesitations until the free action detaches itself from it like too ripe a fruit . . .. Deliberation cannot be conceived as an oscillation in space; it

consists rather in a dynamic process in which the ego as well as its motives are in a continuous stage of becoming.

Our free choices affirm the subjective quality of all action.

The freely chosen project, that future desired state of affairs as anticipated when action is begun, is also called the actor's 'in-order-to' motive. All individual in-order-to motives are fragmentary means within a preconceived life-long plan. This life-project provides criteria for subjectively determining the 'best' choice in particular situations. The weight we attach to alternative in-order-to motives is directly related to this higher order system because we will choose only those advancing our overall life-long goals.(34) There are, in other words, no isolated projects. We may choose to go to work tomorrow morning, for example, but we do so only in order to pay for the apartments where we pursue our more primary goal of writing. All personal in-order-to motives and life-projects are subjectively constituted by each free actor.

Actors define their situations and choose their projects in the context of their own unique, subjective existences. The unity of any individual act depends on the scope of the corresponding project, and this is freely chosen. We can never 'objectively' describe an act in a meaningfully complete manner because in so-doing we ignore, and possibly impugn, subjective qualities distinguishing this action from other, unconscious conduct, such as reflex movements. Yet a scientific study of social action depends on generalization. How do we generalize without distorting reality, which is subjectively defined? Schutz admits that in trying to understand another's decision to pursue a course of action, the observer can never be sure as to the actor's decision-making process. Even if the actor and observer are situated in a 'we-relationship,' the biographically determined situations, the selection of relevant elements among all the open possibilities of both actor and observer, must be different. We can never fully understand past actions or predict future decisions of any individual actor.(35) If this is true, on what basis does Schutz construct his scientific method? He is now down to the last, irreducible unit of social analysis: the individual ego. The viability of his theory now depends on his reconciling this ego to a scientific method stressing generalization.

4 THE SOCIAL DETERMINANTS OF INDIVIDUAL ACTION

Schutz forms his argument by introducing the ambiguous notion of a 'because-motive.' Whereas the 'in-order-to' motive is oriented towards the future and is subjectively constituted, the 'because-motive' refers to the past and deals only with those preceding phenomena that brought about the specified action. Each act has both an in-order-to and because-motive. The in-order-to motive is an integral part of the action itself. To uncover the because-motive we exert a special effort to reflect on the possible reasons because-of-which the act was performed, which means a because-motive becomes significant only after an in-order-to motive is freely chosen. Projects, then, are not determined by some pre-existing because-motives, but can be understood in terms of causal relations by our submitting them to retrospective analysis. The project itself will determine which past experiences are to be considered because-motives, and therefore knowledge of because-motives presupposes knowledge of in-order-to motives. Despite this, once they are uncovered, because-motives constitute objective causes of our free, subjectively defined projects.(36)

Just as in-order-to motives exist as part of a higher order system, because-motives are similarly grouped into systems, and are not randomly expressed in concrete actions. However, these motives are not systematized by a goal for the future, but are included under the category of 'personality.' Elements of our own personalities objectively cause us to behave as we do, though they do not determine the quality of our actions. In Schutz's words:(37)

> The self's manifold experiences of its own basic attitudes in the past as they are condensed in the form of principles, maxims, habits, but also tastes, affects, and so-on are the elements for building up the systems which can be personified. The latter is a very complicated problem requiring most earnest deliberation.

Unfortunately, Schutz never does 'earnestly deliberate' on this topic. Instead, we are left with a concept of motivation allowing us to freely choose subjectively defined projects which are, themselves, causally related to aspects of our personalities. Apparently Schutz assumes our free actions will always correspond to the inevitable, personality-caused behavior each of us is fated to exhibit. This concept of individual freedom is restrictive and ambiguous.(38)

But even with this questionable interpretation of freedom Schutz has not yet explained how we can understand social action, still performed by unique individuals, by applying generalized concepts. The because-motive must somehow become socialized, so that our subjective personalities can be replaced by a more general social force which will similarly affect everyone. To do this, Schutz turns once again to the concept of typification.

Projects and acts are based on our stocks of knowledge at hand when acting, including knowledge of experiences, previously performed, similar to the present project. We utilize these particular experiences to guide us in bringing about those consequences which were also experienced and now desired. Consequently,(39)

> all projecting involves a particular idealization, called by Husserl the idealization of 'I-can-do-it-again,' i.e. the assumption that I may under typically similar circumstances act in a way typically similar to that in which I acted before in order to bring about a typically similar state of affairs.

Every in-order-to motive presupposes a stock of experience characterized by an 'I-can-do-it-again' quality, or else there is no recognizable means of bringing about the desired future state. Though the repeated action will be different because our stocks of knowledge at hand have grown, nevertheless, in common-sense thinking the unique aspects of the two different acts are ignored and the similar ones emphasized. In the common-sense world, whenever we act, we use part of our pasts as models for leading us to expected goals.

If our intended projects are expected, and our actions take place in an intersubjective common-sense world, there must be some method for our predicting how alter egos will react to our initiatives. Such a method does, in fact, exist and is based on what Schutz calls 'the reciprocity of motives.'(40) Since we abstract from our pasts typical experiences to guide us in bringing about intended goals, and the Other is structurally similar to us in all ways, we can reasonably conclude everyone in society makes use of the 'I-can-do-it-again' idealization. This means all social interaction is based on the reciprocal expectation that the Other will behave in a predictable manner, just as he or she has under similar circumstances in the past. Our actions in a particular situation will bring about the same response the Other exhibited in a preceding similar situation. All our social behavior, then, is closely, inseparably, interconnected. We expect the Other to behave in a predictable way, and we determine our own actions according to this expectation. There is an interlocking of motives between ourselves and our fellow human beings: what we do will, under given circumstances, 'cause' them to behave in an expected manner. Social interaction in the common-sense world is based on the idealization that our in-order-to motives become the because-motives of those we are dealing with. All social interactions presuppose a series of common-sense constructs based on this idealization. If I ask you, 'Which way to the subway?' I am presupposing my desire to reach the subway, my in-order-to motive, will cause you to perform an action furnishing me this information. By your answer, 'Go one block and turn left,' you are presupposing your desire to tell me how to reach the subway, your in-order-to motive, will cause me to go in that direction, i.e. will become my because-motive. Though we are never sure of the Other's higher in-order-to motives (do I want the subway station so I can go uptown or so I can rob the teller?), the idealization of the reciprocity of motives allows us to meaningfully interact in the common-sense world.

The experiences comprising our stocks of knowledge at hand are organized, according to this idealization of the reciprocity of motives, into a system of ideal types. We assume if we act in ways typically similar to previous actions, under typically similar circumstances, we will bring about typically similar states of affairs. This implies we also ideally typify the course-of-action motives of those we interact with, since we assume these actors will be motivated to act in a typically predictable fashion. There results a system of ideal personal types ranging in character from the closeness and informality of the 'we-relationship' to the anonymity of our relationships with contemporaries, predecessors, and successors. But we have already seen that ideal typifications, both functional and personal, characterizing our stocks of knowledge at hand, are not individually constituted. They are prescribed by society, especially the 'in-group' sub-culture we are part of, and unquestioningly accepted by each of us in the everyday world. Our actions in this common-sense reality are based on our adopting ideal typifications enabling us to bring about states of affairs we find desirable. These socially prescribed and approved typifications are the basis for our in-order-to motives, in that, to continue the previous example, my desire to find the subway (my in-order-to motive) is based on my unquestioned acceptance of the social recipe prescribing the subway as a means of public transportation which will get me where I'm going. My in-order-to motive, in turn, becomes the because-motive of those with whom I interact, and causes them to freely choose an expected response, emerging as another in-order-to motive. This repeating process is the essential quality of the common-sense world. Since because-motives are synonymous with their corresponding preceding in-order-to motives, and both are derived from unquestioned socially prescribed ideal typifications, we have in these ideal types general, impersonal criteria for understanding and predicting individual action in society. The more standardized and institutionalized these ideal types become, in terms of law, rules, regulations, customs, habits, etc., the greater is the possibility our actions will bring about our desired states of affairs, and the easier it will be for an observer to understand and predict action related to these types.

This completes Schutz's philosophical anthropology of human beings in everyday life, a necessary prelude to his developing a specific sociological method. Though Schutz himself apparently came to realize social action in the common-sense world is not simply an interaction of because and in-order-to motives, his hesitating reflections on the subject deal more with the sociology of knowledge than with a methodology of social science.(41) In any case, these ideas are too vague and incomplete to seriously affect the analysis, the primary focus of which has been on describing Schutz's efforts at creating a philosophical rationale for the scientific explanation of free, subjectively meaningful social action. With this argument now established, it is relatively easy to outline the specific operational method Schutz proposes. Not surprisingly, this method is both a reflection and consequence of his underlying philosophical ideas.

5 A SOCIOLOGICAL METHOD

Schutz has thus far talked exclusively of the common-sense world of everyday existence, but it is glaringly apparent to us all that we do not always operate in a pre-reflective sphere of consciousness. There are times we submit either ourselves or perceived objects to careful scrutiny in order to uncover facts not observed quickly or easily. This procedure does not take place in the common-sense world because it requires our abandoning the non-questioning, pre-reflective attitude. It is, in other words, impossible for Schutz to develop a scientific method for explaining social behavior without somehow replacing the natural attitude with a mode of consciousness more amenable to reflective intellectual effort. He recognizes this in admitting the world we normally experience can be articulated into 'multiple realities,' different ways of perceiving corresponding to different levels of consciousness. Each reality, or 'finite province of meaning,' attains the status of an unquestioned, real world simply by a conscious act to do so. Schutz finds it necessary to begin re-defining the reality of the common-sense world, what he now calls the 'paramount reality.'(42)

Our in-order-to motives, we have seen, take place within a higher order system, the life-plan. We all have definite long-term goals we intend on realizing by means of the specific projects that compromise our everyday activities. We do this because, within the paramount reality of daily life, all individuals experience a 'fundamental anxiety': I know I shall die, and I fear death.(43) From this vivid experience of our own mortality springs the realization that all our hopes and expectations must be actively pursued in the world by means of our projects and actions. With human life so brief, it is imperative we give it personal meaning by attempting to master the world in our own interests. The paramount reality is founded on this implicit grasping of one's own mortality and the explicit commitment to realize oneself in the world through action. We express this commitment to action in our respective life-plans.

The paramount reality is therefore a world of working, one characterized by our bodily movement and our manipulating objects and things in order to realize specific projects. It is a world in which we succeed or fail in achieving these projects and share this success or failure with others who are doing the same. Within this reality, where we give our full attention to life and its requirements, we are constantly experiencing severe tension. Consequently, our states of consciousness within the paramount reality are characterized by their alertness and 'wide-awakedness.' We must always remain aware of what goes on around us, for only with a continually changing and relevant strategy can we hope to successfully work our life-plans in the world.

We remain within the paramount reality, the common-sense world of our pre-reflective, everyday lives, for as long as we choose to cognitively perceive the world in this way. 'As long as our experiences of this world - the valid as well as the invalid ones - partake of this cognitive style we may consider this province of meaning as real, we may bestow upon it the accent of reality.'(44) Periodically, however, we submit ourselves to a 'subjective experience of shock,' a radical modification in the tension and attention of consciousness by means of which we escape the paramount reality and enter a new province of meaning.(45) By altering the cognitive style of our consciousness we not only perceive the world differently, but also unquestioningly accept a new reality removed from the common-sense world we formerly experienced. There are many examples of shocking experiences that shift the accent of reality from the common-sense world to other finite provinces of meaning: the shock of falling asleep removes us from the paramount reality into the reality of dreams; the shock of empathy removes us into the reality of the stage-play; the shock of an aesthetic experience removes us to the world of art; the shock of a mental illness could remove us to the world of insanity. Each of these new finite provinces of meaning, as well as any other we might experience, has its own particular cognitive style which organizes and co-ordinates all possible experiences.(46) Cognitive styles are situated somewhere within the polar extremes of the paramount reality (where consciousness is fully alert and tense) and the reality of dreams (where consciousness is totally passive and relaxed).

Husserl felt our worldly experiences are epistemologically validated only by means of a systematic purification of consciousness, the phenomenological reductions. The most important element in this process is the epoché, suspending our belief in the reality of the world and everything in it in order to uncover that kernel of scientific or universal knowledge embedded in pure experience. Schutz adopts the epoché as the key to developing a method of scientifically understanding the social world. Everyone, in the paramount reality, makes unquestioned use of the epoché in suspending all doubt of the world, its objects, and other living beings, never questioning that the world we perceive might not be, or might be different than it appears. This is 'the epoché of the natural attitude.'(47) Since it is only by performing the epoché that we achieve scientific certainty, Schutz intends to practice an epoché on 'the epoché of the natural attitude.' By phenomenologically investigating the common-sense world, performing an epoché on the constitutive theses of the life-world itself, we are able to scientifically understand social behavior. But such an analysis is not performed from within the paramount reality, for it requires systematically doubting everything the cognitive style of the paramount reality unquestioningly accepts. Science is a province of meaning attainable by any one willing to divorce himself from the common-sense world. It is, in this sense, a level of consciousness, though one differing in important respects from that of the paramount reality.

All theoretical cogitations, including those of science, are types of actions, because they are spontaneous behavior carried out and performed according to a project. Consequently, scientific theory has in-order-to and because-motives and is one element of a hierarchy of life-plans. It is, furthermore, purposive, because it intends to find a solution for a specific problem. However, the similarity between the worlds of common-sense and science ends here: 'Scientific theorizing . . . does not serve any practical purpose. Its aim is not to master the world but to observe and possibly to understand it.'(48) The theoretical cogitations of science are not part of the working world because scientists are interested only in obtaining knowledge, not in actively expressing themselves as committed subjects. They are involved in the observed situation with only a cognitive interest, totally avoiding feelings of personal attachment. Scientists contemplate the common-sense world, they don't act in it, even though contemplation itself is a form of action.

Scientists must detach themselves from their biographical situations within the social world and abandon those project-oriented systems of relevances prevailing in the natural attitude. The positions or statuses they occupy in society are irrelevant to their scientific undertaking. Whereas the stocks of knowledge at hand of social actors consist of culturally determined typifications, that of scientists consists only of the corpus of their particular science, including accepted scientific procedure. Within the world of science actors 'put in brackets' their own physical existences, and thereby ignore the system of spatial orientation characterizing the common-sense world: scientists have no 'here' within the social world, and do not layer that world around themselves. Furthermore, objects of scientific contemplation exist only within objective time, the durée being similarly bracketed. Only the current project at hand defines the present; previous information relevant to this project constitutes the past, while the anticipated outcome defines the future. We relate to others in the scientific world only through our projects, with no possibility of achieving the spatial and temporal interaction native to the we-relationship.

'The theorizing self is solitary; it has no social environment; it stands outside social relationships.'(49)

Finally, scientists must free themselves from the fundamental anxiety governing the hopes, fears, and aspirations of people in the natural attitude. With space and time defined in objective, disinterested terms, there is no fear of death and no attempt at subjectively defining oneself through commitment to a life-plan, nor is behavior any longer motivated by a desire to advance subjectively meaningful, personal goals. By transposing themselves into the disinterested attitude, scientists have likewise detached themselves from that state of wide-awakedness experienced in the common-sense world. The strategy for a successful life, which in the common-sense world stressed the constant, attentive, tense search for practical solutions to personal problems, is more measured and systematic in the reality of science. Instead of being self-centered, the scientist 'is interested in problems and solutions valid in their own right for everyone, at any place, and at any time, wherever and whenever certain conditions, from the assumption of which he starts, prevail.'(50)

Within this world of scientific contemplation, actors choose their systems of relevances according to the problems they are concerned with, and accept these problems as their primary projects. Though the precise level of study and the selection of the particular problem may be decisions rooted in actors' personalities, once embarked on the actual enterprise they function disinterestedly, in a correct scientific manner prescribed by the logic of science and the methodology of the relevant branch of study. At a minimum, the results of scientific endeavors must satisfy three conditions: they must be consistent and compatible with other scientific propositions and with the common-sense world; they must be derived from immediate experiences of actual, worldly facts; they must be clear and concise.(51) How is this last condition met if the scientific reality is an isolated one, where meaningful interaction between the self and others is impossible? How, in other words, do we communicate the results of our scientific research to other scientists? Finite provinces of meaning are merely categories for the differing tensions of a constant, enduring consciousness. Though all actions are unique to the respective provinces where they are experienced, we can communicate results of these actions to those in a different sphere of reality. Of all possible finite provinces of meaning only within the paramount reality do people meaningfully interact; it alone serves as a common denominator through which we communicate results of our scientific observations. By using our everyday language to symbolically represent these observations, we integrate scientific knowledge with the social stock of knowledge unquestioningly accepted in the common-sense world. The results of our experiences in all other provinces of meaning (for example, our dreams) are similarly communicated by our using ordinary everyday language.(52)

Scientists, then, utilize common language to communicate scientific facts to the social world. But what distinguishes a scientific fact from a social fact? All thinking, regardless of the finite province of meaning it takes place in, involves intellectual constructs: in the common-sense world we depend on our stocks of knowledge at hand, consisting of socially engineered generalizations; in the world of science we depend on the appropriate scientific method and the corpus of previous scientific knowledge. There are no 'facts' existing isolated and objective, apart from conscious human life. Facts are experienced by a thought process which excludes and admits elements from the universe according to implicit, preconceived criteria. All facts are therefore interpreted facts because they are detached from the universe through subjective mental processes. In the common-sense world, facts consist of those elements of the universe we perceive as relevant to our lives, as expressed in our past experiences, our present actions, and our goals for the future. Scientific facts, on the other hand, are only those phenomena perceived as relevant to, and consistent with, the accepted rules of disinterested, objective thinking known as scientific method. A scientific fact differs from a social fact in that it is abstracted from the world by means of intellectual constructs which are intersubjectively defined and accepted and are devoid of any unique, subjective motivations.

It is relatively easy for natural scientists to communicate natural scientific facts, for they are just that, facts, totally apart from all subjective implications other than their occurring within their field and method of observation. Social scientists have a more difficult task. They must recognize that social scientific facts are part of a structured world consisting of living human beings who think and act according to their own particular subjective points of view. Each 'fact' social scientists discover means something to those participating in or comprising it, for all social action depends on ideal constructs which are subjectively interpreted. The problem lies in devising a way of describing such subjectively meaningful action factually, i.e. relating them to the impersonal, explicitly non-subjective constructs of science. Schutz feels this can be accomplished by having social scientists define their method, a principle component of the ideal construct determining the quality of social scientific facts, in direct relation to the way social actors define their worlds in the natural attitude.(53) By so-doing they are creating a series of second-order constructs modeled after the first-order ideal constructs social actors themselves use in defining the world and guiding their own actions in it. The objective, scientific context of meaning these second-order constructs represent refers directly to the subjective meaning contexts exhibited in the socially derived typifications comprising our stocks of knowledge.

These second-order constructs appear in the guise of artificially recreated ideal types which, because they are constructed and programmed as though they could perform working actions and reactions, are analogous to puppets. In reflecting first-order constructs, the derivative, puppet-like ideal types reveal actual subjective meanings actors experience in their social relationships. Since the social world is defined and given meaning by actors in the natural attitude according to the generalized typifications inherent in society, it is necessary that social scientists, in constructing ideal types, utilize knowledge of typically similar patterns of interaction occurring in typically similar situational settings characterizing the common-sense world they are investigating.(54) The ideal types are, in effect, models of rational action for any typical actor in the common-sense world.(55) Schutz means by 'rational action' all action taking place within the framework of unquestioned type-constructs involving setting, motives, means and ends, courses of action and personalities. He equates the process of progressive typification with the rationalization of society.(56) In the common-sense world actors behave rationally by analyzing their states of affairs, contemplating the best possible projects for their future well-beings, and deciding the most efficient means of attaining these projects - always guided by an unquestioned set of socially generated, relevant typifications. Social scientists abstract from society and recreate only one such rational behavior pattern for each constructed ideal model by developing a scheme of reference limiting the behavioral scope within which available information is considered relevant. Such a scheme, for example, may refer only to mailmen, in which case only information relevant to understanding the typical behavior of a typical mailman under certain typical circumstances is included in the model. This important procedure of limiting the scope of relevant information, based on what Schutz calls 'the principle of relevance,' is fundamental to constructing workable ideal models.(57)

Social science, in sum, is concerned primarily with rational action, and aims at constructing relevant models or ideal types. Schutz names these models 'homunculi,' and means by this designation that each is an artificially recreated typical behavior pattern, of a typical actor relevant to the purpose of our inquiry, in similarly relevant typical circumstances.(58) Our synthetic construction of homunculi is an idealization of those typifications and self-typifications practiced in everyday life, and the homunculi themselves will interact with each other in the same way actors interact in the common-sense world. Among the homunculi, the theses of reciprocal perspectives and corresponding, interlocking motives operate just as they do among real actors in society. However, whereas in society people interact in this manner because they unquestioningly accept socially dictated rules, the homunculi exhibit such behavior only because social scientists have determined they should, based on their observations of typical social actors. Each homunculus, therefore,(59)

> does not assume a role other than that attributed to him by the director of the puppet show . . .. It is he, the social scientist, who sets the stage, who distributes the roles, who gives the cues, who defines when an 'action' starts and when it ends and who determines, thus, the 'span of projects' involved. All standards and institutions governing the behavioral pattern of the model are supplied from the outset by the constructs of the scientific observer.

All the difficulties facing a real actor in the common-sense world are eliminated: for humunculi, rational acts, choices, and motives are assured.

There are three principles or postulates to be followed in constructing useful homunculi:(60) 'the postulate of logical consistency' implies, simply, that the model makes sense to those in the scientific community who will use it; 'the postulate of subjective interpretation' requires the model to explain the meaning an observed action had for the actor; and 'the postulate of adequacy' prescribes the model to explain how, if the act were performed in real life according to the construct, it would be understood by the actor and those with whom he or she interacts. If social scientists fulfill the criteria of these three postulates, we can be sure they will construct epistemologically valid models of rational behavior patterns. This is what Schutz means when, in referring to a valid and useful homunculus, he states:(61)

> an actor in the life world would perform the typified action if he had a perfectly clear and distinct knowledge of all the elements, and only of the elements, assumed by the social scientist as being relevant to this action and the constant tendency to use the most appropriate means assumed to be at his disposal for achieving the ends defined by the construct itself.

If the three postulates are carefully followed, each step involved in constructing ideal models can be verified by empirical observation, provided we mean by this not only the recording of sensory perceptions of objects and events but also the 'experiential forms by which common-sense thinking in everyday life understands human actions and their outcome in terms of their underlying motives and goals.'(62)

Constructing homunculi constitutes the vital core of Schutz's method, though actual working procedure is a little more complicated.(63) Social scientists first observe selectively chosen interactions of the social world and begin establishing course of action patterns for use in typifying the action. They co-ordinate with these patterns a personal type, or model, of an actor gifted with a consciousness restricted to those elements relevant to the observed course of action pattern. To this fictitious consciousness social scientists attach typical in-order-to motives (corresponding to the apparent goals of the observed course of action patterns) and because-motives (based on relevant preceding actions that prompted the observed actor to behave in this way). Both types of motives are assumed invariant and entirely determining in the imaginary actor-model. Observers then bestow on the model such segments of life-plans and stocks of experiences as appear necessary for making the imaginary horizons and backgrounds of the homunculus consistent with the observed action. With this accomplished, they associate the fictional actor with other similarly constructed personal ideal types exhibiting motives evoking typical reactions to the first model's typical act. All constructed models are then inserted into a setting which includes only those elements relevant for performing the observed typical act. What emerges from all this is an empirically verified scientific model for explaining specific social actions, and, within certain vaguely defined limits discussed in the following chapter, predicting future actions of individuals in society.

Schutz's method, like Weber's, is intended to scientifically explain social action in terms of the meaning this action has for involved actors. Weber employs the concept of 'Verstehen' to operationalize this intention. Schutz accepts the notion of interpretative understanding in principle, but criticizes Weber's weak analysis of foundational terms such as 'meaning,' and 'action.' Without an explicit and systematic theory of subjectivity, 'Verstehen,' as a method of understanding society, remains an unrealized goal. We are now prepared to analyze exactly how Schutz has modified 'Verstehen' to satisfy his phenomenological epistemology. There are, embedded in his arguments, three different meanings for 'Verstehen,' each corresponding to a different analytical level.(64) First, and primary for the rest of his theory, is the meaning of 'Verstehen' defined 'as an epistemological problem.' Schutz here refers to those fundamental issues of philosophy dealing with the nature of valid knowledge and conditions necessary for its constitution. Before we can understand anything or anybody there must exist philosophical criteria for judging what is true and building a reliable body of knowledge. In this context, Schutz accepts as valid the philosophical ideas expressed in Husserl's phenomenology. Next, there is the meaning of 'Verstehen' as it relates to our 'experiential form of common-sense knowledge of human affairs.' How do we orient ourselves in society so that we 'understand' and effectively participate in it? The answer to this question, the meaning of 'Verstehen' when used in this sense, is given in Schutz's philosophical anthropology of the life-world. Finally, 'Verstehen' also connotes 'a method peculiar to the social sciences.' Social scientists must somehow assimilate subjective interpretations of social acts into an empirical, scientific context of meaning. Schutz describes how this is done in his sociological method. Obviously, the last two meanings of 'Verstehen,' Schutz's philosophical anthropology and sociological method, are totally dependent on Husserl's epistemology, the phenomenological understanding of valid knowledge. An actor's understanding of the common-sense world, as well as a scientist's understanding of society, are both founded on a phenomenological assumption that knowledge reveals itself in the consciousness of unique, meaning-endowing subjects. Weber's failure to distinguish the three meanings of 'Verstehen' is predictable given his non-phenomenological - non-existent - epistemology.

SUMMARY AND CONCLUSIONS

This chapter has described the major components of Alfred Schutz's social theory. Schutz is concerned with a problem that dominated the efforts of Germany's major scholars from Dilthey to Weber: how can we scientifically understand the social interaction of free, creative actors. By utilizing Husserl's phenomenology as an intellectual framework for re-structuring Weber's interpretative sociology, Schutz feels he has solved this problem.

1 Schutz deals primarily with the naive, unquestioning mode of consciousness characterizing people in the common-sense world. His major premise is that subjectively meaningful action is shaped by an unquestioned acceptance of socially derived and approved 'recipes,' prescribing typical behavior used in typical circumstances. The validity of this premise is assumed, not proven, in Schutz's description and analysis of culture, intersubjectivity, and social interaction.

2 Schutz must confront the ambiguous quality of our subjective, yet socially determined, action when he analyzes the isolated social actor. The explanation emerges in his identifying our freely arrived at in-order-to motives, or projects, with our because, or causal, motives, related to relevant preceding action. Put simply, my project is caused by your project, which was caused by his project, and so on . . . .. The connecting link in this process is the system of socially derived typifications, which maintain a precarious position as existing independent of social actors, but also, through our naively accepted stocks of knowledge at hand, are identically experienced by everyone.

3 Schutz's sociological method is derived from these arguments. The potential existence of various provinces of meaning, or modes of consciousness, permits us to consciously abandon the natural attitude for the more dispassionate, non-involving world of science. As scientists, we duplicate first order constructs - which, in the form of actors' stocks of knowledge at hand, shape their actions in the common-sense world - in second-order ideal constructs removed from the world of action and therefore more objective. These emerge as artificially created and programmed models, called homunculi, that

accurately reflect observed rational behavior patterns occurring in society. The models enable scientists to understand and predict rational social action.

There is little doubt Schutz has included in his methodology that dimension of subjectivity he found lacking in Weber's. However, he has, in the process, added to his burden: an explicit interpretation of subjectivity must be explicitly adhered to and defended, there is no curtain of ambiguity to hide behind. When confronted with the rigorous demands of empirical scientific logic, any concessions in the case for subjectivity will be very noticeable. Consequently, whereas Weber's ideas appear vague, it is more likely Schutz's will be viewed in more extreme terms. The next chapter examines this methodology to determine which seem most applicable.

3 Phenomenology, free action, empirical social science: some theoretical and practical problems

1 THE TENSIONS WITHIN SCHUTZ'S PHILOSOPHICAL ANTHROPOLOGY

A phenomenological approach to social science maintains, as one theorist sees it,(1)

> that what is needed above all is a way of looking at social phenomena which takes into primary account the intentional structure of human consciousness, and which accordingly places major emphasis on the meaning social acts have for the actors who perform them and who live in a reality built out of their subjective interpretation.

Alfred Schutz's social theory is oriented towards developing a scientific method which meets these criteria. Like Weber, Schutz realizes the social sciences are interpretative, analyzing the actual meanings actors experience when acting. Schutz builds his interpretative sociology on the more basic epistemological principles contained in Husserl's phenomenology. Since a subject's constitution of worldly objects, at least initially,(2) is a function of experience, social scientific method deals exclusively with the experiences of individual actors interacting in society. These are unalterably subjective, results of actors' defining all worldly objects and events according to their own perceptions. For both Husserl and Schutz, therefore, individual action is free, in that it is self-determined. In defining subjective experience as a filter through which the world reveals itself to us, it is impossible to even conceive an extra-personal variable determining meaningful behavior apart from our subjective interpretation of it. We all act at our own initiatives, according to our own definitions of the world, and in the context of our own visions of the future, for there is no valid knowledge existing independent of perceiving, thinking subjects. Were this not so, phenomenology would be devoid of substance and logical consistency. Schutz's primary problem, as we have hinted, is to develop a method honoring the subjective status of reliable knowledge but, simultaneously, analyzing society in objective terms. The substance and logical consistency of Schutz's argument likewise depends on his having not sacrificed either of these two aims.

Schutz himself succinctly sums up his task in asking, 'How is it, then, possible to grasp by a system of objective knowledge subjective meaning structures? Is this not a paradox?'(3) His answers have, for the most part, already been described. The thought-objects created by social scientists in the homunculi do not refer to free actors' subjectively meaningful acts occurring within the context of specific, biographically-determined environments. These actions are understandable only when observer and actor share a we-relationship, enabling each to experience the other as a unique subject. Social science, however, is knowledge of contemporaries and predecessors, never referring to personal or face-to-face relationships. It replaces first-order thought-objects of actors in the common-sense world with a constructed model of a specified, limited sector of the social world, containing typical rational action patterns for certain types of actors. These artificial models, the objective meaning contexts of our scientific analysis, reflect actual subjective meanings experienced by typical actors behaving rationally under specified, typical circumstances. The self-determining quality of individual action is apparently preserved by these scientific models: in being meaningfully adequate they reflect subjective experiences of typically rational actors, and in no way hinder their freedom by, for example, substituting impersonal determining variables for subjective initiative.

But meaning adequacy alone is not sufficient to qualify the ideal constructs as scientifically valid explanations. For this, the homunculi must also be causally adequate: they must describe, in addition to subjective meanings experienced by actors, the impersonal patterns of events within which the act systematically occurs.(4) Each homunculus, consisting of abstract, rational action patterns not directly related to any one, concrete individual, nevertheless is modeled after the action free individuals do exhibit in the common-sense world. While the model is not a person, the described action is the self-determined result of meaning-endowing individuals perceiving their world and acting in it. Schutz's contention that homunculi are also causally adequate implies that in spite of their being derived from the action of free, self-determining actors, when used to scientifically explain this action they elicit data acceptable as causal proof. The homunculi, in other words, are causal explanations of the behavior they express.

But how is action which is self-determined also caused by rational action patterns contained in a relevant homunculus? Perhaps the answer lies in the way we define 'causality':(5)

> When we formulate judgments of causal adequacy in the social sciences, what we are really talking about is not causal necessity in the strict sense but the so-called 'causality of freedom' . . .. A type construct is causally adequate then, if it is probable that, according to the rules of experience, an act will be performed . . . in a manner corresponding to the construct.

Schutz now distinguishes between what he calls the 'causality of freedom' and 'causal necessity in the strict sense,' with only the former relevant to his analysis. Yet this 'causality of freedom' is too vague and questionable a notion to be considered seriously in its present form. Any observed act for which we construct a model is likely, sooner or later, to re-occur. This is not necessarily caused by, or even related to, action patterns described in the model: the new act may just be coincidentally related to the old one, or, perhaps, it is a causal result of action patterns totally different from those we considered. Schutz apparently intends, in developing this notion of the 'causality of freedom,' to integrate seemingly opposing theses of 'freedom' and 'causality' into one, logically viable concept. Obviously, he must now modify his definition if it is to have any theoretical or practical meaning for social scientists.

Schutz, in fact, quickly supplements his previous interpretation of causality:(6)

> If I am going to construct a personal ideal type in a scientifically correct manner, it is not enough that the action in question probably take place. Rather, what is required in addition to this is that the action be repeatable and that the postulate of its repeatability not be inconsistent with the whole body of our scientific knowledge . . .. A construct is appropriate and to be recommended only if it derives from acts that are not isolated but have a

certain probability of repetition or frequency. In order for an homunculus to be causally adequate the described act is not only performed again, but, more importantly, the ideal action pattern should guarantee the same act reappears with 'a certain probability of repetition or frequency.' The regularity and frequency with which the described act re-occurs in society, confirmed by empirical observation, validates the construct's causal adequacy. Causality, as Schutz uses it here, is an empirical, not a logical, concept. There is no necessary or 'a priori' relationship between a cause and its effect, only the generalization, based on our observation of the social world, that one act regularly and frequently follows another.

This revised formulation of the 'causality of freedom' is, in certain respects, much more informative and useful than the earlier one. In particular, social scientists are provided with explicit criteria for creating causally adequate homunculi and applying them as scientific explanations of social action. However, in refining the concept of causality Schutz also assumes the concomitant responsibility of reconciling it to the idea of individual freedom implicit in any phenomenological analysis. If action is free, in its being determined solely by actors themselves, how does Schutz explain the constantly re-occurring patterns of behavior evident in society, the subject matter of causal analysis? On what basis does Schutz causally analyze social action and simultaneously maintain we still act freely? Are we all free, but only to a degree consistent with the 'probability of repetition'? Or, rather, do we all coincidentally choose to act according to a pre-existing pattern of expected behavior? Since action is self-determined, Schutz must explain how and why it manifests itself in impersonal, repeating patterns.

This was a key problem plaguing Schutz's whole social theory. Throughout his analysis of culture, intersubjectivity, and society, Schutz assumes free individuals voluntarily accept the social recipes that are part of society and appear in their stocks of knowledge at hand. People in the common-sense world, as Schutz sees it, unquestioningly accept and obey rational action patterns characterizing the surrounding social environment, but, at the same time, do so freely, always determining for themselves what they accept and obey. This is the hub of his argument: we can validly understand free action by subsuming it under general, impersonal concepts that introduce an element of objectivity into our analysis. It is easy enough to accept this conclusion, as Weber did, and develop a scientific method based on the ideal type concept. Schutz, however, is under an added burden of having to reconcile his acceptance, and his corresponding method, to an explicit, undeniable vision of subjective freedom that is the epistemological foundation for all his ideas. Weber is unaware of such abstract, philosophical premises, and was justifiably criticized. Schutz's efforts are now judged by how well he accomplishes the goal both he and Weber share, but he must do this by diligently adhering to the principles he defends in rejecting Weber's own contributions.

Unfortunately, this explanation is not forthcoming. When Schutz can no longer ignore the issue, when he is face to face with the individual as an isolated unit who must choose his or her course of action, here: he solves the problem by simply defining it out of existence. We choose our projects by referring to our stocks of knowledge at hand, consisting of socially derived and approved typifications. This much appears self-evident, given the fact we do exist within a social world not of our own making. The important question concerns what role these typifications play in our choice. If we are all free because we determine our own actions, then the typifications appear as constituent elements of our backgrounds, of concern to us during our subjective decision-making processes. The eventual action is determined by the free actor, functioning as a subject in the context of those surrounding social forces. The social world, including idealizations engineered in it, appear to us through the filter of our own subjectivities. Although we don't ignore this world, our subjective perceptions allow us to respond in our own ways. There can be no determining relationships between our actions and socially engineered typifications, for our subjectivities first mediate the two. Alternatively, if socially derived typifications do determine our behavior, then there is little more than hypocrisy in contending we are free, self-determining, meaning-endowing actors. Our behavior, in this case, is the determined result of variables existing independent of us, and the problem of reconciling freedom and science is eliminated. How does Schutz chose between these two divergent alternatives? He doesn't. Instead, the action we freely choose to perform is identical to the behavior we would exhibit if this were impersonally determined by social typifications. My project is both the freely chosen goal of my in-order-to motive and the determined result of my because-motive. Since the latter is identical to the in-order-to motive of the person I am responding to, and this person chose to obey the social typifications that are part of his or her stock of knowledge at hand, I am, in a sense, 'forced' to 'choose' a project consistent with these typifications. In the common-sense world I am free only to obey. But since freedom is defined as the actualization of a pre-existing, pre-determining motive, this is all I will ever choose to do anyway.

Schutz's analysis is not meant to 'prove' his case. On the contrary, it is based on a two-fold assumption that all observable social action is free action, and all free action is consistent with socially engineered rational action patterns. When describing the interlocking of actors' motives, Schutz ignores logical problems concerning the relationship of freedom to science we have just outlined. There is absolutely no reason for identifying succeeding because- and in-order-to motives other than as a rationale for the two assumptions. Can we really conclude our free, subjectively determined projects are always identical to objectively determined courses of behavior, without the prior assumption that observed social patterns are freely chosen? The converse, in fact, appears more plausible: based on what we observe, social behavior is apparently caused by factors independent of the subject. Schutz's task is painfully evident, to actively demonstrate how our senses are deceiving us into minimizing the role of subjectivity in influencing social behavior. This, given his phenomenological bias, is accomplished only by explaining how the concept of freedom inherent in his epistemology is reconciled to the apparent uniformity of behavior empirically confronting us. What we get, instead, is a redefinition of freedom tailored to eliminate even the need for this explanation. If subjective and objective necessity coincide, they don't have to be reconciled. The reason for this coincidence is that socially (i.e. objectively) determined action patterns are adhered to by free actors. We choose, by and for ourselves, to act as these patterns prescribe, even though they have been imposed by society. Why do we freely choose to do this? Because by 'freedom' we mean the coincidence of subjective and objective necessity. Schutz's entire social theory is founded on a phenomenological world-view: with cognitive experience the ultimate criteria of knowledge, actors define the world themselves, and choose projects accordingly. Thus, in trying to explain how patterned social behavior is also free action, Schutz already assumes all social behavior is self-determined. By assuming what he is attempting to prove, it is easy for Schutz to avoid those arguments which question the assumption itself by doubting whether behavior determined by social forces is also self-determined. The re-formulation of freedom is perfectly acceptable provided we adopt this underlying assumption. We purchase this acceptance, however, at an extremely high price, for it appears to contradict empirical evidence, and, in any case, leads us to a definition of freedom so broad as to include behavior determined by factors originating outside the actor.

Schutz's unique doctrine of freedom applies to all actors carrying out their goals in the common-sense world. He uses this world as the sugar-coating for a presentation which, if this analysis is correct, has failed to even consider relevant and vital issues. People in the common-sense world are characterized by a mode of consciousness unquestioningly accepting, or taking for granted, everything it perceives. Schutz uses this naive attitude as a connecting link between the two antagonistic elements in his definition of freedom. By never questioning socially derived idealizations we are confronted with in our daily routines, we, as actors, assimilate them into our stocks of knowledge at hand and naively obey them in choosing our projects. This unquestioning, voluntary acceptance of idealizations originating in society, independent of the actor, guarantees the continual correspondence of subjective and objective necessity.

The actual nature and extent of our freedom in the common-sense world is difficult to comprehend. If Schutz means that conscious, willing action is, in fact, determined by social recipes because we unquestioningly (blindly?) accept the life-world, then in what sense is free action actually initiated and controlled by a willing actor? Our abilities to freely choose a project in the common-sense world are illusions, for, as Schutz himself implies, we could not do otherwise than what is expected of us. This is certainly a strange notion of freedom not only limiting what we are socially able to do but actually prescribing the one course of behavior we must voluntarily choose. Freedom, when defined in this manner, cannot be distinguished from its opposite, and surfaces as a meaningless concept of little practical importance. If individuals are free and action is subjectively meaningful, then social institutions and culture - analytically distinct phenomena into which conscious actors are thrown - cannot shape or mold them in some vaguely objective sense. When one adopts a phenomenological approach to social science, as Schutz has, he cannot, simultaneously, analyze culture and society as objective phenomena having a determining influence on human action. That Schutz has done this remains, with one exception, unnoticed by his commentators.(7) In a broader sense, Schutz's entire theory is flawed by his uncritical acceptance of Husserl's ideas on the 'Lebenswelt,' and their relationship to a phenomenological interpretation of human nature. Molina has commented:(8)

> Further thought will serve to show that these may in fact be potentially antagonistic themes; for we have as a starting point of departure an ultimately non-critical commitment to the fact of the reality of the world, while at the same time we have a commitment to the fact of the absoluteness of consciousness and to a decided relativity of the world vis-a-vis the fact of this consciousness.

These antagonistic themes are vividly, though unintentionally, illustrated in Schutz's analysis of individual freedom.

So freedom in the common-sense world is a totally engrossing, totally de-personalizing submission of willful individuals to those socially derived and approved idealizations prescribing expected, 'correct' attitudes and behavior. Whether or not this is a logically valid construction, the fact remains Schutz formulates his sociological method to scientifically explain all social interaction included under its rubric. Though Schutz's definition of freedom is ambiguous, by focusing our attention on that part of the social world he is, in fact, referring to, we can perhaps clarify what he means. To fully delineate the precise locus and nature of this world, it is necessary we supplement Schutz's treatment of the common-sense world with a presentation more relevant to our actual daily experiences. As Gurwitsch and Natanson have astutely recognized, Schutz's conception of people in the common-sense world closely resembles Heidegger's interpretation of the anonymity of 'das Man.'(9) A brief description of this theory will not only clarify our understanding of Schutz, but also unearth some hidden premises contributing to Schutz's strained expositing of free action.

2 THE IMPERSONAL WORLD OF 'DAS MAN'

Heidegger's analysis of 'das Man' relates to the same everyday world of daily routines concerning Schutz. However, whereas Schutz describes the mode of consciousness characterizing the common-sense world as practical and necessary for social interaction, Heidegger sees it as the most obvious expression of our alienation from ourselves and the world. A crucial difference, then, between these two presentations is Heidegger's presupposing, in theory at least, the possibility that meaningful social interaction can take place even when actors somehow remove themselves from the natural attitude. The idea of perfectability, the belief there is a better way for each actor in the everyday world to communicate with society, is implicit in Heidegger's analysis. It allows him to circumvent many of the dilemmas endemic to Schutz's philosophical anthropology.

Heidegger's life-long efforts are devoted primarily to uncovering the essential nature of being ('Sein'), that underlying, taken for granted quality without which the being ('Seiendes') we experience as particular human beings is impossible. His ontology, expressed in 'Being and Time,'(10) attempts to describe how being is manifested in the essential character of man ('Dasein'). Because being reveals itself only to human beings, Heidegger's ontology means to awaken humanity to the indisputable truth of being and the possibility individuals have of exhibiting this truth in and through their own existences, ultimately achieving their utmost potentials of actually living the truth of their beings, what Heidegger calls 'ecsistance,' or authentic existence. Only when we stand in the enlightenment ('Lichtung') of this fundamental quality of being are our actual existences truly authentic to the beings that we are.(11)

Maintaining an authentic existence requires the constant effort on our parts of continually recognizing our beings, and living accordingly. Unfortunately this often proves too trying for those of us looking for an easy, simple way of going through life that will provide many paths of escape from the whole burden of our existential responsibilities. When we go out of ourselves, submerging ourselves in entities and ignoring the ontological aspects of being exhibited in 'ecsistance,' we enter the realm of 'existence,' where our lives are tainted by inauthenticity. Inauthentic life reveals itself when we forget our 'ecsistance' is a reflection of being, and instead concentrate on those external objects and things of only superficial, or ontic, significance. The profound life-experience of recognizing the actual quality of their beings is sacrificed by inauthentic individuals to the ephemeral, constantly changing joys and pleasures of the external world.(12) This world of inauthentic existence is recognizable in Schutz's description of common-sense reality. The naive, unquestioning attitude that concerns Schutz is analogous to our total, inauthentic absorption in external phenomena. In both, our mode of consciousness is focused entirely and uncritically on the external, or social, world, where the quality of subjectivity is impersonal and pre-determined. It is not surprising that even the terminology Schutz and Heidegger use is similar. Schutz emphasizes phrases such as 'common-sense world,' and 'everyday life' to describe the mode of consciousness he is interested in; Heidegger chooses 'average everydayness' to describe us in our inauthentic states.(13) These all refer to the same phenomena: Heidegger's inauthentic actor is known to Schutz as an individual living and working in the common-sense world.

Our 'fall' ('Absturz') into inauthenticity does not mean we totally, irretrievably, lose our beings in the process. Just as Schutz's conception of multiple realities allows us, in our on-going lives, to experience many different modes of consciousness, so Heidegger implies in his theory of inauthenticity that this type of existence is also just one possibility we choose to live. In fact, in choosing to lead an inauthentic existence we actually confirm our own beings, the peculiar quality of this choice hiding from us the very being it confirms.(14) Consequently, the amount of time we live inauthentically does not affect our 'humanity,' or our status as human beings existing in the world. For both Schutz and Heidegger, all individuals who act in the world, no matter the mode of consciousness they choose to experience, are thinking, choosing human beings affirming their own humanity even in their denying it.

Our fall into inauthenticity is marked by a turning away from being and a turning towards objects and things of the external world, the ontological recognition of being replaced by a concern for worldly superficialities. By ignoring being, we begin to objectify ourselves and others, and soon those external objects and things we orient ourselves towards begin to resemble the objectified human beings we interact with. Eventually, we inauthentically treat all individuals as if they were like inert implements, and, in turn, begin to experience ourselves similarly. By losing ourselves in experienced objects and things we deny not only our humanity but that of others as well, and the whole world, including ourselves and others, is perceived as consisting solely of lifeless tools manipulated for our own inauthentic, material purposes. The human condition, in this state, is analogous to that of a beast.

In objectifying humanity, our own and others, we deny our existences as thinking, choosing subjects capable of forging unique life-experiences. Objectified individuals are not capable of freely choosing courses of action because they are unable to go 'beyond' themselves in search of alternative possibilities, dynamically synthesizing the experienced world with their ontological potentialities. In becoming inauthentic we therefore forfeit our freedom and accept the guidance and control of those social forces signified by the impersonal pronoun 'one' or 'people,' which in German is 'das Man.' While, as inauthentic actors, we try to live our lives independent of others, in reality we are in a docile state of subservience, allowing 'people,' 'das Man,' to determine all behavioral, emotional, and intellectual aspects of our lives. We internalize 'das Man,' and in so-doing reject our personal responsibilities to life, assuming instead a mode of existence Heidegger calls decadence ('Verfallensein'). In society, our inauthentic lives reflect the rule of 'das Man' by appearing average, apart, afraid to differ from 'everyone.' We are afraid to be unique, fearful of straying from the average; there is a hesitancy to surge ahead for fear of what 'people' will say. Thought is unoriginal, for the maintenance of personal security requires we avoid upsetting ideas. Language is vague and often meaningless, with colloquialisms such as 'This is killing me!' and 'I was scared to death,' taking the place of meaningful communication. We all try to 'escape' into the average and the supervised. Our intellectual efforts are characterized by a superficial curiosity, belying any real interest in learning or understanding.(15) Life, under these conditions, is blighted with cowardice and fearful acceptance of socially approved values and expectations. With the mass media and the powerful force of anonymity serving as enforcers, 'das Man' imposes its rule with an iron-willed discipline. Yet, in the last analysis, it is us, as inauthentic individuals, who ensure this rule with our unwillingness to confront the obvious: 'das Man' is obeyed because it resides in the mind of the victim. This passive life-style continually feeds on individuals lacking conviction and direction:(16)

> One does not care for what is original; originality is levelled down to familiarity. What is most profound and really secret loses its original distinction and becomes popularized or vulgarized; correlatively what is originally superficial is made profound - levelling is a two-way process. In this public world - this world of publicity - all is really unclear, ambiguous, hazy, yet everything is presented as if it were clear and well-known. We are afraid to ask questions which are not superficial for fear that One will think we are ignorant; in the realm of public life, ignorance is un-bliss. In the everyday world of the One, everything takes on a hue of soporific optimism: One always feels better, and things are always getting along well with One, things are always 'fine.'

This frightening description of inauthentic life is, in its own right, sufficiently penetrating to make each of us ponder the significance of all those radio, television, and hi-fi buttons hanging so alluringly close to our fingers.(17) What is perhaps even more frightening is the fact a person of Schutz's intelligence and knowledge can devote a lifetime to studying this very same life-world and conclude the behavior he has observed fulfills the only possibility we have for free, meaningful social interaction. The inauthentic life-world Heidegger presents in such foreboding terms, and the common-sense world Schutz describes as the context of our free social interaction, are one and the same. Heidegger sees routinized social life imbued by the dominance of 'das Man'; people, in the everyday, common-sense world, are marked by inauthenticity. Schutz defines our everyday, naive, unquestioning acceptance of socially derived and approved typifications as expressing our freedom and individuality; people, in everyday life, are characterized by a naive attitude permitting them the freedom to obey. Both Schutz and Heidegger similarly describe the everyday social world, but differ in prescribing the quality of life men and women actually experience in it.

To understand why this is so, we must reconsider certain of Heidegger's premises. In recognizing how being is expressed in existence, we actualize the possibilities inherent in us as human beings. Heidegger believes all individuals are potentially capable of freely formulating, and choosing from among, various possible courses of action. Since the quality of being reveals itself to us only through our actual beings, and this defines each of us as a free, creative actor, we live to our potentials only by recognizing the 'open' quality of our free human existences.(18) This self-awareness is the trademark of an authentic human life and alone grants us that freedom we are always potentially capable of achieving. Our fall into inauthenticity implies a turning away from this concern for being and a turning towards the material, external world. Because this fall is actually a choice, in its fulfilling one possibility of our being - that of living inauthentically - it confirms the free, creative quality of our beings and upholds our humanity even in this fallen state. The choice, however, has paradoxical consequences: it inhibits our recognition and understanding of being, without which our freedom remains an unfulfilled possibility. In falling into inauthenticity we have freely chosen to give up our freedom. Consequently, our behavior within the inauthentic state is not free because, under the conditions of our original acceptance of the inauthentic possibility, we have given up further responsibility for our actions, choosing instead to rely on the impersonal 'das Man' for guidance and approval. Our freedom exists only as a possibility in the common-sense world, where our actual behavior is determined by impersonal external forces originating apart from our potentially creative human abilities. The inauthentic individual, that person living in the everyday, common-sense world, is mollified and secure - but not free.(19)

This assessment of our inauthentic condition in the social world is accepted by phenomenologists of a less radical, or existential, viewpoint than Heidegger. Strasser, for example, contends our behavior in the social world exhibits an 'aspect of unfreedom of the human situation,' over which we have no control.(20) This does not deny the inherent, potential freedom embedded in, and defining, our humanity. Rather, Strasser is saying our freedom in the social world remains an unfulfilled possibility, it is 'held in abeyance' but always implicitly supposed.(21) What, then, is the difference between Schutz's description of free action in the common-sense world and Heidegger's analysis of unfree behavior in inauthentic existence? If, as claimed, they are both referring to the same phenomena, how can there be such a divergence of opinion concerning their human quality? The difference, it seems, is primarily one of terminology. Schutz means the same thing, in defining our unquestioning freedom in society, as Heidegger does in defining decadent, inauthentic behavior. Schutz's freedom is a freedom to obey only. There is no possibility of choosing among competing alternatives, for such a procedure necessitates abandoning the naive, unquestioning attitude. When Schutz refers to free social action he is referring to phenomena impersonally determined by factors originating independent of the creative human faculties of social actors. Heidegger offers a less ambiguous notion of freedom by introducing the concept of perfectability: in the common-sense world we are characterized by a potential to originate alternative courses of action and choose from among them. In this sense, in its being an unfulfilled possibility, are we free. Until we consciously choose this possibility our behavior is not free, it is determined by factors Heidegger includes in his description of 'das Man.' Heidegger, unlike Schutz, is able to preserve the integrity of free, meaning-endowing actors without distorting the quality of behavior characterizing the common-sense world.

What Schutz calls the common-sense world, therefore, is a place where free individuals, who have both the inherent ability to choose their own courses in life and the responsibility to accept the moral consequences of their actions, instead hide behind a facade of social mores and institutions. They act as 'expected' and do what is 'proper,' but, in the process, sacrifice their initiatives to anonymous social pressures.(22) Schutz's sociological method is applicable only to this reality; we utilize it exclusively to investigate acts exhibiting actors' non-questioning acceptance of their surrounding social imperatives. As a result, Schutz's social science is relevant only to social behavior not an outcome of thoughtful choice. Schutz means this when asserting a member of an 'in-group' surveys a situation and 'immediately' sees the ready-made recipe appropriate to it. 'In those situations his acting shows all the marks of habituality, automatism, and half-consciousness. This is possible because the cultural pattern provides by its recipes typical solutions for typical problems available for typical actors.'(23) Rational, non-impulsive behavior that is 'habitual, automatic, and half-conscious' is obviously instigated and determined by forces independent of the actor. Schutz's analysis is relevant to social behavior of what Natanson calls an 'anonymous personality': one lacking a sense of personal identity and unable to transcend the social and natural 'determinants' of his or her situation.(24)

Is this type of social behavior the limit of our capabilities? Is Schutz correct in claiming social interaction among contemporaries takes place only within these inhibiting parameters? If so, then, paradoxically, he eliminates the only possible rationale for a phenomenological approach to social science. With all social behavior a product of naively internalized directives, there is no longer a conflict between our need for scientific generalization and the ideal of individual freedom. Freedom - a self-conscious awareness and choice of alternatives - is not actualized by unquestioning actors whose behavior is determined by impersonal social forces internalized and accepted. Since these actors' social values are primarily unquestioned consequences of their belonging to influential subgroups, then 'in general . . . a person's basic valuations are no more the result of careful scrutiny and critical appraisal of possible alternatives than his religious affiliation.'(25) If this is so, why should social scientists even bother with a burdensome phenomenological emphasis on consciousness when they can, simply by studying impersonal social phenomena each actor unthinkingly reproduces, know all that can be known of the common-sense world. What advantage does Schutz's phenomenological approach to social science hold over a more traditional empirical approach? Granted, this latter method sacrifices the humanity of social actors to the demands of objectivity, yet Schutz admits his own method is not applicable to particular, unique subjects. If the everyday social world really does consist only of socially determined, naively internalized behavior patterns, it appears easiest and clearest for social scientists to focus their efforts primarily on uncovering empirically valid generalizations, or 'laws,' inherent in these patterns. These generalizations are useful in explaining and predicting social behavior, while their degree of accuracy is at least as high as Schutz claims for his ideal models, for both are derived from the same empirical evidence. The pure empirical approach has an added virtue of not interjecting an elaborate, self-defeating, and empirically unverifiable argument based on principles of phenomenology. The natural attitude, Kockelmans points out in another context, is better studied by means of an empirical realism, 'inasmuch as . . . it makes a pre-given objective world prevail over consciousness, which in the last resort is passive in respect to the world.'(26) Schutz's illogical and ambiguous analysis of the quality of social behavior is an attempt to obscure this fact.(27)

Are we then to conclude Schutz's analysis confirms the validity of a traditional scientific approach to studying society? When referring to determined behavior of the common-sense world, this conclusion is largely justified. If one subject's social behavior is determined by forces identically affecting behavior of others, there is little need to distinguish between subjects. But it is also naive to assume society consists only of this type of interaction.(28) Schutz, in his theory of multiple realities, maintains social actors are inherently capable of transcending social forces comprising their existential situations. There is nothing to prevent one's consciousness from changing itself, making a new choice in its way of being, acting differently towards its environment. Freedom does exist even within the common-sense world, but only as an unfulfilled possibility potentially attainable by everyone. To achieve this, social actors must liberate themselves from an attitude of naive obedience, without unknowingly divorcing themselves from society. By freeing themselves from a routine, habitualized, impersonal mode of perceiving, actors constitute a self-consciously realized intersubjective world where their dealings with others manifest those qualities of freedom and responsibility inherent in their phenomenologically-defined existences. The common-sense world is not the limit of social participation. It is within our abilities to communicate and interact with the rest of the social world as free, creative actors, influenced, but no longer suppressed, by our environments.

It is not what we do that transposes us into this world of self-realizing independence, but *how* we act. Schutz's common-sense world consists of habitual, routinized, mundane activities actors never even think about. We behave automatically, without self-consciously reflecting on the relevant, internalized social recipe. The social consequences of such behavior are expected. How often have we been self-consciously aware of mailing a letter, stopping at a red-light, answering a telephone?(29) These are standard behavior patterns in our everyday worlds, definitely important to our functioning in society, but also extra-personally initiated, amenable to behavioral analysis of a traditional, naturalist kind. In contrast, how often do we 'automatically' submit to induction in a time of war, protest an official policy, participate in or support a strike, demonstration, or other organized movement, join a socially or politically active organization, or (on a different level) promulgate an official directive adversely affecting thousands of constituents? The personal and social consequences of these acts are too great to be naively taken for granted. We usually carefully consider social recipes relevant to these types of acts before deciding to accept, reject, or modify them in our actions.

These contrasting types of social acts usually parallel similarly contrasting modes of perceiving and acting. The first group is usually performed by a naive, unquestioning actor, automatically responding to internalized social dictates. The second, by a self-consciously aware actor critically considering and evaluating the circumstances (including social recipes) he or she acts in. As social actions qualitatively approach the second group, consequences appear more subjectively meaningful to involved actors, and Schutz's method appears increasingly irrelevant. Significantly, however, even with routine social behavior, we are potentially capable of exhibiting a quality of awareness invalidating the usefulness of Schutz's homunculii. One example: empirically speaking, most of us still accede to basic sexual stereotypes in our personal behavior. The important question, from a scientific point of view, is why we do so. As we become increasingly aware of consequences of even routine stereotyped sexual behavior, especially as a large number of citizens demand our attention to alleged injustices, our *naive* acceptance (not necessarily our acceptance) of social recipes declines, and the explanatory adequacy of the homunculii decreases. Who is to say whether pride, prejudice, pique, spite, or an infinite number of other possibilities are decisive in shaping a self-consciously aware social actor's 'conforming' to his sexual stereotype. Thus, though empirically valid, homunculii may be meaningfully inadequate - even to the extent of deceiving observers as to why we act as we do. On the level of international political decision-making studies (public officials being even more sensitive to consequences of their decisions than most others), this fault can have adverse, tragic consequences for policy-makers assuming the validity of such generalizations.

The important point is this: once actors stop, even if just for a moment, to think about the situation in which they find themselves, the eventual decision is no longer unthinkingly determined by a social recipe. They then decide, by themselves, and for their own subjectively meaningful reasons, what to do. Schutz's artificially created homunculus adequately explains the action in question only when the actor does it automatically, without thinking. It becomes increasingly useless, and very possibly misleading, when applied to social actions of increasing complexity and meaning for those involved. The element of subjectivity thoughtful consideration entails eliminates, according to standards Schutz has established, any possibility the actual social act can be scientifically explained.

Schutz's method is now seen in a more revealing perspective. Originally, it was his intention to clarify Weber's methodology by introducing an explicit, unambiguous notion of subjectivity. Schutz is forced to sacrifice the clarity of this principle as his own analysis proceeds, making one wonder if perhaps the philosopher in Weber accepted the terminological ambiguity as a necessary price for a scientific approach to society. In any event, Schutz's zeal for clarification apparently blinds him to an extremely important element of Weber's argument. It is theoretically possible, in Weber's opinion, to use natural scientific methods in an epistemologically valid study of society. This is not desirable because, when transplanted from the study of nature to the study of society, this method focuses only on those regular, mechanistic-type behavior patterns characterizing our unthinking mundane lives. Weber feels this automatic social behavior is of little interest to most people and, in any case, is so obvious and uncomplicated it is understood without using an elaborate scientific method. Our study of society should focus on problems important *from a social point of view*, that clarify issues uniting and dividing a people trying creatively to come to terms with their environment. Yet these are precisely the problems beyond the reach of both Schutz's phenomenological method and the method of the natural sciences. It may be interesting, for some, to scientifically explain why we mail letters, use telephones, or stop at red lights, but it is more useful and significant for society as a whole to understand the origins, nature, and possible correctives for the 'seamy' aspects of our democratic system, the problems of poverty, violence, corruption and oppression that so many of us experience. If science is to contribute to the survival of our society it must prove itself relevant to the problems upon which this survival depends. Schutz, unfortunately, is satisfied with much less.

These inadequacies make it unlikely Schutz's method can have an important impact on our attempts at social inquiry. It does not afford us any useful tools to facilitate either the understanding or solving of society's major problems, while the scope of social phenomena it is related to is amenable to scientific analysis by another, more accepted method. Its adoption by any particular branch of the social sciences should, if this analysis is correct, evolve into a dead-end venture merely confirming the virtues and vices of a traditional naturalist approach to social science. By describing the method of political investigation known as decision-making theory, the oldest approach to empirical social science accepting basic elements of Schutz's methodology, we will see if this is, in fact, the case.

3 THE OPERATIONALIZATION OF PHENOMENOLOGICAL SOCIAL SCIENCE IN DECISION-MAKING THEORY

Decision-making theory, in its 'classical' version, originated as a theory of economic and administrative behavior postulating the undeniable rationality of significant decision-makers. According to its central thesis, all possible alternatives and all possible consequences of these alternatives are examined and placed in a rational hierarchy of preferences by rational decision-makers, who proceed to choose the 'best' possible course of action. This classical approach has come under much criticism from contemporary social scientists, most notably Herbert Simon and Joseph Frankel.(30) Their critique is based on two obvious difficulties permeating the classical approach: first, it is logically incorrect to assume all possible solutions to a problem have been discovered by an actor; and second, it is psychologically incorrect to assume we all can perform the complex mental activity each ideal rational actor must perform. Instead, they claim decisional behavior is characterized by a sequential consideration of conceived alternatives until one is found that actors feel best meets the requirements of their respective situations. This process may well be affected by emotional and irrational factors fundamentally influencing the nature and quality of observed decisions.

The decision-making model we are now concerned with is formulated by Richard C. Snyder and his associates, H. W. Bruck and Burton Sapin.(31) Despite its shared goal of scientifically explaining decision-making - specifically, decisions of national political actors(32) - Snyder's model is not a direct continuation of the debate between new and classical approaches to this subject matter. While not ignoring the controversy, it focuses primarily on integrating the work of David Truman and other interest group theorists into decision-making analysis.(33) Interest group theory, however, is not accepted at face value. Snyder rivets his attention on actors themselves, hoping to measure the real influence of social groups by the perception actors have of them. It is, therefore, an attempt to understand decision-making by synthesizing psychological and organizational factors into a theory united around the central importance of individual perception.

Snyder's attempt to supplement the exclusively empirical approach to international relations with an emphasis on the subjective perspectives of national actors has met with general approval. Since its publication in 1954, decision-making terminology and actor-oriented concepts have infiltrated numerous scholarly works and political speeches. It has been professionally recognized as a valid approach to scientific political inquiry by its inclusion in respected anthologies,(34) and it is a rare occasion when a new text dealing with international relations or political methodology ignores significant issues related to the formation of relevant subjective perspectives. Additionally, the decision-making approach has been utilized, though not always consciously or with proper credit given Snyder, as a theoretical basis for many diverse political studies having the limited aim of exhibiting general relationships between particular actors and select environmental phenomena strongly influencing their perceptions. These are, for the most part, not methodologically oriented, and of a much more limited scope than Snyder's model, isolating only one or two variables and trying to show their special relationship to an actor's subjective point of view. As such, they don't claim to have discovered 'why' decision-makers act as they do, but are content with uncovering partial explanations of selected events.(35)

Despite the apparent enthusiasm within the discipline towards Snyder's work, a closer examination unveils the quixotic nature of this popularity. For the first time a scientific method had been formulated giving equal footing to thinking, meaning-endowing actors and the environmental and psychological factors determining their behavior. Undoubtedly, this emphasis on subjective perspectives of political actors is greatly needed and long overdue in a discipline that, until recently, has shared with the other social sciences a rigid commitment to traditional, naturalist methods. These had left very little room for dealing with individual actors themselves, capable of subjectively experiencing their political environments and reacting to them in subjectively meaningful ways. The feelings generated by Snyder's ideas reflected this newly awakened concern for the actor and the important role he or she plays in society. Snyder was dealing with a topic that had previously been neglected, and now had to be directly confronted if the discipline was to avoid a self-imposed sterility unalterably removing it from the human beings it was intended to study. There was a need for decision-making theory and, with its appearance, the mood has been one of satisfaction.

However, this mood is a result not of Snyder's model itself, but of its intent of coming to terms with the thorny problem of reconciling subjectivity and science. In practical terms, Snyder's conceptual scheme has been left absolutely untouched. There has been no effort to improve upon or modify the model Snyder claimed could integrate subjectivity into a scientific method. The newly motivated books, articles and speeches stressing the importance of actors' perspectives in explaining a political decision have not been concerned with those methodological issues constituting the bulk of Snyder's model. In the field of international relations, methodologists have reacted to decision-making theory, generally speaking, in one of three ways.

The most common reaction has been one of bewilderment and helplessness at the immense task Snyder set for himself. There are simply too many variables to take into account in attempting to scientifically explain subjective perspectives of decision-makers.(36) Thus, as Wolfers contends, we must overcome this difficulty by limiting the number of necessary variables which conceivably influence decision-makers, primarily by disregarding unique national organizations that complicate our testing hypotheses, and specific psychological categories tending to over-emphasize subjective aspects of unique individuals.(37) The Sprouts, who are more in sympathy with Snyder's goals, nevertheless conclude the study of national policy formation is a matter of psychologically analyzing decision-makers, whose own ideals and motivations are products of their perceptions of the milieu within which they function, and are not causally dependent on any outside forces. Only by shifting our analytic focus from the decisions themselves to the operational results of these decisions do we achieve scientific explanation. Political science, contrary to Snyder's claims, must limit itself to identifying and evaluating both those structures of the environed unit and those factors of the milieu setting limits to performance, and to discovering the achievements, actual or potential, relevant to a given undertaking or strategy.(38) These two approaches to politics and international relations, and others like them,(39) reject the possibility of our ever objectively explaining unique perceptual processes. As such, they limit themselves to impersonal, empirically verifiable variables.

Others walk the opposite path and concentrate on the 'subjective, emotion-gilded perceptions' of national decision-makers. There is no pretense to scientific objectivity; they deal with historical generalizations and exceptions, emphasizing the possible influence of certain environmental factors in shaping personal conceptions of the world, while purposefully avoiding scientific formalism. The nature of the subject matter (i.e. the unique decision-maker) eliminates any realistic hope of attaining scientifically valid explanations.(40)

A third reaction to Snyder's model, most clearly illustrated in the work of Joseph Frankel, implies a type of benign acceptance avoiding all critical issues upon which its validity rests. Here, a model for international study is developed closely resembling Snyder's, but written in much simpler language and dealing with much simpler problems. It blithely describes environmental and mental determinants of social behavior without touching on the psychological or philosophical problems involved in reconciling these determinants to each actor's inherent freedom, also postulated. The result is a scientific model which, admittedly, may or may not be applicable to political decisions, apparently depending on whether or not these are 'clearly acts of free will and products of imagination.'(41) The meaning of these last words is also a product of imagination - the reader's.

None of these methodological responses to Snyder's model serves a constructive function. The first two, in opposite ways, deny the grounds for its even existing, while the last ignores those crucial issues motivating Snyder in the first place. All three have left decision-making theory intact: they either naively accept Snyder's attempt at reconciling subjectivity and science, or they reject it.

Just as there has been no conceptual modification of decision-making theory, there has similarly been almost no attempt to validate the model empirically. Notwithstanding certain self-serving, over-optimistic claims,(42) since 1954, there has been only one full-length case study utilizing Snyder's decision-making model as a guide to gathering empirical data.(43)

Why is it that decision-making theory has remained unmodified conceptually and untested empirically? Like Schutz's methodology, from which it is derived, the decision-making model rests on shaky logical grounds. It presupposes, as we shall presently see more clearly, that individuals act according to their own perceptions of their environments and are, therefore, free agents participating in the social process. Yet the whole intent of the theory is to create a scientifically valid model for gathering empirical data to determine the causes of specific national political decisions. The prime goal of this theory, as of Schutz's methodology, is to create an objective context for explaining the willful, thoroughly subjective perceptions of decision-makers. By re-constructing Snyder's argument into four analytical stages we shall see how decision-making theory, despite its admirable syncretistic intentions, is self-defeating and untenable.

1 The epistemological foundation of decision-making theory is located within the borders of phenomenology, especially its emphasis on consciousness as the final source of knowledge. Snyder declares conclusively,(44)

> The situation is defined by the actor (or actors) in terms of the way the actor (or actors) relates himself to other actors, to possible goals, and to possible means . . .. These ways of relating himself to the situation (and thus of defining it) will depend on the nature of the actor - or his orientations . . .. It is . . . one of our basic choices to take as our prime analytical objective the recreation of the 'world' of the decision-makers as *they* view it (emphasis is mine).

The decision-maker's subjectivity is the key variable, all others only helping us discover relevant perceptions guiding the actor's behavior. All external, environmental factors acting as 'potential' limitations on actors' deliberations and results of deliberations, 'gain their significance from the perceptions and judgments of the decision-makers.'(45) 'In accordance with our general phenomenological approach, we feel that the range and impact of limitations should be considered from the decision-maker's point of view . . ..'(46) Snyder's position, for the moment at least, seems clear.

Important principles of method Snyder derives from this epistemology are modeled after Schutz's methodology.(47) Thus, actors are motivated, as Schutz has described, by in-order-to and because-motives, and social scientists devote their attentions to the former because of the meanings actors attach to them.(48) Individual action, therefore, is based on an actor's perceptions of the situation, goals for the future, expectations of the consequences of various modes of behavior, and choices - all taking place in time. The objectives or goals actors project for themselves are 'an "image" of a future "state of affairs" - a "set of conditions" to be fulfilled or a "set of specifications" which when met are to be regarded as the achievement of what was desired by the decision-makers.'(49) We understand why decision-makers act by understanding the subjective meanings the actions had for them. These are determined by the way they experience and define their situations.

2 The actor is, then, an irreduceable unit of analysis and a necessary focus of attention for social scientists. However, all decisions of international political significance are made by actors functioning within a governmental organization that is relevant in their defining the situation. Snyder therefore concludes that a phenomenological line of reasoning suggests 'that we conceptualize two fundamental processes - the intellectual and the organizational - and attempt to discover how the latter conditions the former.'(50)

An organization is 'the outcome of the operation of formal rules governing the allocation of power and responsibility, motivation, communication, performance of functions, problem-solving, and so on.'(51) Since political decision-makers act in the context of organizations they belong to, and the basic attribute of these are the formal rules they institutionalize, Snyder claims significant decisions of sanctioned public officials are governed by these organizational guides to action called rules. Resembling Schutz's description of social recipes, (52) rules affect the actor in two ways: they prescribe the type of response necessary when faced with certain possible situations; and they prescribe the subjectively relevant meaning commonly experienced when confronting these situations.(53) In this sense, decision-makers' actions are governed by the effective rules characterizing their institutional environments.

3 Political decision-makers are also influenced by situations and conditions originating outside of themselves and the governmental organizations to which they belong. These conditions are included in the concept of 'setting,' which Snyder defines as 'a set of categories of potentially relevant factors and conditions which may affect the action of any state.'(54) The setting is sub-divided under two headings: external and internal. The external setting consists primarily of the international system, whose 'modes, rules, and nature of reciprocal influence . . . structure[s] the interaction between states.'(55) Also included in the external setting are all international actions of foreign states, and all external events, conditions, or phenomena of international significance. The internal setting includes the corpus of institutions, social and governmental, characterizing the decision-maker's national environment. As such, the internal setting represents all domestic, political and social pressures decision-makers are aware of before acting.(56) Because national actors always act in, and are at least partially aware of, their internal

and external settings, Snyder feels these settings limit the possible choices open to decision-makers. Political action is not properly explained without investigating how these settings condition an actor's choice.

4 'Decision-making is a process which results in the selection from a socially defined, limited number of problematical alternative projects of one project intended to bring about the particular future state of affairs envisaged by the decision-makers.'(57) Decision-makers work within decisional units or organizations, functioning in internal and external settings. Both organization and setting profoundly influence actors' choices. But what is the extent of this influence and how are we to know the relative significance of the three factors already mentioned: actor, organization, setting? 'We shall consider that all factors which influence the results of deliberation in foreign policy-making can be accounted for by . . . [three] variables.'(58) These include, respectively, spheres of competence, communications and information, and motivation. Taken together, these three factors constitute 'the three major determinants of action in the [decision-making] system . . . .'(59) We scientifically explain why a decision-maker acted by empirically investigating the actor, decisional unit, and internal and external settings in terms of these three determining variables.

a. The decisional unit consists, according to Snyder, of 'a set of competences and relationships among competences . . . . A competence is defined as the totality of those of the activities of the decision-maker relevant and necessary to the achievement of the organizational objective.'(60) In any particular organization, spheres of competence are described by two sets of rules, those officially prescribed (i.e. by a formal constitution) and those informally, or habitually, accepted. These rules detail actors' responsibilities, and their relationships to other actors in the decisional system. In this way each member of an organization knows who his or her superiors and subordinates are.

Although these rules are admittedly subject to the actor's interpretation,(61) 'the pattern of activities is predictable with a high degree of probability to the extent to which it is specified and prescribed in the explicit rules of the organization.'(62) While there appears to be at least a slight difficulty here between the concept of free actors determining their own actions by subjectively perceiving the world, and the predictability characterizing such behavior, Snyder refuses 'to get involved in the sterile debate between the advocates of free will and those of determinism.'(63) On the other hand, because 'there are apparently no data available on the problem of the reciprocal interaction of actor and social structure,'(64) Snyder also refuses to provide empirical evidence which might clarify the issue. Thus, without philosophically discussing the assertion or empirically defending it, Snyder declares meaningful, self-determined action 'predictable with a high degree of probability.'

b. When one speaks of communication he implies 'that the world is constituted intersubjectively; that as a consequence objects, social relationships, and so on, are perceived in terms of a system of meanings, values and preferences; and that, furthermore, these meanings, values and preferences are learned and transmitted to others.'(65) The stability of any organizational unit depends upon the communication occurring along its chain of command. Information, very simply, is 'that which is being communicated by the communicator.'(66) Communication and information, together, constitute a decisional unit's 'communications net.' Each communications net is characterized by distinct channels of communication, procedures and rules governing communication, instruments of communication, and kinds of communication. When studying a decision-maker's action, each of these factors in the communications net must be empirically investigated. This is so not only because the actor needs information in order to act wisely, but also because this information, when perceived, determines what the actor will do.(67)

c. Motives refer to the 'psychological states of the actor in which energy is mobilized and selectively directed toward aspects of the setting.'(68) Motives are always manifest in political behavior. If they refer to the past, they are because-motives; if they refer to future states of affairs envisaged by an actor, they are in-order-to motives. The quality of an actor's motives, what Snyder calls a 'motivational structure,' is determined by this actor's attitudes and frames of reference (consisting of perception, valuation and evaluation). In making a decision, all elements of an actor's motivational structure come into play. Social scientists must empirically define this motivational structure to explain why the act was performed, primarily by developing motivational types which are empirically verified and easy to identify (cf. Schutz's homunculi).(69) Then, after compiling certain kinds of data,(70) we determine which type the actor is, and work with the motivational structure proper to that type. This motivational structure, together with the actor's sphere of competence and the information communicated to him, determines what the eventual decision will be and why it will be so.

The major purpose of decision-making theory is to create a taxonomy from which to derive scientifically valid hypotheses meant to be integrated into a general theory.(71) This ideal is reflected in Snyder's comments on human behavior and decision-makers' actions. In particular, the choices of decision-makers are 'made on the basis of preferences which are in part situationally and in part biographically determined.'(72) The assumption underlying this statement is that investigators are trying to discover causal relationships existing between actors, their environments, and history. Political action, for Snyder, is determined by empirically confirmable factors discovered by our examining all relevant causal variables. Such an analysis, because it creates testable hypotheses and adequate theory, will facilitate prediction.(73)

How well does Snyder's argument, outlined in these four stages, actually achieve this goal? In reconciling a phenomenological understanding of perception with empirical scientific method Snyder must convince us that stage one of his argument is consistent with stages two and three. This will not be easy, a phenomenological emphasis on the important role consciousness has in our perceiving the world seems to preclude the existence of causal factors existing apart from each consciously perceiving actor. If stage one, confirming the phenomenological bias of his argument, is accepted, then stages two and three, both detailing the external factors influencing all decision-makers, no longer generate the meaning Snyder intended. In other words, if the goal of decision-making theory is to develop a model empirically applicable to all political systems regardless of personnel or cultural differences, it is not clear how a basic premise of that model can emphasize the importance of individual perception. Such a postulate distorts the 'objectivity' of decision-making theory's empirical method because individual perception (in the phenomenological sense) is not necessarily molded by any select number of external factors. Stages two and three may adequately define the relevant environment of the decision-maker, enabling us to explain why he acted as he did, but they could just as easily not function in this way if the decision-maker's perception is not subjectively constituted to fulfill our expectations. Thus, the influence of an organizational unit in shaping an actual decision may be significant, but, according to criteria of stage one, it is possible its influence is insignificant or non-existent, depending on the actor's perception. Similarly, information may well be an important component of the decision-making process, but it could, in cases where an actor perceives information differently or not at all, be superfluous and not worth investigating. Other factors not included in stages two and three may influence the actor to such an extent that we can no longer explain an action without referring to them. Perhaps a recently read book, a conversation, a mood, or an overwhelming desire to achieve a subjectively defined project or plan significantly affected the decision-maker. We certainly have no reason to rule these or an infinite number of other possible factors out of our analysis - there are, in fact, as many factors as there are subjectively constituted perceptions. Any attempt at formalism, outlining definite variables necessarily contributing in some way to the resultant act, is wrong simply because the variables may not so contribute if the decision-maker fails to perceive them in the required manner.

If meaningful behavior is somehow determined by objective, empirically verifiable data, then the ambiguity induced by stage one is negated and an objective model, applicable to all decision-making units, can be formulated. Snyder accomplishes this by including stage four. In describing spheres of competence, communication and information and motivation as three empirically verifiable factors determining a decision-maker's action, Snyder eliminates the troublesome element of subjectivity. No longer is there any doubt as to the adequacy of an explanation empirically focusing entirely on these three factors, excluding all others. Since they do, in fact, determine why a decision-maker acts, we are able to confidently predict that by empirically defining them in relation to an actor we can properly explain the act. This model now presupposes that different actors will respond in the same manner to the same objective, empirically verifiable conditions, that each specific decision 'is entirely comprehensible in terms of the perceptions and values which any occupant of the role is likely to have.'(74) Stage four accomplishes for Snyder what the social recipes accomplished for Schutz: shifting our attention from the subject to those objective conditions within which an act is performed.

An important question now is whether or not stage four has forced Snyder to sacrifice the intent of stage one. Can we really use three empirically verifiable determinants of a decision-maker's action as valid indices of this actor's subjectively determined perception? Robert Jervis has described the difficulties that inhere in attempting to correlate objective data of international relations with the subjective intentions underlying them.(75) He illustrates that, because of the complex, subjective nature of the perceiving process, it is impossible to accurately equate most empirically verifiable facts in some way related to perception with perception itself. Since the scientific approach to international relations Snyder accepts requires data organized into objective, uniform categories, 'this [scientific] technique deals less adequately than traditional methods with the concepts of perception and intention and . . . these techniques have not provided accurate and useful comparisons involving what the actors did, what they thought others did, and what they themselves planned to do.'(76) It is unlikely, using this reasoning, Snyder's model will describe a decision-maker's subjectively determined perception, though of course it is not entirely impossible it may do so. The important point is this: guided by stage four of Snyder's argument, if the analysis is to be in any sense scientific we must concentrate not on actors, but on those phenomena existing independent of them. Any coincidence between an actor's actual perception and these empirically verified phenomena is just that: a coincidence.

The tension between stages one and four rapidly surfaces in Paige's case-study. Almost immediately, Paige acknowledges the trouble he experienced in empirically defining subjective elements comprising actor's definitions of their situations.(77) Finding Snyder's analysis deficient, he offers us seven 'more precise' categories by which to organize empirical data in order to determine actors' subjective attitudes.(78) In this case, Paige is investigating attitudes of three American political actors, President Truman, Secretary of State Acheson, and Secretary of Defense Johnson. Chapters two and three, the only ones dealing with these actors' own perceptions of the situation surrounding America's intervention in Korea, consists of a running account of empirical sources that hint at these actors' opinions of their roles, the domestic political environment, public opinion, congress, the role of communism in the world and America's documented official interactions with various countries. The commentary builds an ambiguous portrait of the three personalities, stroked in extremely general terms, about broad topics of interest. Our knowledge of the actors' perceptions of the situation within which they found themselves in 1950, is vague, based on generalizations probably shared by 99 per cent of American public officials holding office in that year. Although this may be of value to those interested in learning how America, as a nation, reacts to this type of situation, the decision-making model goes beyond this in demanding that adequate explanation include an understanding of national actors, *as individuals*. Paige's case-study, the only one of its kind, confirms the inability of Snyder's decision-making model to reconcile stages one and four of its argument. By using only selected empirically validatable phenomena to re-construct a decision-maker's action, Paige has abandoned the three actors he originally intended to study, all of whom, based on stage one of the model, are thinking subjects perceiving and consciously defining the world for themselves. What we get are generalizations concerning values and beliefs prevalent in American society, which may or may not have been significant elements - and in any case are only some of many other possible ones - in Truman's, Acheson's, and Johnson's actual perceptions in those weeks preceding their decision to intervene.

Perhaps realizing the logical hole he has burrowed himself into, Snyder turns to Schutz for a possible way out: 'Since we are dealing with planful actions (rather than random behavior), interaction is characterized by patterns, that is, recognizable repetitions of action and reaction. Aims persist. Kinds of action become typical. Reactions become uniform. Relationships become regularized.'(79) There is an obvious contradiction between stages one and four. Since stage four is necessary for Snyder to achieve his goal of creating scientific theory, either stage one is amended or the whole model falls apart. Meaningful, self-determined action is also patterned, repetitious, persistent, typical, uniform and regularized behavior; Snyder unquestioningly accepts Schutz's argument that these two forms of conduct are synonymous. Only with respect to such habitualized behavior can we assume the categories of data described in the three determinants of action provide significant and complete explanations. Stages one and four are no longer opposed because our freedom to think and perceive is the same as our freedom to obey determinants of our actions. The scope of phenomena relevant to Snyder's model comprises the unthinking, naive behavior of individuals unquestioningly accepting dictates of impersonal social forces.

Because these forces represent an environment equally

affecting all actors functioning within it, it seems reasonable to conclude socially determined behavior of this type can be explained by a more traditional scientific method that doesn't confuse the issue with phenomenological jargon. Snyder at first rejects this as unwarranted. 'The manner in which . . . [the decision-makers] define situations becomes another way of saying how the state oriented to action and why. This is a quite different approach from trying to recreate the situation and interpretation of it objectively, that is, by the observer's judgment rather than that of the actors themselves.'(80) It is important here to distinguish between what Snyder says and what he means. The 'actors themselves' define their situations without even resorting to a 'self-conscious decision process.'(81) Since the behavior Snyder is referring to is unthinking and habitual, he assumes any specific actor, when placed in certain circumstances, will react just as any other actor would, circumstances remaining the same. Determining factors are not located in the actor, but in an environment he unquestioningly obeys. An actor's 'judgments' are therefore not at all subjectively determined. They are inherent in the situation, guiding the actions of any actor encountering them. When Snyder claims the aim of his model is to understand 'how the state oriented to action and why,' the answers to these 'how' and 'why' questions are based on impersonal, and in this sense objective, forces similarly determining for all actors how any one of them will deal with a situation, and why he will choose to do so. Is this really 'a quite different approach' from a more naturalist scientific method which answers the same questions by focusing on the same phenomena and attempting to empirically verify similar idealizations - but without the help of a superfluous phenomenological epistemology?

An answer is found in the spotty history of decision-making theory and in later writings of Snyder himself. The lack of conceptual modification and empirical validation of Snyder's model, already noted, indicates that, because of its inherent features, it simply could not develop further in any meaningful way. If the stress on individual perspective is taken seriously it becomes impossible to understand or accept stages two through four, obviously aimed at circumscribing the significance of subjectivity in constituting perception. Since this (stages two through four) is the body of decision-making theory, there is little room left to modify the model from a subjective point of view. Social scientists, on the other hand, realized that Snyder's goal of creating scientific theory could be accomplished easily by abandoning stage one, which introduced an unverifiable and qualitative variable. But without this stage there is nothing to distinguish decision-making theory from those behavioral studies that had grown up quite apart from Snyder's analysis. It makes very little sense to modify one approach to social science when there is already another fulfilling the requirements. Behavioralism has all the advantages of decision-making theory, from a scientific point of view, with none of its drawbacks. Consequently, one of Snyder's most accomplished students has recently described decision-making theory as being just one front 'in the behavioral revolution in political science,'(82) whose major weakness lies in its over-emphasis of isolated categories not readily enough subsumed under 'if-then' causal relationships.(83)

Snyder's own turn towards behavioralism is not surprising given the fact that, if he is to move at all, this is the only place for him to go. In 'Experimental Techniques and Political Analysis: Some Reflections in the Context of Concern over Behavioral Approaches',(84) Snyder outlines certain rules and procedures for maximizing results of empirical behavioral analyses of political situations, which alone yield valid political knowledge. In 'Some Perspectives on the Use of Experimental Techniques in the Study of International Relations',(85) he utilizes simulation (i.e. a procedure which recreates select situations by exposing human subjects to certain controlled variables) and experimentation to investigate 'the trial and error of everyday political and social life.'(86) Both these procedures are based on behavioral premises that human behaviour is determined and controlled by external variables that scientists can manipulate for desired effects. Neither of the articles contains any reference to the possible significance of individual perspective or subjective meaning, the subject matter of stage one in the original model. There is, instead, a total emphasis on describing techniques that can be used in explaining objective environmental factors determining any actor's frame of mind under specified circumstances. Even the term 'subjective perspective' is replaced by the more objective and empirically verifiable concept 'individual characteristics.'(87) It is much easier to empirically study actors' characteristics than their self-determined perspectives. By focusing on these objective characteristics, social scientists are in a better position to develop good scientific theory, which now must 'describe a causal relationship (directional influence) between one or more antecedent variables and a consequent variable.'(88) National actors' definitions of situations are viewed as 'consequent variables,' causally determined by factors existing independently in society, the 'antecedent variables.' In abandoning stage one, Snyder eliminates the logical ambiguity plaguing his original model, but he also eliminates all pretense that his scientific approach to studying political behavior is in any sense phenomenological. When Paige claims it is the goal of his case-study to utilize empirical analysis in order to derive 'causal explanations' of use in establishing general explanatory scientific theory,(89) we need no longer worry about how this is accomplished without destroying actors' capacities to determine their own courses of action: in the interests of science this issue has been deemed irrelevant. 'To reconstruct the world from the perspective of the decision-maker, the researcher must examine *the world itself* in order to comprehend the dynamics and limits of the decision-maker's perspective . . .. To expect decisional phenomena to provide the . . . basis for if-then propositions about politics is . . . to establish an unattainable goal'(90) (emphasis is mine).

Snyder's model is directed at the common-sense world, where social action is characterized by its unthinking, automatic quality, where political action is patterned and regularized by an unthinking actor. This type of political behavior, termed by some a 'routine,' has been rather carefully studied by Ira Sharkansky.(91) Though the jargon differs, Sharkansky's notion of a routine is entirely consistent with the type of behavior Snyder is concerned with.(92) In both, all actors uniformly obey a set of rules prescribing, under given circumstances, what to do and how to do it.

The bulk of Sharkansky's analysis is aimed at proving that 'routines lend themselves to small explanations in political science.'(93) By 'small explanations' Sharkansky means two things: first, knowing the routine underlying a certain type of decision does not explain all possible conditions under which that type of decision will be made, nor does it explain all possible decisions the actor theoretically is capable of making; and second, the types of decisions routines are capable of explaining are relatively small and unimportant when contrasted with those major, far-reaching decisions national actors are often compelled to make. In the American political process, Sharkansky sees five types of decisions adequately explained by describing relevant routines.(94) All deal with political actors performing types of behavior having no, or very little, political significance to themselves or their constituents, behavior that is not a matter of controversy to anyone even remotely connected to the decision. Such decisions require no contemplation by actors other than an unquestioning acceptance of the relevant routine, which provides an easy and quick way to respond to non-controversial situations that apparently must be dealt with. Since Snyder's decision-making model is concerned with routinized political behavior, these types of decisions constitute the limit of its applicability. Not surprisingly, Snyder at first admits his model should not be used to understand 'big' decisions. It must be applied, instead, to 'lower level responses to ongoing business' that 'may not emerge from a self-conscious decision process at all.'(95) However, even Snyder eventually realizes there is not much call for elaborate decision-making case studies of America's decisions to replace a retiring ambassador, repay a foreign loan, or attend a scheduled NATO conference - these being the types of international political decisions considered routine. Anyone casually interested in international diplomacy normally explains decisions such as these with a reasonably good chance of accuracy, for the explanations are embedded in rules and customs of the world environment unquestioningly accepted by that country's officials, regardless of who they are. There is as much point in devoting great time and effort to studying decisions like these as there is in similarly studying why we put letters in a mailbox when we want to mail them.

In order to avoid this dilemma, Snyder is forced to alter his model, making it more relevant to interests of the scholarly community. He does this by introducing three new variables which must be correlated with the three determinants of his original model.(96) The new variables are aimed at opening up the range of phenomena to include major foreign policy decisions culminating in international crises. Since crisis decision-making 'varies with perceived changes in the amount of threat in combination with the amount of decision time and/or the amount of surprise,'(97) threat, decision time and surprise constitute the new factors in his model.

Snyder is now implicitly admitting his method is inadequate to the major social tasks confronting social science today. He contends the common-sense world of routine social behavior is not a sufficient reservoir for the kind of information needed by an aware, crisis-ridden public. Yet he has already gone too far to reverse himself in any meaningful fashion. The newly revised decision-making model, with its three added variables, offers no great methodological innovations to neutralize those weaknesses inhering in the old one. If anything, the new model has confused matters to an even greater extent: by creating a taxonomy for studying crisis decisions, in effect the result of adding three crisis variables to the original model, Snyder is now confining himself to scientifically studying regularized, habitual, non-thinking behavior exhibited by actors in reacting to crisis situations. The same weakness we found before is present here, but moved to a different level and with more unintended implications. Actors' common-sense worlds disintegrate as they initially experience jolting or shocking turns of events, forcing them to think about their situations and determine, for themselves, how best to react. The perceived shock occurs because things no longer happen 'as they are supposed to,' and the consequences of personal decisions assume a significance far greater than those unquestioned, monotonous ones experienced in the common-sense world. Actors now find themselves thinking about things they used to take for granted, questioning socially-determined routines they formerly naively obeyed. Such perceived shock is implied in Snyder's conception of crisis. Within a relatively short amount of time the normal, everyday happenings we had all come to expect and unquestioningly accept are dramatically altered by a surprising and threatening event. Consequences of our actions have similarly changed, and we now think very carefully about what to do before accepting any particular course of action. As thinking actors, we have injected an undeniable element of self-consciousness into the situation, a quality not manifest in the common-sense world. It is this type of crisis situation that Snyder intends to study with a model developed for, and suited to, the everyday occurrences of the common-sense world.

Snyder's attempt to use his decision-making model in understanding crisis decisions has two important consequences, neither of which can be eliminated by a superficial juggling of terms. First, because actors usually respond to crisis situations as thinking subjects, Snyder can never be certain the empirically verified generalizations he may uncover are in any definite way relevant to actual decisions. All empirical evidence may indeed point to the conclusion that, for example, with increasing degrees of surprise and threat, and decreasing time, a national actor will give less attention to communicated information and more to the explicit perogatives of his role. But, since the actor is presumably no longer unquestioningly experiencing the world, he naively accepts neither the information he receives nor the prescribed privileges of his role in the decision-making unit. Both factors enter into his decision, but neither determines it, for while contemplating what to do, he also filters all these empirically verified factors through his own subjectively constituted perceptions. Decision-making theory adequately describes those factors which would have determined an actor's decision if he were still naively perceiving the world. Since he is not perceiving the world in this manner there is absolutely no way of telling, from Snyder's model, how much importance the actor attributed to the little information he was aware of, the perogatives of his role he knew in such great detail, or to a thousand other topics that may, and probably did, enter into his thinking. When the decision-making model is used like this it offers us explanations founded more on guesswork than on scientific clarity. These can have disastrous consequences if, assuming their correctness by accepting them as valid explanations, we formulate national policy accordingly and later - too late - discover we were wrong. Given the blatant nature of this model's irreconcilability to crisis decision-making, implied in Snyder's own definition of crisis and the principles contained in decision-making theory itself, such consequences are not only possible but likely to occur.

The second difficulty emerges predictably from the first. Since empirically verified findings of Snyder's crisis decision-making model refer to courses of action actors would unquestioningly accept if they were, in fact, experiencing the common-sense world, we can rightfully assume these patterns are based on socially derived and approved idealizations. In other words, evidence we uncover through applying the decision-making model to a crisis situation concerns those impersonal social forces identically affecting (not determining) all possible actors in the same motivational-type group. This evidence consists of uniform, habitual, socially-determined behavior patterns any actor, in 'normal' crisis situations, confronts when deciding how to act. The decision-making approach therefore abstracts from a crisis situation only routinized, mundane information having its origins in the situation itself, not the actor. This is also the information disinterested observers, who are reasonably well informed as to the decisional unit's organization and the general ways it has functioned in past crises, can discover for themselves by simply using their judgment and common-sense. The decision-making model is tailored to understand and explain routine, habitualized decisions. Crisis decisions, on the other hand, are extremely complex and subjective, not necessarily determined by impersonal social forces. When we apply the decision-making model to crisis situations we get simplistic explanations (which in any case may well be misleading) of extremely complex decisional processes. These explanations do not tell the story of the actor or the act, but give us instead very general characteristics of an idealized organization and situation, which a decision-maker, in a time of crisis, will subjectively interpret.

These last conclusions are supported by the type of data accumulated by Paige and two others who have at least borrowed from Snyder's model in their own studies.(98) None of the propositions empirically verified in these studies are contradictory, and many are similar or the same. This is in spite of the many unrelated events they include, ranging from selected aspects of decision-making in the House Rules Committee of the American Congress, to American intervention in Korea, to her many interactions with the Soviet Union in crisis situations around the world. From a behavioral viewpoint, this similarity of data is probably a good sign, indicating factors have been discovered equally affecting all decision-makers acting in similar circumstances. However, from the point of view of Snyder's decision-making model, which all these studies to one degree or another accept, the similar data shows a dramatic inability of the model to accomplish that task it had set for itself: scientifically explaining how and why decision-makers acted in specific crisis situations. Is it really possible that self-determined perceptions of different actors, in different crisis situations, and at different times and places, were the same? This is not very likely. The uniform, obvious, mundane - almost unimportant - quality of most of the propositions indicates that the analysts have uncovered socially derived idealizations most actors in the common-sense world unquestioningly accept, but these actors, because they are in a crisis atmosphere, simply take into consideration. These propositions are therefore neither adequate explanations of the crisis decisions nor adequate indicators of how the national actors perceived their situations prior to acting. Snyder's decision-making model has failed in both its major objectives.

4 ETHNOMETHODOLOGY AND THE 'HUMANIZATION' OF SOCIAL SCIENCE

Schutz's influence in the social sciences is growing, primarily because of an increasing awareness among social scientists and others that traditional scientific method, though suited to technological concerns of an industrialized society, does not adequately deal with human problems of a less quantifiable nature. His phenomenological social science is now seen by many as a reasonable and important attempt at reconciling empirical science to distinctly human social issues, a humanizing force upholding rationality, scholarship and science. Nevertheless, the results of empirical studies influenced by Schutz's method, as the historical evolution of decision-making theory illustrates, are disheartening and a bit ironic.

The precarious balance between subjectivity and science, first evident in Schutz's own methodology, has made decision-making theory too difficult to work with, forcing interested political scientists - Snyder included - into maintaining their credibility as scientists at the expense of their infatuation with phenomenology. Ethnomethodologists, perhaps recognizing the theoretical difficulties Snyder encounters, maintain a purposefully low-key approach to scientific claims of their methodology, in one particular case even denying sociology is a science or amenable to quantification while simultaneously offering quantified scientific explanation as a reasonable goal for practicing sociologists.(99) Though adopting basic principles of Schutz's methodological work,(100) ethnomethodologists are more practical, concerned with empirically studying and explaining normal, structured, everyday activities.(101) Decision-making theory, as first conceived, was so intent on remaining true to both a phenomenological epistemology and empirical scientific method, it yielded only one full-length case study, even this admittedly inadequate to its purpose.(102) Ethnomethodologists, instead, focus almost exclusively on practical matters, methodological theory being foreign to the everyday social activities they study.

Their theoretical complacency, however, limits ethnomethodologists to explaining only that scope of social behavior included in Schutz's common-sense world, the routine, semi-automatic social patterns relevant to his sociological method. Typical ethnomethodological case studies therefore deal with problems which, though distinct, are something less than profound: the first five seconds of 500 taped phone conversations;(103) normal conversation patterns in a Lue tribe;(104) how a policeman on the beat becomes suspicious;(105) general rules for acting like a woman in American society;(106) how we conceptualize, in normal conversation, a place not immediately present;(107) how we make sense out of, and talk about, observable sights in which other persons are apparently active;(108) why we sometimes recognize situations immediately, 'at a glance';(109) an analysis of the art of walking.(110) These, and other similar studies,(111) have given us such sweeping sociological generalizations as: 'describers' interpretations of behavior are not necessarily independent of their interpretations of the behavior's situation or circumstance'; (112) 'in selecting a "right" formulation, attention is exhibited to "where-we-know-we-are," to "who-we-know-we-are," to "what-we-are-doing-at-this-point-in-the-conversation"';(113) we become suspicious of moral character by establishing 'normalities' and looking for 'abnormalities';(114) and the avoidance of collision when walking is the product of concerted work on the part of co-participants, based on socially-accepted navigational rules and constraints related to 'togethering' (walking with others) and 'aloning' (walking alone).(115)

This type of social observation, evidently of interest to some and certainly relevant to our understanding selected aspects of social behavior, concerns us now for two reasons. First, its sociological subject matter and quality of explanation are both clearly irrelevant to an actor's self-consciously determined view of things. Schutz's method is concerned with explaining what any typical actor will do in typical situations under typical conditions. As such, it deals with general social forces equally affecting everyone, e.g. social rules for interpreting behavior, becoming suspicious, knowing where and what we are talking about, walking properly. Ethnomethodologists investigate impersonal, objective forces similarly determining for all actors in the common-sense world how and why any one of them reacts to a typical situation. The naturalist approach to social science, a topic in chapter four, cogently and efficiently accomplishes the same task. It should, consequently, not be overly surprising to hear a noted practitioner call for the computerization of data related to ethnomethodological studies.(116) Still, even the suggestion of computerized phenomenology has to irritate, or worse, anyone familiar with, and sympathetic to, the original aspirations of the phenomenological movement. When a serious scholar can, in good conscience, infiltrate a group of heroin addicts, provoke them into conversation, and then transcribe their at times frenzied remarks in an article he is writing concerning how the word 'pinched' is used by members of the drug culture(117) - when this type of odious, demeaning, impersonal scholarship is encouraged by a group whose heritage is the concern for human subjectivity, then something vital has been sacrificed at the altar of empirical science.

Second, the phenomenological attempt at humanizing social science, epitomized in decision-making theory and ethnomethodology, has circuitously gone nowhere. It deals only with routine, mundane social behavior patterns, accumulating tomes of data about things we normally recognize anyway, and can adequately explain simply by reflecting on our common-sense habits. What about civil disorders, political disaffection, official corruption, war, racial, economic and sexual discrimination, violence - all embedded in a functioning democracy: these are distinctly human problems, more often than not encompassing people self-consciously aware of their situations, creatively coming to terms with society as they see fit. These problems must be understood and solved if we are to improve the quality of our lives, survive as a viable social unit. What hope does social science afford us when even its 'humanized' version scrupulously avoids this crucial task?

SUMMARY AND CONCLUSIONS

This chapter has analyzed Schutz's social theory with respect to its logical consistency and empirical usefulness. Its conclusions include the following:

1 in a logical sense, Schutz has been unable to reconcile each actor's freedom, implied in his phenomenological epistemology, with the totally passive role the actor assumes in the common-sense world;

2 consequently, Schutz's scientific method is relevant only to a scope of social phenomena more efficiently served by the traditional scientific approach Schutz is attempting to repudiate;

3 when Schutz's method is employed in studying a limited segment of social behavior, as it is in

decision-making theory and ethnomethodology, its logical and empirical weaknesses quickly sabotage the effort;

4 Schutz's attempt to 'humanize' social science by injecting a phenomenologically-derived notion of subjectivity into methodology, has altered the rhetoric, but not the reality, of social scientific investigations.

What could Schutz have done to avoid these difficulties? Can we, in theory and practice, integrate a phenomenological interpretation of individuality, stressing our innate abilities to subjectively perceive the world and determine our own actions in it, with a social scientific method? The horizon is still too opaque, our visions obscured, for any definite conclusions. We must now go back to fundamentals, analytically reconstructing the concept of 'science' from both within and outside of the phenomenological perspective, and determining whether or not there are points of contact between the two. Though it appears Schutz has failed, it is not yet clear success is even possible.

4 The 'objectivity' of empirical social science: a philosophical perspective

The phenomenological principles constituting the backbone of Schutz's presentation have emerged as major obstacles to his success. To the degree individuals do actualize the inherent tendencies described by these principles, Schutz's technique appears inadequate and misleading, while, negatively, our suppressing these tendencies eliminates altogether the relevance of a phenomenological approach. Schutz's writings are, in effect, attempts at integrating basic phenomenological concepts, used by Husserl in developing his own notion of science, with criteria of objectivity and empirical verifiability that are cornerstones of contemporary science. Our task now is to outline the epistemologies of these differing philosophical interpretations of valid, objective, 'scientific' knowledge. It will become increasingly evident that Schutz's vulnerability is rooted in these philosophical issues concerning the nature of science.

1 NATURALISM AS A PHILOSOPHY OF SCIENCE

Despite scattered contrary protests,(1) in the last forty years the philosophy of science has been dominated by one 'school' or perspective called, at different times, 'the classical position,' 'scientism,' 'positivism,' or 'naturalism'; the cardinal tenet of this view is the belief that scientific method is the only reliable way of attaining universal truths about nature, human beings, and society. For naturalists, the term we adopt, reality consists only of what science shows us exists, and valid, reliable knowledge results only from our applying scientific technique to selected aspects of reality. Naturalism, from this view, is truly 'the philosophical generalization of science.'(2) The precise content of naturalism will evolve, in quality and quantity, as each particular science matures.

There are, of course, many distinguished philosophers of science in the naturalist movement who have contributed important ideas to the task of outlining an explicit scientific method. We shall emphasize the work of two of the most popular and widely-read of these philosophers, Ernest Nagel and Carl Hempel, in order to represent, in general terms, how scientists today interpret valid scientific method. Though there are many technical differences between Nagel and Hempel, as between these two and others, my purpose here is to paint in very broad strokes a picture of what most contemporary scientists feel is the nature and purpose of their scientific enterprise. The ideas of Nagel and Hempel are used to illustrate this general, widespread agreement, not to emphasize possible sources of internal debate existing within the discipline.(3) Since I am proposing now to theoretically establish the socially accepted naturalist position for Husserl's eventual rejection of it, this slight distortion seems justified.(4)

> It is the desire for explanations which are at once systematic and controllable by factual evidence that generates science; and it is the organization and classification of knowledge on the basis of explanatory principles that is the distinctive goal of the sciences. More specifically, the sciences seek to discover and to formulate in general terms the conditions under which events of various sorts occur, the statements of such determining conditions being the explanations of the corresponding happenings.

This statement effectively summarizes the goals and purposes of science as seen from within naturalism. Science is systematic explanation, which aims at showing how individual objects or events depend for their occurrence on the existence and presence of other relational or structural properties. By isolating selected properties of phenomena and then 'ascertaining the repeatable patterns of dependence in which these properties stand to each other,'(5) scientists develop general laws or theories which systematically explain the observed uniformities. This explanation, because it places observed objects or events in the context of objective, determining relationships, provides the basis for effective prediction (and postdiction) of similar phenomena. Scientific explanations, therefore, in establishing a definite relation of dependence between propositions superficially unrelated, create objective causal patterns which allow us to predict when and how specific states can be expected to re-occur.(6)

Because scientific statements purport to explain real objects and events, they must expose themselves and their claims to the challenge of critical observational data accumulated under carefully controlled conditions. Scientific conclusions, in other words, are empirically verified according to an explicit scientific method, whose function it is to determine what the actual facts are. This method is not a definite set of techniques or rules (such as techniques of measurement employed in the physical sciences) applicable irrespective of subject matter. Rather, it is 'the persistent critique of arguments, in the light of tried canons for judging the reliability of the procedures by which evidential data are obtained, and for assessing the probative force of the evidence on which conclusions are based.'(7) The standards prescribed in these canons assure us that a significant proportion of our empirically verified conclusions will remain in general agreement with additional data we might obtain. Though not unalterably rigid, these canons exist apart from the subjective whims of any particular scientist. Valid knowledge is generated by our adopting these explicit, impersonal standards which, concomitantly, promote the aims of scientific inquiry. Personal assumptions or commitments distinct from those implicit in science as a method of achieving reliable knowledge, are outside the realm of scientific verification. If they actively influence the investigative procedure, it is no longer scientifically valid. Systematic explanations require that scientific inquiry investigate the relations of dependence between things irrespective of human or social values. 'Science aims at knowledge that is objective in the sense of being intersubjectively certifiable, independently of individual opinion or preference, on the basis of data obtainable by suitable experiments or observations.'(8)

The function of science, in sum, is to systematically explain the real world, where 'explanation is deductive subsumption under general laws.'(9) With the guidance of professionally accepted rules of method, aspects of the world are isolated and understood as determined results of a complex system of preceding variables. Scientific laws are empirically verified repeating patterns of events which predictably manifest themselves in the world, each law a general rule covering a select species of objects and events. In the inanimate world it is assumed, based on prior empirical evidence, that every representative phenomenon will react similarly to identical environmental conditions. From one general rule, therefore, we deduce what will occur, under given circumstances, to the whole species of objects. With human beings also part of the real world, the deductive applicability of scientific explanations holds true even when we investigate aspects of individual or social behavior: from one scientific law we are able to deduce the behavior every human actor will exhibit in a defined situation. Inherent in this naturalist position is a theory of perception first enunciated by Hume. Known as the causal theory of perception, it states that what we perceive is ultimately determined by the objects of perception. Objects of the world, real only because they are confirmed by means of accepted scientific technique, act as 'outer' stimuli to individuals coming in contact with them, and, sequentially, provide them with an 'inner' sensory response. Perception results from the subjective process of interpreting the sensation caused by the external objects. The process of perceiving is totally isolated from the objects of perception: my perception of a tree is caused by my inner sensory response to the tree, which, in turn, is caused by the tree itself. In reality, of course, the tree initiates the procedure by causing the sensory response which causes me to perceive it. Perceptions are always determined by sensations; sensations by outer stimulii. Consequently, the same external object will cause all individuals to perceive the same thing. Scientific explanations of individual or social behavior, because they are based on empirically verified objects and phenomena of the real world, are therefore deductively applicable to all human beings.(10)

The naturalist conception of science is based on this desire to provide systematic, empirically supported explanations which take the form of general laws that are applied deductively to the real world. However, the diverse qualities of existing worldly phenomena make it improbable that scientific explanations will always be expressed in the same manner. Stars, water and people are all alike in their being part of the real world, yet their qualitative differences make it difficult to study each in the same way or understand each to the same degree. For this reason naturalists claim there are different kinds of systematic explanations, all of which are scientific.(11) Deductive models, applicable to situations and subject matters easily verified by accepted scientific procedure, are, from a scientific viewpoint, the most desirable and perfect forms for explanations to take. Such models provide empirically verified general laws from which a whole class of objects and events are deductively explained. Not surprisingly, Nagel and Hempel claim their respective deductive models characterize scientific research done under the most ideal conditions, where the quality of observed phenomena facilitates our accumulating a maximum of information from which relational or structural laws can be abstracted. Research conducted in the natural sciences is generally of this kind. Does this now mean objects and events constituting the subject matter of the historical and social sciences are not scientifically explainable? If deductive models ideally fulfill the naturalist requirements for adequate explanation, how can other models, relevant to all objects and events not included in the natural sciences, be considered scientific?

These questions are based on a faulty assumption, for the various models described by Nagel, Hempel and other naturalists are actually not as different as they first appear. In fact, the ideal of scientific explanation is hidden, in one form or another, in all of them. Probabilistic or statistical explanations are, for example,(12)

> uniformly deductive in pattern; at least one premise in such explanations must be statistical in form; and the degree of statistical dependence assumed in at least one premise must be greater than the degree of dependence stated in the generalization for which the explanation is proposed.

Statistical laws are therefore analogous to deductive laws because they 'assign to the explanandum event described by the explanandum statement the logical probability called for by the logical relation between the explanans and the explanandum statements.'(13) Both Nagel and Hempel indicate in these statements that the occurrence of a class of phenomena can be inferred with a high degree of probability by applying laws of statistical form to specific circumstances. Thus, even statistical explanations are assumed to possess a high degree of deductive applicability. Prediction is therefore as much a quality of statistical explanations as it is of more strictly deductive ones.(14) There is, however, an even more important connection between statistical and deductive explanations. Inherent in the naturalist position is the following thesis:(15)

> for every set of attributes (or variables) [in the real world] there is some system which is deterministic with respect to that set . . . .[F] or every set of human actions, individual or collective characteristics, or social changes that may be of

> concern to the historian, there is some system which is deterministic with respect to those items.

All objects and events in the world, including those related to human behavior, are theoretically subsumable under one or another general law that is deductively applicable to a whole class of phenomena. This means that statistical laws are useful not because the phenomena they explain are in any sense unpredictable or unscientific, but rather because we simply do not have enough information - which is there, waiting to be discovered - to recognize the systems deterministic with respect to them. The more evidence we accumulate, the greater likelihood of developing valid statistical explanations.(16) Because all phenomena are determined by some system, once we accumulate enough evidence to recognize the one relevant to our needs statistical explanations will evolve into explanations of the deductive type. This is why Nagel claims that, even though the empirical social sciences are characterized by statistical explanations, the development of strictly universal deductive laws of social behavior is not inherently impossible.(17) Hempel puts it bluntly by stating:(18)

> I think that all adequate scientific explanations [including statistical explanations] . . . presuppose at least implicitly the deductive or inductive subsumability of whatever is to be explained under general laws or theoretical principles . . .. And the covering-law model [i.e. deductive-nomological explanations] represents . . . the basic logical structure of the principle modes of such explanatory subsumption.

Though some naturalists, criticizing Nagel and Hempel on their treatment of statistical laws, feel these are not explanations because they fail to meet the predictive criteria of deductive laws,(19) there is no disagreement in principle. Statistical laws are valid when, in the light of available information, deductive laws can not yet be discerned. As our information increases, statistical laws become more dependable. When all necessary information is ours, statistical laws become 100 per cent dependable, i.e. strictly deductive. For naturalists, statistical explanations are merely an indication that further information is needed if we are to understand the underlying unity of statistically connected phenomena.

Teleological explanations present no greater problems for naturalists, for, as Nagel puts it, 'the use of teleological explanations in the study of directively organized systems is as congruent with the spirit of modern science as is the use of nonteleological ones.'(20) The case for this claim is a relatively simple one. A standard teleological statement declares 'The function of the heart in animals is to enable animals to circulate blood to all parts of their body,' or, more technically, 'The function of X in a system S with organization Y is to enable S in environment E to engage in process P.' Naturalism 'unpacks' these statements to read: 'All living animals, under normal bodily conditions, circulate blood throughout their bodies; if animals have no hearts, even though they have all other bodily organs, they do not circulate blood; hence, animals contain hearts;' or, 'Every system S with organization Y and in environment E engages in process P; if S with organization Y and in environment E does not have X, then S does not engage in P; hence, S, with organization Y, must have X.' Naturalists contend only the form of the first, teleological, explanation has been altered, that the quality remains, though translated into nonteleological terms. The difference between teleological and equivalent nonteleological explanations is the difference between saying 'P (i.e. the circulation of blood) is an effect of X (i.e. the heart)' and 'X is a cause or condition of P.' 'In brief, the difference is one of selective attention, rather than of asserted content.'(21) There is nothing unique about phenomena that are explained teleologically; by slightly shifting the focus of our efforts we can use deductive explanations to accomplish the same task. This is done by analyzing what appear to be goal-directed systems into constituent parts which are causally relevant to the maintenance of some feature of those systems, and which, in relation to each other and to environmental factors, exhibit determinate relations capable of being formulated as general laws.(22) Teleological explanations therefore presuppose the existence and relevance of general laws which can be, potentially, deductively applied to explain the same phenomena.(23) Since humans, according to the causal theory of perception presupposed by naturalists, react to stimuli in a manner similar to the way natural phenomena do to controlled environmental variables, teleological or functional explanations used in the social sciences are not logically different from those used in the natural sciences.(24) 'There are, then, no systematic grounds for attributing to functional analysis a character *sui generis* not found in the hypotheses and theories of the natural sciences and in the explanations and predictions based on them.'(25)

A genetic explanation interprets observed phenomena as

final stages of a developmental sequence, the successive stages of which account for what is observed. The logical structure of a genetic explanation requires our describing various events that chronologically separate the state of affairs being explained and the occurrence that originated the sequence culminating in this state. The logical progression from one occurrence to another is accomplished through the use of statistical and, if possible, deductive laws, connecting one to the other. 'In a genetic explanation each stage must be shown to "lead to" the next, and thus be linked to its successor by virtue of some general principles which make the occurrence of the latter at least reasonably probable, given the former.'(26) Consequently, genetic explanations of particular events can be analytically broken down into sequences of probabilistic explanations whose premises refer to events happening at different times rather than concurrently. Probabilistic explanations, we have seen, are deductive in nature because of both their logical make-up and epistemological assumptions. Naturalists therefore conclude that genetic models, like teleological and statistical ones, fulfill the requirements of a valid scientific explanation.(27)

Our brief survey of various models of scientific explanation illustrates each of them is reconcilable to the naturalist demand that valid scientific explanation be 'deductive subsumption under general law.' Deductive laws expressing causal relationships and applicable to a whole species of phenomena are the most complete and useful form of scientific explanation. For one reason or another not all aspects of the real world are amenable to such orthodox understanding. Scientists come to terms with these types of phenomena, usually related to historical and social behavior, by using statistical, teleological and genetic models of explanation. These closely resemble the ideal deductive model because all aspects of the real world, including natural and social phenomena, exhibit some system which is deterministic with respect to themselves. Each model attempts to elicit these deterministic systems in its own manner, but each fulfills the same scientific task. When this is achieved, the models will merge with the deductive ideal on which their separate logics are now based.

Since scientific explanation aims at uncovering the causal order of the universe, the naturalist conception of human freedom will, predictably, focus on impersonal, objective conditioning factors. Both Nagel and Hempel, while lauding the moral responsibility characterizing men and women in society, also believe:(28)

> a person is correctly characterized as a responsible moral agent if he behaves in the manner in which a normal moral agent behaves; and the characterization remains correct even if the organic and psychological conditions that make it possible for him to function as a moral agent are *not within his control* on any of those occasions when he is acting as a responsible person. (emphasis is mine)

It would be illogical for naturalists to define human freedom as being in any sense unique or subjectively determined because scientific understanding entails our recognizing those general laws or theoretical principles encompassing the subject matter. Our behavior, if it is to be understood and scientifically explained, must be placed in the context of its relevant, impersonal determining system.(29)

If this is so, if human behavior can be studied in a manner consistent with the ideals of scientific method, why have the social sciences thus far so conspicuously failed in developing empirically supported laws of the type distinguishing the natural sciences? Naturalists, for obvious reasons, feel this deficiency represents a failure of technique rather than theory. For the purposes of science, human beings must be considered as complex, but understandable, variants of a quality inherent to all worldly phenomena - inhuman and human. The philosophy of social science is therefore the philosophy of natural science applied to the study of social products of human interaction. Five major arguments have evolved to refute this claim, each seeing in the relative failure of contemporary social science a more fundamental conflict between the quality of individual action in society and the criteria of scientific method. These, with the naturalist critique, follow.

1 'Because social interaction is a spontaneous process taking place in a realm impervious to an observer's control, there is no way to reproduce those laboratory conditions of controlled experimentation so necessary to the discovery of valid scientific law.'

Naturalists find two significant weaknesses in this argument.(30) First, there is nothing unique about the social sciences in their inability to reproduce laboratory conditions of controlled experimentation. Disciplines such as astronomy and embryology, both solid members of the natural sciences, share this same characteristic and yet have contributed significantly to our body of scientific knowledge. Second, 'controlled investigation,' entailing 'a deliberate search for contrasting occasions in which the phenomenon is either uniformly manifested . . . or manifested in some cases but not in others, and the subsequent examination of certain factors discriminated in those occasions in order to ascertain whether variations in these factors are related to differences in the phenomena,'(31) does not require we reproduce or manipulate variables in satisfying the logical function of experimentation. Science requires controlled empirical inquiry. This is accomplished either by using controlled experimentation, in which one variable is manipulated by an observer, or controlled investigation, where the fluctuation of many variables is observed in the repetition of a real phenomenon.(32) The social sciences present no insuperable problem in the quest for controlled empirical inquiry.

2 'Social behavior has a "culturally determined" and "historically conditioned" character, and will therefore vary with the society and historical period we choose to study. Because of this, scientific generalizations dealing with society and history are valid only within a limited time and locale.'

Since all real phenomena, including human actions, are the caused results of one or more relevant deterministic systems, naturalists contend 'all human actions must involve physical and physiological processes whose laws of operation are invariant in all societies.'(33) Apparent differences in the organization and modes of behavior of different societies are consequences not of qualitatively incomparable patterns of social relations, but simply of variations in the explicit manner universal truths are manifested separately, where specific social values may obscure the relationship between these separate variables and the common pattern they really exhibit. Different cultural patterns that characterize our world do not preclude the existence of common universal variables, and are actually the stage upon which these truths parade in disguise. Social scientists must abstract the real from the apparent.(34)

3 'Because human beings can modify their behavior when in possession of new knowledge, the public espousal of scientific technique and general transcultural social laws may both alter the behavior they are intended to explain. This dilutes the value of social scientific investigations.'

Naturalists propose four solutions to this difficulty.(35) First, though experimental technique may alter the behavior of observed subjects, this also happens in relation to non-human objects studied by the natural sciences. Precautions, such as observing the subjects without them knowing it, can be taken to neutralize such undesirable side-effects. Second, scientific laws are, in a logical sense, conditional. They are based on the supposition that 'if' described antecedent conditions are present 'then' there will occur predictable consequences. If action based on knowledge of such a law is not one of the conditions that law mentioned in its antecedent clause, then it is not necessarily shown to be erroneous if a situation is discovered in which the stated conditions occur but the predicted consequences do not take place. The law is valid only for the antecedent conditions it has specified. Third, it is possible, using accepted scientific method, to uncover social laws that take into account the social knowledge we possess as a variable in the determination of an event. Finally, it is easy to exaggerate the role of deliberate choice in the determination of human events. Social habit and other uncontrollable factors usually work to inhibit such 'radical,' 'over-all' changes in social behavior feared by those who support this argument.

4 'The subject matter of the social sciences includes purposive human action, directed at individually conceived "ends" or "values." It therefore has a "subjective" or "value-impregnated" quality. Valid social knowledge must reveal what the actors themselves think, rather than what can be intersubjectively verified through accepted scientific techniques. A purely "objective," social science is impossible.'

This argument, which we have been studying in relation to the presentations of Weber and Schutz, is the most important challenge to naturalist hegemony in the social sciences. Yet, based on those principles of science already enunciated, naturalists have very little difficulty defending themselves. In the first place, because subject matter not familiar to actors is very often vital in explaining why they behaved in a certain way, many factors relevant to a scientific understanding of social phenomena are not at all subjective. Scientific explanations of social behavior cannot always be reduced to a special class of statements about individual conduct. By limiting the understanding of social events to an interpretation of action in terms of its subjective meaning, we eliminate all social behavior not directly related to subjectively meaningful motivational concepts. Obviously, explanations in terms of meaningful categories can illuminate social processes, as Weber's discussion of the rise of capitalism has. However, it is absurd, for naturalists, to claim such explanations completely account for all social processes, or are always more useful than explanations in terms of other variables (e.g. the state of technology, form of political and economic organization, population density, or physical environment) often exhibiting at least as much predictive and systematizing power.(36)

> Accordingly, although methodological individualism and interpretative social science rightly emphasize that social phenomena are constituted out of interactions between purposive human agents, neither of these essentially similar approaches to social inquiry possesses the unqualifiedly pre-eminent merits that are claimed for it.

The same can be said for the ideal type method Weber and Schutz claim is unique to the interpretative social sciences: in developing a valid ideal rational behavior type we must know more than the subjective motives and beliefs constituting a rational act for an actor. Because we are attributing to a typical actor the tendency to uniformly behave in a characteristic way, we must carefully delineate the conditions within which this typical act will occur. Since we are often unaware of variables affecting our behavior, these conditions must include information not only about a typical actor's objectives and beliefs, but also about other aspects of the psychological and biological state he is in, and about his environment.(37)

> To explain an action in terms of . . . [a typical] agent's reasons and his rationality is thus to present the action as conforming to those general tendencies [described in the conditions relevant to the ideal type] or as being a manifestation of them. According as the sentences expressing the tendencies in question are of strictly universal form or of a statistical form . . . the resulting dispositional explanation will be deductive or inductive probabilistic in character. But in any event it will subsume the given particular case under a general uniformity.

As we gather more information relevant to the typical behavior pattern in question, the probabilistic nature of our ideal type construct will evolve into a more clearly nomological explanation. With regard to methods of classification (i.e. ordering, measurement, empirical correlation and theory formation), ideal type explanations are entirely compatible with deductive explanations of the kind all empirical scientific inquiry aims at.(38)

Apart from its being inapplicable to large segments of social conduct and its lacking a distinct method, there are even more cogent reasons for rejecting the interpretative conception of society as an independent and competing approach to social science. Scientific method is a set of professionally tested and accepted standards that supply us criteria by which to separate real facts from unverifiable - and therefore unreal or imaginary - notions. These criteria prescribe that the subject matter of scientific investigations be objective in the sense of being verifiable through the controlled (by means of accepted scientific techniques of measurement) sensory observation of anyone prepared to make the effort. Scientists, when performing their professional tasks, will not concern themselves with abstract notions such as 'ghosts,' 'love,' or 'ideals,' unless these can somehow be operationalized in the real world according to the canons of scientific method. Though this process is somewhat easier for natural scientists, whose objects of study are usually readily identifiable and measurable, 'the crucial point is that the logical canons employed by responsible social scientists in assessing the objective evidence for the imputation of psychological states do not appear to differ essentially . . . from the canons employed for analogous purposes by responsible students in other areas of scientific inquiry.'(39) Scientific knowledge must be based on objective evidence, whether this knowledge deals with trees, stars, animals, or human attitudes. Behaviorism is a methodological approach that places a premium on objective, intersubjectively observable data. It doesn't necessarily deny subjective consciousness, it just contends such states can be revealed and studied by means of overt manifestations of individual behavior (acts, words, expressions, etc.). As reprehensible and incomplete as behaviorism appears to some, it is necessary if we desire to understand human behavior scientifically, for it is only by means of behaviorism that intersubjectively verified - scientific - generalizations are found.(40) This point cannot be over-emphasized: though attitudes and beliefs may exist in a subject's mind or consciousness, they cannot be scientifically explained apart from their objective manifestations in the real world. Thus, behaviorism, the naturalist method for studying human behavior, is an irreplaceable component of any valid scientific study of purposive human action. All projected emotions, attitudes, or purposes must be supported by evidence gathered in accordance with accepted canons of empirical inquiry. They must be defined by means of a systematic organization of data obtained from overt human responses to a variety of conditions, hopefully leading to our finding regularities in such responses and our constituting scientific explanations of them.(41) These explanations reveal that, though we act according to meaningful categories comprising our motives, our behavior, in specific instances, is caused not by subjectively defined goals or motivations, but by antecedent impersonal conditions determining both our initial subjectively-experienced desire and the courses of action through which we mean to satisfy this desire.

5 'The social values of scientific observers control their assessments of evidence and influence their conclusions. Scientific knowledge of society is therefore biased in favor of the scientist's own beliefs.'

Naturalists parry this argument with relative ease.(42) First, though of course scientists study what they are interested in, this does not necessarily affect the objectivity of the investigation itself, which must reflect impersonal principles of scientific method. Second, because facts and values differ, they are easily distinguished and practical steps can be taken to eliminate value bias. This is one important function of scientific debate and a free scientific community. Finally, we must distinguish between 'characterizing value judgements,' which state a given characteristic is in some degree present or absent, and 'appraising value judgements,' which conclude some state of affairs is worthy of approval or disapproval. Social scientists must make characterizing value judgments, or else there is no basis for limiting the subject matter of their inquiries. This type of value judgment is consistent with the logical canons of science, for it in no way interferes with accepted scientific procedure. Appraising value judgments, on the other hand, cannot be scientifically verified. Since these are the kinds of values the proponents of this argument are referring to, they must be assiduously avoided and weeded out of our body of scientific knowledge. Objectivity is guaranteed in social science as long as we adhere to principles the scientific community itself has found satisfactory.

These arguments illustrate the utter confidence naturalists exhibit that only their approach to reality is worthy of the prestigious label 'scientific.' They are, in effect, contending the weakest link in the chain of scientific knowledge, our inchoate science of social interaction, can be strengthened by more of the same. There is nothing so exceptional or unique about human beings that their social behavior cannot be exposed to the same type of analysis that has been so productive for natural scientists. Approaches to society which feed off the apparent differences between human and non-human phenomena are living in a world of illusions - or at least unverified generalizations. They are all doomed to inconsequential and fanciful existences unless they accept the indisputable principles of science upon which all valid knowledge is founded. With this acceptance will come the realization that they are each tributaries leading into the same river of scientific truth. To naturalists, these approaches have been nurtured on the mistaken premise that, because the world is large enough to accommodate many divergent methodologies, more than one can be scientific.

In sum, there are five epistemological principles defining naturalism and distinguishing it from all other organized attempts at explicating the philosophy of science:

1 scientific knowledge consists of our explaining each phenomenon as a constituent element of an objective system of relations that is existent in the real, external world;

2 there is no reliable knowledge apart from scientific knowledge;

3 scientific knowledge is drawn from all kinds of subject matter, natural and social, non-human and human;

4 all these phenomena are scientifically explained only by our using an explicit method, though some more easily than others;

5 scientific investigations are conducted according to methods of empirical verification that are in accordance with contemporary criteria of objectivity.

Differences of opinion among naturalists concerning the logic of scientific explanation do not question the substance of these five principles, but are directed at their increasing actualization in scientific research. We now adopt these principles as a yardstick for measuring the phenomenological effort at coming to terms with the same issues of truth and falsity.

2 PHENOMENOLOGY AS RIGOROUS SCIENCE

The philosophical foundation for Husserl's critique of naturalism has already been established. Whereas naturalism claims all things in nature are understood and empirically studied as conditioned in their existence or occurrence by causal factors within an inclusive system of nature, Husserl feels that in the act of consciousness are elements not reducible to nature. This feeling is at the root of Husserl's doctrine of transcendental phenomenology. The phenomenological conception of science is a logical outcome of this epistemology.

As Husserl sees it, the basic weakness of naturalism lies in its theory of perception.(43) The causal theory of sense perception implies there is an external physical world, and this world is real, i.e. defined solely in terms of the physical. Because there is only one real world in which phenomena exist in one or another system of determined relations, and human beings are part of this world, all individuals perceive the same thing when placed in the same system of determining environmental events. Placed in front of a tree, every observer perceives it identically. Husserl claims this central thesis of naturalism is based on naive assumption. If knowledge is derived from sense impressions, as naturalists contend, then all we know for sure are our own sense perceptions. Though our culture interprets them as objectively valid, this does not alter the problem from an epistemological point of view: 'objective' empirical science is built on a subjectivism falsely 'reduced' to a physical objectivity by social convention. We believe the causal principle of sense perception is true, and, consequently, we believe there is an objective world. In actuality, all we really experience is our subjective sense perceptions of the world we assume is there. Everything except our own experiences are taken for granted and accepted, not validatable unless we invoke more unprovable statements. This becomes increasingly obvious as we recognize the reduction from sense perception to physical objectivity as failing to adequately convey private and subjective knowledge we know, but cannot easily express in physical terms. At these times especially we realize contemporary empirical science depends on a subjectivism it is incapable of expressing. Its claim to objectivity is false because its principles are really ideal and hypothetical, confirmable only by naive assumptions not directly related to our actual experiences. These, the subject matter of our own unique perceptions, are the only means we have for confirming scientific knowledge. Self-conscious experience must support the claim to objectivity of any intellectually honest interpretation of science. Since naturalism, though inadvertently justifying it, explicitly hinders our studying consciousness, we reject naturalism as a defendable path to science.

Consciousness is the focus for any justifiable theory of objective knowledge. It is also a unique attribute of human beings, distinguishing them from every other kind of animate or inanimate phenomena we perceive in the world. It is, consequently, impossible for us to categorize consciousness as a 'natural' phenomenon, in the same sense that non-human objects and things are considered part of the world of nature. Consciousness is not a natural event, but is a product and consequence of our irreducible subjectivity. We do not, therefore, equate nature with all of reality, for what is most profoundly real in the life of each human subject is unalterably distinct from the non-human world of unthinking, mindless phenomena. But this naturalization of consciousness is precisely what scientists assert when they demand all scientific investigation be based on a method proper to the study of nature. Contemporary scientists, unaware an inherently subjective, completely irreducible quality of consciousness must support any responsible claim to objectivity their discipline offers, are thus powerless to epistemologically justify their own scientific method. Since this method is the result of specific subjective mental activities (e.g. observing, inferring, theorizing, revising, etc.), how does naturalism, ostensibly objective, account for itself on its own terms? Put differently, what is the objective rationale for our accepting the naturalist belief that scientific method includes professionally accepted, impersonal and objective, intersubjectively verifiable (by means of empirical sense-data) criteria of validity? Husserl answers there is none - there can be none - given the limits naturalism sets for itself. Each scientist simply accepts the 'a priori' truthfulness of naturalist criteria of objectivity, unaware even this conscious process of acceptance illustrates the inadequacy of these criteria. If naturalism is to epistemologically justify what it presents as objectively valid, without falling into the dead-end trap of merely asserting its truthfulness, it must elucidate the subjective process of our consciously experiencing the criteria. This is beyond its scope or capability, so naturalism remains an unjustified, and unjustifiable, philosophy. It assumes there is a social world where scientists and philosophers share intersubjective methods of communication, but is powerless to study the actual nature of this world or critically evaluate social criteria of objectivity. It is unaware that, 'true nature in its proper scientific sense is a product of the spirit that investigates nature, and thus the science of nature presupposes the science of the spirit.'(44)

Contemporary science is a product of this inadequate naturalist view of the world. Scientific disciplines therefore find themselves in a state of crisis, their 'genuine scientific character, the entire manner in which they have posed their problem and have devised their method for . . . [solving] it . . . [becoming] questionable.'(45) Scientific knowledge, universal, pure and absolute, is still attainable, but is not derived from a method distorting the quality of our subjective experiences and isolating consciousness from the world it perceives. Knowledge is scientific only if scientists themselves, and anyone else willing and capable, consciously perceive it as universal, pure and absolute. It is not in the natural world of non-human phenomena that we uncover scientific knowledge, but in the world of subjective consciousness, where all we can and do know originates. Husserl feels it is left to philosophy to delve into this world of consciousness, searching for the process by which knowledge is subjectively constituted, and eventually searching for knowledge itself. Genuine science is, in this view, synonymous with philosophy, while scientific method coincides with a body of rules or procedures facilitating our ascent into the world of consciousness. When Husserl terms his philosophy a 'rigorous science,' he means something quite different than the refined methods of the natural sciences. Primarily because contemporary scientific thinking starts from unclarified and ambiguous premises, philosophy, to be truly, 'rigorously,' scientific, leaves nothing unsolved. It explicates all primary presuppositions, which become immediately evident to us, and thus true. Philosophy is rigorous science in its uncovering universal elements of knowledge, the building material for derivative, empirical scientific explorations.

With scientific knowledge a product of philosophy, and this concerned mainly with consciousness, valid scientific knowledge is derived from, and continually brought up before, consciousness. There is no body of scientific knowledge independent of the consciousness of reflective individuals. The method of constituting scientific knowledge is characterized by a multiplicity of independent cognitions, all built on the transcendental phenomenological reduction. The truths of science, for Husserl, are not to be inferred from each other, but rather are linked together at their source: the universality of transcendental subjectivity. The objectivity of this knowledge is assured through our communicating it to others, though its purity is maintained only if identically reconstituted in each separate individual through a similar reflective procedure. The precise method of subjectively constituting scientific, or 'eidetic,' knowledge is thus an integral part of a phenomenological philosophy of science.(46)

Husserl's quest for scientific knowledge is marked by a special emphasis on human initiative and intellect. By performing the series of intellectual processes known as reductions, we elevate ourselves to successively purer states of consciousness, culminating in the universal subjectivity of the transcendental ego. This is the purest state of consciousness we experience, pure enough to be marked by a transcendental merging of subjectivity and objectivity. The transcendental ego objectifies an actor's reflective consciousness, assuring him the ability to constitute absolute knowledge, from which all contingent facts of the empirical world are derived. Such knowledge reveals itself in the form of 'eidé,' or essences, the apodictic truths manifested in, and giving meaning to, all particular factual phenomena we perceive in the everyday world. Knowledge of these essences, what Husserl calls eidetic science, is the only means of attaining the objectivity and universality that has traditionally been the distinguishing feature of science. The naturalist notion of science flounders in a derivative world of constantly changing empirical facts, never fulfilling its scientific responsibility to reveal indubitable, objective knowledge. Transcendental phenomenological method, on the contrary, probes directly into those essential invariants necessarily remaining unchanged, comprising the real subject matter of science.

Eidetic knowledge is constituted by transcendental egos through a process of imaginative and continuous variation of a given empirical sample. Let us take, as an example, a brown wooden table we readily perceive in front of us. Our problem is to scientifically investigate this table to uncover the objective, apodictic essence making it appear to us in this empirical form as a table. Our perceptions of the table in the normal, everyday world we usually experience are subjective and contingent. It is undoubtedly perceived differently by different people, depending on numerous and unpredictable factors such as mood, expectation, position, lighting, etc. Similarly, we can empirically quantify the physical characteristics of the table, but these figures are arbitrary and easily changed without necessarily producing a change in our perceptions: we can re-paint the table red and cut its legs in half, and still perceive a table. A valid scientific explanation reveals objective, universal criteria prompting each of us to perceive this particular empirical phenomenon as a table.

We attempt, first, to consciously abandon our normal mental states by performing a succession of phenomenological reductions culminating in our constituting ourselves as transcendental egos. From this vantage point we are able to constitute the universal knowledge we are searching for. Next, we transform the perceived object in our imaginations, by successively and uninhibitedly varying its features: its color, size, material, perspective, illumination, surrounding, background, density, weight, etc. This intellectual transformation should be as complete as possible, guided only by the broad scope and creative quality of our imaginations. The set of characteristics, unchanged among all the imagined transformations of the concrete thing perceived - in a sense, the 'kernel' of all possibly imaginable tables - are essential characteristics of the table, its 'eidos.' All imaginable tables must have these essential features. Conversely, all other qualities not included in the perceived table's 'eidos' are not essential for its being perceived as a table. We utilize this eidetic method to scientifically study any other quality or thing, making sure to imaginatively transform the selected phenomenon to the fullest extent possible. Had we instead chosen to investigate the perceived color 'brown' or the perceived material 'wood,' we would have varied everything but the color or material to uncover their respective 'eidé.' It is free, continuously modified variation that abstracts from a perceived phenomenon its unchangeable, objectively valid essence.

The essence of an empirical object determines the limits within which its contents vary in our imaginations. Consequently, the essence represents necessary conditions to be realized for an object to exist as an empirical fact. These are not all conditions of the object, only those making it what it is to those perceiving it. Scientific knowledge, then, is independent of the objects it explains, existing in a reality of its own. The 'eidos' of the table we observe exists as objective knowledge apart from this particular factual object, and would exist even if this object had never been built. Its mode of being, the mode of being of all scientific knowledge, is independent of external, empirically verifiable appearance. Naturalists construct a law of nature, the logical foundation of what they consider a valid scientific explanation, from results of their intuiting specific empirical facts. Husserl feels this total concern for the factual renders naturalist laws of nature contingent and inexact. They are based on facts, and it is of the very nature or essence of a 'fact' - revealed through eidetic research - that it is contingent and inexact. Husserl's concept of science refuses to reduce scientific laws developed by naturalists to laws 'a priori.' Naturalism, in this view, emerges an unscientific, arbitrary philosophy. For Husserl, 'the element which makes up the life of phenomenology as of all eidetical science is "fiction," [and] that fiction is the source whence the knowledge of "eternal truths" draws its sustenance.'(47) Fiction, not fact, is the basis of science. Since naturalism is concerned only with facts, it is unscientific.

A body of scientific information is formulated after eidetic constitution has already taken place. Husserl often utilizes the science of geometry to illustrate how this process unfolds.(48) At some point in history the 'eidos' of geometry was constituted by one transcendental ego. At that moment it was not quite ideally objective, for it was still based on a purely subjective awareness, not yet intersubjectively verified. As often happens, the original evidence, based on transcendental perceiving of eidetic knowledge, may have passed over to the observer's retentional consciousness, and finally faded into forgetfulness. It was eventually awakened by a directed effort of this observer's will. The re-awakening of this nascent 'eidos' was followed by its embodiment in words and its communication to others. It now became possible for many people to re-constitute, through their own mental activities, the original experience revealing the 'eidos.' As the spoken word is translated into writing, the science of geometry assumes a truly objective character. However, as this last historical stage is reached, words begin to hide the original significance of that transcendental act they are derived from. The original mental activity, the foundation of eidetic knowledge, is not and cannot be adequately reproduced in our actual communications. The original experiential evidence has faded, but not disappeared, underlying our scientific understanding in a sedimented form. Sedimentation, for Husserl, is analogous to forgetfulness, and the historical growth of a science is always accompanied by such forgetfulness. Original experiential evidence must be reactivated so its historical objectivization does not lose significance. Husserl's goal is to disentangle sedimented layers of science so we can all recognize the objective nature of its 'original' foundations,' or 'roots.' In criticizing naturalism, Husserl is claiming sedimentation is so thick that contemporary science, in general, is almost barren of significance. Eidetic knowledge is not intended to replace the results of empirical research, but rather to make this accepted body of information 'scientific.'

Husserl's concept of science is thus complete and unambiguous. It is universal in scope: all scientific laws are valid only to the extent they are intentionally constituted by reflective egos. The establishment of a body of scientific knowledge, if it is to be, in fact, truly scientific, must be accompanied by its relevant subjective process of constitution. Science and phenomenology are inseparable.

3 TWO ORGANIC VIEWS OF 'SCIENCE'

Naturalists claim there is a real, objective world consisting of a wide variety of phenomena, ranging from inanimate things to human subjects. This world, and all the phenomena it is composed of, is accurately measured by any scientist willing to adhere to an explicit method, or body of rules, professionally tested to insure objectivity. If it is properly performed, the measurement process reveals the existence of systems of determined relations actually causing all worldly phenomena - including individuals and societies - to appear as they do to the naked eye. These systems of determined relations are abstracted into generalizations, or laws, and are used in scientifically explaining whole species of phenomena each is relevant to. Laws constitute the body of our scientific knowledge; there is no reliable knowledge apart from them. Knowledge, for most contemporary philosophers of science, lies in an objective reality that is empirically confirmed and impersonally understood.

Opposing this view is Husserl's contention the world exists only through our perceptions. We subjectively perceive objects and events by extending ourselves outward and intending them with our conscious awareness. Within the scope of intentionality lies everything we have come to associate with the 'external world.' Since the reality of this world is actually located in conscious awareness, we impute a meaning to it ourselves, according to our own values and feelings. We define the world and determine our own courses in life - there is no other possibility given the subjective nature of reality. Scientific knowledge is not drawn from the objective world, for this world is an illusion, a consequence not of objective determining forces but of our self-imposed alienation from our own conscious processes. Knowledge exists, but it is individually constituted by a successively purified consciousness, able to transcend subjectivity and merge with the absolute. Science is an awareness of essences originating in the non-empirical world of the transcendental ego and percieved as contingent facts on the empirical level of reality. Scientific knowledge lies originally in an ideal world of universal subjectivity, not in the empirically confirmable environment.

If by 'empirical fact' we denote knowledge developed through an analysis of our observing and experiencing the world, then both phenomenology and naturalism can justly claim to be empirical: both strictly adhere to the use of empirical evidence. However, the intrinsic presuppositions of phenomenology and naturalism used to evaluate experiential data preclude our identifying empirical phenomenological evidence with empirical evidence as described in the naturalist scheme. While both phenomenological and naturalist knowledge are validly termed 'empirical,' empiricism in the former has a radically different meaning from that which it has in the latter.

Phenomenologists assume the world is given only through their conscious experiences, while naturalists assume their conscious experiences are given in, and only one element of, the external natural world. From a phenomenological point of view, the world is given to us as a direct and conscious sense-experience. On the other hand, though naturalists also experience the world through their senses, the sensory qualities of their experiences merely signify the communication of events and objects from the external world to their own minds. Phenomenologists experience worldly objects and events as cognitive constructs derived entirely from their conscious awareness, while naturalists assume their conscious sensory experiences are evidence for the existence of phenomena not merely as consciously perceived sense-objects, but also as representing physical objects existing in the world, apart from consciousness, only reflected in perception. To phenomenologists, objects and events meaningfully exist only when conscious experiences they are conceived in are given; to naturalists, the consciously experienced object or event is significative of a physical counterpart present in the natural world and existing even in the absence of an observer's experiential awareness.

As long as inquiries are restricted to actual experiences these differences between phenomenology and naturalism amount to no more than differences in terminology. When inferences are drawn from experiences, in particular, when knowledge derived from such experiences is used to build a body of universally or scientifically valid truths, the differences become paramount. If sense-data represents for conscious subjects the effective presence of physical objects, naturalists can use such data, gathered according to explicit and generally accepted rules, in building a body of scientific knowledge. If only the reality of the data of personal experience is assumed, as it is by phenomenologists, a system of scientific knowledge cannot be constructed from empirical data alone, for there is present no criteria of universality. This is why, as a philosophy of science, Husserl's phenomenology is non-empirical. It suggests that criteria of objectivity transcend any one subject's conscious experiences, occupying an ideal realm the observer can and must become conscious of to universalize his own data of experience. Naturalism is therefore the philosophical basis of empirical science, while phenomenology, also 'empirical' by its own criteria, as a philosophy of science describes a realm beyond empirically verifiable subjective experience.

Husserl thus 'humanizes' the social and natural sciences by substituting one idealism for another, countering scientists' alienation from humanity with a humanism that leap-frogs from consciousness to absolute, universal, 'objective' subjectivity.(49) The apotheosis of both empirical fact and an elusive transcendental ego are polar points in the self-consciously aware actor's search for Self. Husserl's scientific method leaves this actor grasping for a mode of consciousness that is subjectively meaningful and universally determining - a project more suited to theology than methodology.

Which of these two opposing concepts of science, naturalist or phenomenological, is 'real'; which is actually 'scientific,' which mere fancy? The answer depends on whether we consider ourselves naturalists or phenomenologists, the point being each interpretation of science is 'scientific' according to its own stated criteria. Naturalism and phenomenological idealism can both be defended as living up to their own norms of rigorous objectivity, provided they are recognized as organic positions in which various internally consistent principles are closely interconnected in such a way that they mutually supplement and support one another. Neither of the approaches is dependent on the other, and both, based on their respective premises, are logically tenable. Though each criticizes the other and claims to 'include' it within its own broader scope, clearly these criticisms are justified only from within their respective epistemologies. When considering empirical science and eidetic science together, each is 'right' or 'wrong' only in relation to the other. Taken separately, each offers a compelling argument.

Thus, it is perfectly acceptable, from a phenomenological point of view, to solve the verification problem with 'more and better subjectivity, more discriminating subjectivity, and more self-critical subjectivity, which will show the very limits of subjectivity.'(50) Similarly, for phenomenologists, scientific statements are proved 'only by the affirmation of everyone who, without prejudice, directs himself to the phenomenon in question.'(51) These statements are scientifically reliable only from within the definition of science phenomenologists offer us. From a naturalist viewpoint, however, they are almost meaningless: scientific knowledge is empirically confirmed through a method that is objective, in its being independent of any personal experience or consciousness. What does 'better,' 'discriminating,' or 'self-critical' subjectivity mean when there already exists an impersonal, objective method waiting to be used, not interpreted? Does 'without prejudice' imply scientific statements are validated apart from explicit objective criteria? If there really is an objective world of nature and an objective method for understanding it, why play with terms that scientists can interpret differently? On the other hand, if the world is subjectively defined and constituted, scientists will constitute for themselves, through subjectively meaningful procedures, the body of valid scientific knowledge. The irreconcilable quality of this conflict is effectively summarized, from the naturalist side, by Abel:(52)

> [I]t is difficult to see how the scientific validity of the phenomenological method can be maintained. Its claim for absolute certainty alone is unscientific. It furthermore rests upon the assumption of a 'pure ego' which is a metaphysical postulate. It implies uniformity of mental life that cannot be proved. Its criteria - the inner evidence - is only a subjective test, which unjustifiably claims objectivity. Its judgements, which are arrived at through contemplation of the nature of 'things,' are not susceptible of proof. Thus, if a statement made by the phenomenologist is not accepted as 'evident' by another person, the phenomenologist can only accuse his opponent of inaccurate contemplation but has not means whereby to convince him of the validity of his

> assertion . . .. Sociology cannot be a phenomenology of society and an empirical science at the same time. A body of scientific knowledge cannot include side by side theses that are derived by opposite methods. The results of the 'perception of essences' are unacceptable to the empiricist who cannot test these results by scientific methods, and, as Husserl says, the empirical discoveries are irrelevant to phenomenology since a phenomenological reduction has to exclude all judgements about empirical reality.

Consequently, there is, and has been, a general lack of communication among 'scientists' of both persuasions.(53) Naturalists, in fact, still use the word 'phenomenology' to denote the explanation of basic concepts of physical theories by description on the basis of direct physical experiences, an interpretation not directly related to Husserl. The extent of their 'recognition' of phenomenology as a competing philosophical approach to science is pointedly illustrated in one naturalist's warning to his colleagues that '"phenomenological" suggests description of phenomena (experiential facts) rather than of objective facts; it even suggests a theory cast in phenomenalistic language - the non-existent language of "sensa" dreamt by some philosophers.'(54) A notable lack, from both sides, of more sensible, dispassionate claims, indicates this statement accurately describes the mood surrounding the non-existent dialogue between naturalists and phenomenologists.(55) It is not too surprising that phenomenological efforts at dealing with methodological problems of the natural and social sciences are in key respects related to Husserl's transcendental idealism, distinct from those of naturalists. By examining these phenomenological forays into methodology, Schutz's ideas will be seen from a broader perspective, enabling us to approach their weaknesses from a more commanding analytical position.

4 PHENOMENOLOGY AND THE METHODOLOGY OF NATURAL AND SOCIAL SCIENCE

The phenomenological approach to natural science is relatively straightforward and explicit, primarily because non-human subject matter does not exist in a conscious, meaning-endowing state. Phenomenologists readily accept most knowledge comprising the corpus of natural scientific research at its face value: as quantitative descriptions, based on explicit criteria of measurement, of a limited segment of phenomena. What they do not accept are the implications of naturalist epistemology, isolating scientists from their world and rendering their quantitative descriptions 'objective' in an absolute sense. They propose replacing it with a more critical epistemological stance, describing the role of natural scientific knowledge within an inclusive totality of meaning, philosophically defined. Phenomenologists attempt to situate natural science, and all contingent empirical knowledge expressed within its disciplines, in a larger context of meaning reflectively constituted from within our own conscious experiences. Empirical scientific method, from this phenomenological perspective, is then interpreted as an instrument developed and utilized only to facilitate specific investigations, having no necessary or 'a priori' value in itself.

A typical argument from a phenomenologically-influenced natural scientist might unfold in the following manner.(56) Human beings, because they are intentionally-oriented towards the world and capable of reflectively defining all its subjectively meaningful qualities, must be central to any philosophical interpretation of science. Natural science, as now practiced, is deficient in not recognizing or understanding the subjectively constituted essences underlying empirical objects, and in blindly neglecting an ontology for relating natural scientific knowledge to the essential knowledge it is derived from. Phenomenology provides natural science with this ontology. It permits observers the realization that all science begins from an original self-determined project, delimiting, or thematizing, phenomena of the world into one select group, within which only beings of a well defined kind can figure, such as those having either countable or measureable characteristics. These are not 'objective' properties of 'objective' things existing in and of themselves, but are subjectively defined and chosen by those wishing to systematically encounter empirical phenomena. A subjectively limited set of mundane phenomena, insofar as they are countable and/or measurable, constitute for an empirical science the region of its scientific investigation. Each discipline projects its own scientific region. Within a discipline, empirical 'facts' are placed in the context of 'rules' and 'laws.' Since the facts are only expressed quantitatively (i.e. by measuring or counting), and the laws furnish relations between those numbers, mathematics is a useful tool for methodically comprehending observed objects. But numbers, rules, and laws do not provide 'objective' qualities of isolated objects. They have arisen only through scientists' intentional involvement in the world, their own thematizing of perceived phenomena. They are, as a result, valid only within the typical mode of intentionality (i.e. the scope of the original project) identifying each empirical science. An assertion is empirically valid only as long as scientists examine selected phenomena in the correct manner, based on criteria expressed in the relevant intentional mode. Experiences and experiments confirm or deny these assertions. Phenomenology thus removes the 'objectivity' of empirical natural science from internal relations of explanatory concepts or from the hypothesized reflection of a pre-given order of facts belonging to an isolated, objective world 'in itself.' Empirical scientific knowledge is a conscious awareness of phenomena the scope and quality of which have been subjectively determined by our conscious thematization. This knowledge is different from the philosophical verities we constitute through the reductions: without the latter, empirical knowledge is meaningless.

Supplementing natural science with a phenomenologically-inspired ontology is obviously justified only if naturalism lacks a proper philosophical foundation and is unable to account for itself according to its own epistemological criteria.(57) This position is defendable only if the basic principles of naturalism are rejected as inadequate to the task of constituting reliable knowledge. The phenomenological approach to natural science is constructed on precisely this assumption. Yet there is nothing inherently inadequate to the naturalist position, the principles of natural science themselves constitute a positive philosophy provided they are accepted as valid by observers.(58) The two positions, to repeat, are mutually exclusive and self-justifiable, each a logically consistent and organic philosophy. The phenomenological re-definition of natural science is scientifically accurate - consistent with, and oriented towards, intersubjectively verifiable knowledge - only from Husserl's transcendental phenomenological point of view.

Practically speaking, it is inconsequential whether or not phenomenological natural scientists fully accept Husserl's doctrine of transcendental essences. Once an epistemological emphasis on consciousness is posited, empirical natural science is logically derivative, detailing consciously defined measurable and countable aspects of a subjectively limited scope of phenomena.

Quantifiable results always occur within another framework: our consciousness. If Husserl's eidetic analysis is completely adopted, empirical facts of natural science are placed in the context of subjectively constituted absolute knowledge and given meaning from their relationship to it. But even if the extra-worldly existence of eidetic knowledge is denied, still remaining within a general phenomenological outlook, natural scientific facts are still situated in another context - the subjective consciousness of beings intentionally oriented to the world - and are meaningful only in relation to it. In this last case the possibility of our ever achieving absolute, scientific knowledge of any kind is denied, but empirical (i.e. contingent) natural science is still conceivable.

The situation is quite different when human beings become subject matter for phenomenologists, since phenomenology is itself based on the radical distinction of conscious subjects from non-conscious, non-human phenomena. Measurable and countable aspects of reflective human beings are often illusory, making it extremely difficult to quantify or objectify consciousness without abandoning its subjective quality, and thus denying its importance in the first place. In this respect, phenomenologically influenced methodologists of social science have a much more difficult task than their counterparts in the natural sciences. They have responded to the challenge in three distinct, recognizable ways: by accepting Husserl's eidetic analysis, and conceding real scientific knowledge of society is necessarily non-empirical;(59) by rejecting eidetic transcendental knowledge and abandoning the contention phenomenology, apart from a naturalist framework, can ever uncover social scientific knowledge;(60) and by rejecting both Husserl's transcendental 'eidos' and naturalist epistemology, but still contending phenomenology and empirical social science *are* compatible. This last category is most interesting, for it consists of methodologists, including Schutz,(61) attempting to integrate basic principles of two organic philosophies into one method.

5 SCHUTZ'S ATTEMPT AT SYNTHESIS

Husserl wished to apply consistently his method of systematically doubting the 'external' world without falling victim to a groundless negativism, denying everything but subjective whim. His description of a transcendental ego, pure epistemic consciousness, is intended as a new approach to constructing reliable knowledge, originating independently of consciousness, but not recognizable apart from conscious awareness. This presentation, evolving a notion of universal knowledge from consciousness, is analytically vulnerable. A defendable phenomenological argument must illustrate how a method epistemologically grounded in the primacy of consciousness consistently leads to a theory of apodicticity. As Laszlo points out,(62) Husserl's transcendental ego appears to be

> axiomatically projected to the argument in the form of a methodological assumption which, however, is never verified by the application of the method . . .. A truly consistent universal doubt cannot operate on the assumption of a transcendence of experiential events given to 'transcendental consciousness' without circularity and inconsistency. In a consistent 'argument from consciousness' transcendental consciousness cannot be a legitimate postulate, for nothing can be found in the analysis of the contents of consciousness which would warrant the notion of transcendence.

When he wrote 'The Phenomenology of the Social World,' Schutz accepted, in principle, Husserl's transcendental reduction as a necessary principle for phenomenologically deriving the important concept of intersubjectivity, from which all social experience is constituted.(63) As years passed, however, Schutz evinced a cynical appreciation more in tune with his sociological profession, finally rejecting it as a valid approach to intersubjectivity.(64) In this later view, Schutz contends intersubjectivity is not a problem of constitution to be solved in the transcendental sphere, but a basic attribute of our life-world, adequately described only by phenomenologically analyzing that life-world. His rejection of phenomenological idealism culminates in 'Type and Eidos in Husserl's Late Philosophy',(65) where he argues knowledge derived from Husserl's transcendental phenomenological reduction has its roots in the empirical sphere of reality. In other words, ideation, accomplished through Husserl's eidetic procedure, and induction, the procedure Schutz adopts for developing empirical types, are systematically related. Ideation represents a more exact and rigorous expression of the inductive types operative in our encounters with society. Eidetic consciousness originates in structures of typification we all experience in the common-sense world, and develops through an extensive survey of particular empirical possibilities, not through transcendental self-contemplation. What Husserl sees as a transcendentally constituted concept of 'table,' for example, Schutz sees as founded in our typifications of empirical objects perceived as tables, and formed by our extensive consideration of many similar empirical objects. Husserl's 'eidos' resembles and is genetically related to inductive types; it differs in degree only, rather than in kind, from the inductive type. Its superior quality is solely a result of its representing a broader dimension of empirical evidence. Because 'eidé' are genetically derived from empirical typicalities and never free themselves from their empirical origins, eidetic variation is not distinct from induction as a method of analysis.(66)

Schutz's concept of science is significantly different from Husserl's own. Husserl held that the transcendental reduction allows us to perceive apodictic knowledge, essentially independent of empirical objects but constituted subjectively.(67) Facts, meaningfully perceived in the empirical world, are reflections of this transcendental body of knowledge. Schutz, on the contrary, contends the 'eidos' is directly connected with facticity in the form of empirical types. The apodictic knowledge Husserl claims is universal in scope and yet independent of particular facts is, for Schutz, entwined with factual reality. Apodicticity, for Husserl, requires our separating facticity from necessity, but Schutz explicitly rejects such separation, thereby implying there is no 'a priori' knowledge underlying - and defining - empirical reality. He thus accepts the naturalist contention that objective scientific knowledge is located in empirical reality, not in a world constituted by transcendental egos. Similarly, he accepts the naturalist judgment that Husserl's transcendental phenomenological reduction is too subjective, even solipsistic, to comprise a method for uncovering scientific knowledge.(68)

Schutz's methodology provides no transcendental foundation for his objective criteria of scientific knowledge, relying instead on an inductive compilation of empirical facts that takes the form of ideal type explanations.(69) The scientific method appropriate to studying society describes second-order ideal type constructs, modeled after the primary idealizations actually influencing social actors, and explaining typical, regularly performed interaction. These ideal type models, the homunculi, when empirically verified, explain this interaction scientifically while simultaneously remaining true to actual meanings experienced by actors in typical encountered situations. Schutz's attempt at re-invigorating subjective aspects of a non-idealistic phenomenological methodology is an uncertain amalgam of two philosophical views of science, part of what I have called his 'dual vision.' It proclaims scientific, objective knowledge inherent to the empirical world, independent of subjectively constituted transcendental reality. Yet all knowledge must be consciously perceived and subjectively defined, for there is nothing apart from consciousness. Objective knowledge is therefore subjective knowledge - but why? Evidence is needed to show us that what we perceive and subjectively constitute *necessarily* corresponds to what is empirically confirmed. Schutz has rejected both Husserl's idealism and the naturalist's epistemology. The burden is his to somehow transcend the perennial gap separating unique individuality from scientific knowledge *without* ever leaving the world of empirical facts. As Laszlo remarks in another, related, context, the conclusions of a non-transcendental phenomenological investigation 'cannot signify other than private knowledge, and by "private" I do not mean knowledge that is incommunicable, but one that does not admit evidence (in the light of the adopted criteria) of any mind or object existing independently of its experience, to whom or which information could be communicated.'(70) Such conclusions, though grounded in subjective reality, are in no apparent sense scientifically - universally - valid.

Schutz intends to confront this issue in his analysis of motivation. However, in describing patterns of social behavior as products of systematically related 'because' and 'in-order-to' motives, he merely introduces a new vocabulary without solving the fundamental problem of finding objective criteria in an empirical world peopled by phenomenologically-defined subjects. Indeed, given the organic nature of the two philosophies of science he is pretending to integrate, the task itself is misconceived. If a phenomenological epistemology is accepted, objective knowledge must be constituted by the subject, through his subjectivity. In this scheme it is logically necessary that there exist a super-subjective, transcendental realm in which the actor subjectively perceives objective knowledge. Such a realm cannot correspond to empirical reality because, if it does, perceived empirical facts can be scientifically (i.e. objectively) confirmed impersonally, without necessarily referring to subjective perception. Naturalists claim objective knowledge does exist in this empirical world. But because of this, it is necessary they disregard subjectivity or consciousness, which in any case exists within the empirical world and, like all other natural phenomena, is determined by empirically confirmable forces. If Schutz contends empirical reality is the locus of objective knowledge, as he does, then he cannot uphold consciousness as the ultimate source of all knowledge, which he also does. Schutz's concept of science and his sociological method are both irreconcilable to his more basic epistemological premises.

He is thus forced into assuming what he cannot prove. Abstracting from empirical evidence surrounding a limited segment of social interaction, he attributes to the social actors involved a set of typical, subjectively meaningful motives. These are the basis of second-level constructs serving as scientific explanations of the social behavior being observed. Clearly the motives are attributed to the social actors by the observer, on the basis of impersonal empirical data. If actors really do subjectively constitute knowledge, then there is no necessary correlation between empirical data and scientific certainty; those second-level constructs represent only the observer's undirected, fact-filled, descriptive guesswork rather than objective explanations. Conversely, if the empirical data actually is objectively valid, then we are only fooling ourselves in believing it must also be subjectively meaningful: objective empirical knowledge is not contingent on subjective awareness. Confronted with the Scylla of recognizing the dubiousness of his method and the Charybdis of fooling himself into accepting it, Schutz apparently opts for the latter. His analysis of the unquestioning, naive attitude characterizing our existence in the common-sense world is, at best, a feeble attempt at reconciling his epistemology to his method, solving the problem by defining it out of existence. By interpreting the non-thinking, automatic kind of mundane behavior we exhibit in certain social situations as free, self-determined and meaningful action, Schutz is admitting that, within the bounds of universally accepted meaning, he cannot prove his case. Only by offering freedom as an ability to unquestioningly, non-thinkingly, automatically conform to what is empirically confirmed, can he twist his method into his epistemology. Doubtless, he is accepting the objectivity of empirical data while trying to salvage as much of the subject as this data will permit. Unfortunately, there is little remaining. This is why, within the scope of mundane phenomena comprising

Schutz's common-sense world, a naturalist-oriented empirical method does the explaining job just as well and without this unfulfilled pretension.(71) This is also why meaningful, subjectively defined and determined social action is scientifically explained by *neither* naturalist empiricism *nor* Schutz's phenomenological method.

SUMMARY AND CONCLUSIONS

This chapter has described the philosophical issues relevant to an understanding of Alfred Schutz's methodology. Its conclusions support the argument advanced in chapter 3, that Schutz's method is inadequate to its stated purposes. The most important of these conclusions include:

1 naturalism and Husserlian phenomenology are two organic, mutually exclusive philosophies, whose different criteria of knowledge result in correspondingly different conceptions of science;

2 phenomenologists interested in methodological problems of the social sciences generally base their own arguments on the epistemological principles of either naturalism or phenomenology, not both;

3 Alfred Schutz's unique and daring methodology has attempted a synthesis of fundamental aspects of both naturalism and phenomenology. Unfortunately, the organic nature of these philosophies has rendered his argument logically indefensible, and has doomed it to those weaknesses already described.

The question now arises whether the potential role of phenomenology in studying society is limited to either recording empirical expressions of abstract, metaphysical truths, or capitulating to a naturalist epistemology. The final chapter offers some preliminary thoughts on this complex, provocative issue.

5 Epilogue: an alternative phenomenological approach to socal inquiry

In the last two decades, despite what I have argued is a blatantly illogical and illusory theoretical development, there has been a gradual but persistent increase in the popularity of phenomenology as a philosophical framework for empirically explaining aspects of social behavior. There are probably many reasons for this phenomenon - some already alluded to - but three stand out now as worthy of special mention: students today find it easier to find excellent English translations of Edmund Husserl's important studies establishing phenomenology as a major philosophical movement and laying the groundwork for a new approach to social science focusing on the everyday, common-sense world we live and work in, the 'Lebenswelt'; scholars are increasingly, and uncritically, recognizing important contributions to social science methodology made by Alfred Schutz, undoubtedly the single most influential figure in the growth of 'humanized' phenomenological approaches to methodology, and the 'father' of decision-making theory and ethnomethodology; and the existential culmination of Husserlian phenomenology, especially in the writings of Heidegger, Sartre and Merleau-Ponty, has convinced a new crop of dissatisfied but hopeful social scientists that in existential phenomenology they have finally discovered a legitimate approach to methodology which, working from within explicit principles of empirical method, is also 'radical.' Through it all, phenomenology has been systematically and consistently integrated with methodology only by those accepting the idealist leanings of Husserl's philosophy of science.(1) Our challenge now is to see whether and how phenomenology is related to methodology, without recoiling into a transcendentalism that is basically antithetical to the spirit and intention of a subject-oriented epistemology. In this chapter I will outline an alternative phenomenological approach to social inquiry, one avoiding the difficulties Schutz encounters while preserving a stress on the uniqueness of human experience. In the process, I will investigate further the relationship between phenomenology and empirical social science and, additionally, weave in the concepts of existential phenomenology and radicalism.(2) Hopefully, this will illustrate the fundamental relevance phenomenology has to our studying and understanding society, and the heuristic potency of ideological commitment in an alternative phenomenological presentation.

1 PHENOMENOLOGY REVISITED: AN EXISTENTIAL VIEW

We begin by defining those philosophical terms related to the methodological discussion. In particular, an insight into the subtle but important distinctions between existential and Husserlian brands of phenomenology will reveal new and potentially fruitful avenues to social theory. With this in mind, we see three fundamentally different perspectives distinguishing these alternative approaches to phenomenology.(3)

1 Husserlian phenomenology defines subjectivity exclusively in terms of consciousness: our conscious experiences are the only feasible subject matter for phenomenology. Husserl finds objective criteria for his phenomenological studies in the apodictic knowledge subjectively constituted by an irreducible pure or transcendental ego. Schutz, rejecting Husserl's idealism, also contends phenomenology is verifiable objectively, the locus of objectivity situated in a tenuous correspondence between consciousness and empirical reality. Both agree our beliefs are 'scientifically' justifiable only through self-conscious awareness, the ultimate foundation of knowledge. All philosophical concepts, including 'being' or 'existence,' are therefore merely 'by-products . . . of investigations bearing upon and concerned with subjective conscious life.'(4) We approach being and existence only by studying consciousness, from which everything else is derived. Existential phenomenologists reject this claim, defending instead the proposition that existence, not consciousness, is the proper subject matter for phenomenology. All human beings consciously perceive their worlds, as Husserl contends, but far from being an irreducible given, consciousness is actually an attribute of a more basic level of reality defining our humanity. In other words, consciousness is only one aspect of an

encompassing structure of existence. Phenomenology, which deals only with consciousness, must be put to work revealing essential structures of existence. Since these appear inextricably bound to the everyday world we subjectively perceive and act in, evidence either transcending this world or limiting itself to empirically confirmable aspects of it is not fully descriptive, incapable of meaningful explanation. In brief, the phenomenology of Husserl and his more orthodox disciples has an epistemological focus, it seeks philosophical criteria for uncovering knowledge about humans as conscious subjects. Existential phenomenology has an ontological focus, it wants to know what our being is and how we consciously philosophize within it.

2 Husserlian phenomenology, because it deals only with consciousness, runs the risk of being solipsistic unless it can justify its method objectively, establishing a rationale for the 'scientific' validity of its findings. Essentially, then, Husserlian phenomenology is forced from within to evolve into a philosophy of science, thereby creating a problem that is logically solved only through transcendentalism. Existential phenomenology avoids this dilemma by adjuring all claims to scientific objectivity, while, at the same time, carefully building its argument with non-solipsistic knowledge. The philosophical tool making this possible is ontology. By describing how we *can* consciously act, rather than *how* conscious people act, existential phenomenologists eliminate the burden of having to find criteria of objectivity in a world peopled by self-determining conscious subjects. Existential phenomenologists use phenomenology to describe criteria of being within which our subjectivities are accounted for. In capturing ontological reality, not ontic consciousness, they avoid dangers of solipsism without in any way diluting the uniquely subjective quality of human existence in the world. Although they simultaneously eliminate the basis for 'objective' empirical knowledge related to subjectively meaningful human interaction, more importantly, existential phenomenologists also eliminate the tension between our inherent subjectivities and the necessity of a concomitant objective foundation that has rendered phenomenological social science unworkable in any but the most undemonstrable, idealistic terms.

3 Finally, Husserlian phenomenology is based on faithful description of phenomena exactly as they appear to a philosopher's intuiting consciousness. Existential phenomenologists agree, sharing the belief that phenomenological evidence is valid only to the extent it

accurately describes what is consciously experienced. However, since being, not consciousness, is the proper focus of philosophy, and descriptive phenomenology adequately explains only consciousness, it is necessary to offer phenomenology in the service of ontology, using it as a method for a more inclusive inquiry into being. The object of existential ontology is a human quality underlying and explaining our consciousness, and therefore not vulnerable to phenomenological description. Evidence for our ontological conclusions must always remain rigorously phenomenological, but this evidence goes only so far. Being itself, the object of existential ontology, is in some sense prior to consciousness, transcending self-conscious perception without ever determining or limiting its content. Being reveals itself to consciousness through our interpreting the body of phenomenological facts in a manner conducive to this end. This is what existential phenomenologists mean when they call for 'hermeneutic' method to supplement the more strictly descriptive method of Husserlian phenomenology.

These existential modifications of Husserlian phenomenology eliminate the tension between subjectivity and objectivity that is a root cause both of Husserl's turn to idealism and Schutz's mis-conceived methodology. Further, they accomplish this without violating basic principles distinguishing phenomenology from other non-phenomenological approaches to philosophy. In particular, there are two vital points Husserlian and existential phenomenologists agree upon, but all other philosophical 'schools' reject.

1 All phenomenologists, Husserlian and existential, are committed to the epistemological primacy of immediate experience. What is perceived by a conscious individual adequately reveals what is. Though being, for existential phenomenologists, hermeneutically reveals itself to consciousness, nevertheless, like Husserl's own description of apodicticity, it is only through our subjective experiences that it is confirmed as existing. It is just idle chatter to suggest an objective world exists apart from our conscious experiences. The most distinctive and important principle uniting all phenomenologists is this shared thesis that valid knowledge must be subjectively verified.

2 A related principle, also shared by all phenomenologists, is the belief that, despite the subjective quality of valid knowledge, philosophical analysis must somehow reveal essential structures of reality. Husserl accomplishes this with a transcendental idealism; Heidegger, Sartre and Merleau-Ponty with existential ontology.(5)

In sum, existential phenomenology, though of course not identical to Husserlian phenomenology, does share with it certain principles serving to distinguish both from all other approaches to reality and knowledge. Existential phenomenology also has an added virtue of eliminating the 'subject-object' tension making Husserl's phenomenological approach to social inquiry indefensible without a prior commitment to transcendental idealism. If we are to use phenomenology to construct a method of studying society, while simultaneously renouncing both Husserl's idealism and Schutz's inconsistency, we must abandon our hopes of finding an objective reality ordering, or coinciding with, our free, subjectively determined social actions. A phenomenological social 'science' free from either of these two unacceptable consequences is inconceivable. Since the philosophies of both Husserl and Schutz tend towards solipsism if deprived of their epistemological roots in objective, scientific knowledge, it is similarly inconceivable they could be applied to studying society in a form other than they now appear. The implication is now clear: if we are, in fact, capable of satisfactorily studying and understanding society from a non-idealistic phenomenological point of view, it will have to be from within the ontological borders of existential phenomenology.

2 EXISTENTIAL ONTOLOGY

The path to an alternative methodology must be marked with still more philosophical information. Particularly important to our present needs are the results of applying phenomenological method to an analysis of being. This information is available in the existential ontologies of Heidegger, Sartre and Merleau-Ponty, which are too intricate, lengthy, and oft-repeated to be summarily oulined here. These ontologies have been subjected to volumes of critical analysis, for each is the product of a lifetime of thinking and research by an important twentieth-century philosopher. But our purposes are more easily approached: we are searching for broad characteristics of existential phenomenology as a philosophical movement, generalities which might help in formulating a phenomenological method for understanding society.

The existential phenomenologist's interpretation of being is built squarely on the premise that, in certain essential ways, human beings are spatially and temporally 'open' to the world. This fundamental concept, being's openness to the world, culminates an evolutionary philosophical process set in motion by Descartes and crucially influenced by Husserl. Existential phenomenology is inextricably involved with the historical development of the concept of intentionality.

The appearance of Husserlian phenomenology constitutes a rejection of the traditional Cartesian formula for dichotemizing the world into mind and matter.(6) It takes the radical step of directly associating consciousness with the object of which it is conscious. The mind works by projecting itself outward and 'intending' the perceived object, not by passively receiving stimulii or expressing an ambiguously inherent thought or idea. Through intentionality, actors impart meaning to all worldly phenomena they experience. Consciousness, in this view, is 'beyond itself' by nature, and therefore the mind is no longer conceived as a compact, enclosed substance within the limits of an individual whole. Descartes' notions of the enclosed mind and the whole individual, unquestioned tenets of western thought, are now subjected to a criticism directed at its foundations. If a mind perceives things by intending objects beyond itself, then these objects, definitely outside the body, are 'inside' the mind. An individual, obviously possessing both mind and body, is no longer seen as a whole, spatially enclosed unit. An essential element of this individual is, by definition, beyond itself and therefore uncircumscribable.

Existential phenomenologists develop Husserl's notion of the intentionality of consciousness even further. Where Husserl uses it to outline a method for imparting meaning to the world, existential phenomenologists adopt it to characterize structures of existence. Just as Husserl describes consciousness as intending its object, existential phenomenologists describe being as intentionally oriented towards space and time. Despite their particular differences, the philosophies of existential phenomenologists merge in this shared conviction that intentionality is vital to understanding being. The intentionality of being, the spatial and temporal openness of being to the world, is a distinguishing characteristic of existential phenomenology. Human existence as Being-in-the-world: this existential phenomenological thesis is an ontological expression of Husserl's notion of intentionality. It provides us one approach to an alternative phenomenological method.

3 SOCIAL ONTOLOGY

As Beings-in-the-world, we are confronted by socially sanctioned values, attitudes and behavior patterns constituting a pattern of objective behavior and belief which is integrated into our respective lives. We react to these objective forces in one of two ways: by abandoning ourselves to them, automatically obeying their dictates at the expense of initiating our own free actions, our potentials as Beings-in-the-world; or by existentially committing ourselves to a course of action self-determined and meaningfully oriented towards these social phenomena. Only the first category of social behavior, usually associated with mundane, routinized tasks we naively accept and perform, is adequately explained through an exclusively empirical method. Though empirical science does not meaningfully explain self-consciously aware social action, we can, instead, focus on phenomena constituting the social world of each free Being-in-the world, achieving insights into what a particular society means to its inhabitants and what each citizen, potentially, subjectively reacts to. This is what an existential phenomenological approach to social inquiry offers.

I will now unfold an ontology of society based on the significant, distinguishing principles of existential phenomenology. The premise that human existence is Being-in-the-world implies that actors are not intellectually conceivable apart from the social environments constituting their 'worlds.' What is this society that is so intimately part of us, and how do we study it? As Beings-in-the-world, what are the social aspects of this 'world' we are in? Our answers may not causally explain why we act as we do in particular situations, but they will describe the socially-derived meaning context that is part of being and a background for unique projected actions. Just as existential ontology illustrates how individuals potentially act as unique, self-determined subjects because of their essential natures, social ontology will reveal the essential nature of a social world that is part of us and the meaning context upon which we project free actions.

The society expressed in our Being-in-the-world consists of people sharing universally-approved values, attitudes and behavior patterns. From a phenomenological point of view, these social characteristics are not abstract, isolated from individuals internalizing them; their existence is merely an expression of actual values, attitudes and behavior patterns exhibited by individuals in their social interactions. Society consists of thinking, willing individuals, not abstractions. While bearing in mind that society, as such, has no thinking mechanism capable of conscious perception, since it does consist of a group of actors somehow united by intersubjectively accepted rules, its essence will reflect the human quality comprising it. Existential phenomenology is a philosophical attempt to fix boundaries of human existence. In asserting each individual in society is essentially 'beyond himself' in being ontologically open to time and space, we now likewise assert society - consisting of numerous individuals living in close proximity to each other - is also essentially 'beyond itself,' transcending its apparent temporal and spatial limits in the same way that the being of its citizens transcends the 'here' and 'now.' From this viewpoint, society exists as the reciprocal interactions of a number of factors: history; current events and behavior patterns; existing physical resources, institutions, structures and processes; ideals, values, expectations and goals for the future; and a world environment within which all these take shape. The self-defining interactions of these social dimensions make their separate identities dependent on the dynamically interrelating whole, just as, on a different level, are the temporal and spatial elements of Being-in-the-world. Society is now, to put it plainly, its past, its future and its interactions with its world environment.

We have seen that in the history of western thought existential phenomenology has evolved into a radical critique of a naively accepted Cartesian world-view, which separates reality into distinct elements of mind and matter. An existential phenomenological understanding of society critically rejects the Cartesianism implicit in contemporary social science. Let us take an example, to illustrate this point, the study of politics, which today is predominantly 'scientific' (from a naturalist viewpoint) in method. Within political science there are at least five important approaches to limiting the scope of its subject matter, each stipulating defined boundaries beyond which lies an area of social phenomena distinctly 'non-political.'(7) Political science, as a discipline, examines a segment of human behavior and institutions distinguished and analytically separated from the sum-total of human behavior and institutions constituting the life-style of a particular social unit. The precise scope of these social phenomena is debated, but few deny political science is autonomous, distinct from related, but separate, disciplines similarly studying circumscribed areas of human behavior and institutions.

Social interaction, to be properly explained, must be chopped into numerous qualitatively distinct categories,(8) and the whole society is intellectually reconstructed with the combined data of all social disciplines. Just as Cartesian man exists in the present as mind within bodily matter, Cartesian society exists within the 'body' of its physical borders as a phenomenon, cast entirely in the present, that is a patch-work of its disciplinary pieces. Armed with an unquestioned Cartesian approach to life, political scientists have interpreted society as something temporally and spatially enclosed, and amenable to analytic fragmentation. Existential phenomenology, in rejecting Cartesianism and positing instead an essential openness of human existence to time and space, critically rejects what it perceives to be a naive view of society. We do not isolate society's present from its past and future because society *is* its past, present and future; it is open to the ecstacies of time just as is the being of its citizens. Similarly, given our ontological openness to space, we do not isolate one level of society, such as the 'political,' and expect to understand it as something pure, distinct from other concrete levels. Members of society *are* the social world they perceive. When they behave 'politically' they are simultaneously expressing all the social relationships they are open to: one dynamically expresses and defines the other. Society is open to the world and to temporality because its citizens are Beings-in-the-world, and society is not conceived apart from its citizens. The social world actors express in their actions is not explained merely by taking into account factors of the 'here' and 'now' coinciding with their bodies. Understanding society requires our recognizing the dynamic interrelationships fixing its multi-dimensionality, realizing select social phenomena are not meaningfully explained when isolated from other phenomena present in a social world actors share, or cut off from the past and future they are oriented towards. Society 'as a whole' is not the sum of its qualitatively distinct analytical parts: there are no parts distinct from the dynamic society they are abstracted from.

Should political science, then, be abandoned along with the other archaic social disciplines? Studying a 'political reality' leads us into an abyss of Cartesianism by implicitly assuming a whole society is the sum of its separate analytical components. This creates a situation, like the one we now find ourselves in, where elaborate disciplinary research projects and volumes of specialized data barely scratch the surface of society's most pressing and critical problems. Conversely, a political study of social reality might facilitate adequate explanation that remains humanly relevant. The distinction drawn between the phrases 'a study of political reality' and 'a political study of social reality' is not a pun. Involved in the latter is a belief that a social discipline, however one prescribes its boundaries, is a man-made, artificial device, useful only for gathering information to explain a dynamic society. There is no ambiguity regarding the function of 'political' analysis: it is a totally heuristic, intellectual exercise not necessarily mirroring existing social reality. Studying politics affords us many interesting facts and hypotheses, but does not offer meaningful explanations if it stays within the boundaries of its prescribed scope. Our search for a concrete, political level of society leads only to our discovering interrelated patterns.

If studying society from a disciplinary point of view is actually analogous to studying a distinct subject matter abstracted and isolated from its social roots by observers in order to justify their own efforts at analysis, how can it pretend to yield knowledge describing society as it really is? How, in other words, does it fulfill its heuristic function? An existential phenomenological methodology impells us to recognize that all those disciplines we create to facilitate social inquiry be characterized by one preponderant quality: they must be interpretative. Perceptive observers reveal society's essential openness to time and space and its reciprocally interacting levels of meaning by directing themselves at reconstructing the social maelstrom from which their discipline emerges. It is not enough to chart the scope of this discipline and then describe subject matter included within its borders. An arbitrarily defined and delimited social reality cannot convey meaningful human experiences apart from other interacting realities lying outside its scope, or apart from time, emerging outside the discipline as tradition and a vision for the future. Political analysis, then, creatively interprets, using information gained from other disciplines, a picture of society explaining what has been called 'political' in terms of what has preceded and is expected to follow, and in the context of the 'non-political,' the core of our original subject matter. The study of politics interpretatively reaches beyond itself in order to adequately deal with a subject matter defined by its interactions with the rest of society. Each synthetic social discipline is similarly born into this methodological imperative.

4 PHENOMENOLOGY, SOCIAL SCIENCE AND RADICALISM

Interpretative social analysis, based on principles of existential phenomenology, is not 'objective' in the same way naturalist empirical explanations of impersonal, socially determined behavior are.(9) From a fully systematic existential phenomenological point of view, causal, unilinear explanations of self-consciously meaningful social behavior, based on empirical criteria of verifiability, are too simplistic. Though pretending to explain the actions of human beings, empirical social scientists naively ignore the richness of human being, thereby distorting a good portion of social reality.

While implications of existential phenomenology in relation to empirical social science are rather obvious, we are faced with a complex and subtle entanglement of this philosophy with Marxism. Though Sartre may be overstating his case in asserting 'there is no doubt, indeed, that Marxism appears today to be the only possible anthropology which can be at once historical and structural'(10), his point must be confronted.

Contemporary radical, or 'left' phenomenologists eagerly refer to Marx's early assertion, 'To be radical is to grasp things by the root. But for man the root is man himself.'(11) Taken literally, these words supply a theoretical common ground necessary for the evolution of a synthetic phenomenological-Marxism. The goal of Marxism, from this perspective, is to expose (to human perception) the truth of man and history, which has remained latent, hidden and grossly distorted, in the machinations of capitalist society. The phenomenological effort to reveal 'things themselves' so that humanity can move toward a more reliable knowledge of the world is now intellectually linked to a Marxist critique of western capitalism. Both attempt the dis-occlusion of society, the return to a purified human awareness of those naively experienced social structures constituting our own oppression and alienation. The liberation of the working class from their social enslavement corresponds to the enlightenment of a newly awakened, reflective humanity, no longer submitting to those de-humanizing categories of economic, social, artistic and intellectual reality created by and for an elitist society. There is a certain irony to history, as these phenomenologists see it, for at some point in time - perhaps even in the later writings of Marx himself - Marxism was unthinkingly separated from its foundation in humanity and turned, with brutal effects, into a set of inflexible abstract categories. The resulting 'crisis' of Marxism, represented by a sclerosis in Marxist thinking and a general climate of disillusion among Marxists in post-Stalinist western society, has offered us the unique opportunity of reinvigorating the Marxist social critique with subject-oriented principles of phenomenology. Marxists and phenomenologists must now join and work together, for the social liberation of the masses is also the reflective emancipation of each citizen: the two perspectives include each other.

There is more than rhetoric in this argument, and if we return to our existential phenomenological perspective this will become clearer.

The spatial and temporal qualities of being, as seen by existential phenomenologists, are easily assimilated into certain Marxist categories, particularly as these categories have evolved in the writings of recent commentators. Our ontological openness to space means our existences are permeated by the material conditions of society, including our relationships to the means of production. We each are, to a great extent, defined by our objective position in economy, society and polity, by our class, status, and power. The multi-dimensionality of society does preclude any view offering a unilinear sequence of social causation between economic sub-structure and cultural super-structure. But this 'vulgar' understanding of economic determinism has already been surpassed by modern Marxists in favor of a view stressing the numerous mediations between material conditions and the quality of social life, a view entirely consistent with an existential phenomenological understanding of society.(12) Further, the historicity of being implies an historical unity is present in the evolution of society. To the extent that our existences are historical, all human operations take place in a context conditioned by past occurrences, which equally affect all actors sharing a common heritage. There is, consequently, a distinctly intersubjective flavor to existence, formed as it is by the shared material conditions of society and its common historical sedimentations. We thus integrate a materialist understanding of life in society with an historical interpretation of the quality of this life and these material conditions. Material aspects of the world we are open to are seen as culminations of historical trends, as expressions of present conditions and as seeds of future material forms of society. Our objective positions in economy, society and polity, all three of which are reciprocally interrelated because of the multi-dimensional texture of society, play major roles in determining the quality of life we experience. If life in society is in any way adjudged to be de-humanized, alienated, or oppressed it is in large part because the material social conditions are de-humanizing, alienating and oppressive. Thus, a Marxist stress on the class struggle as constituting the driving force behind capitalist society, provided naive economic determinism is replaced by an awareness of the complexity and importance of social mediations, is compatible with an existential phenomenological point of view.

Based on these shared notions, it is now also apparent that when we refer to 'interpretative' social inquiry as a necessary consequence of an existential phenomenological approach to methodology, when the social disciplines are seen as heuristically useful rather than objectively real, we are merely asserting that all social inquiry be dialectical. Once again, this Marxian notion of dialectics must not be defined in a naive, vulgar sense as some sort of unstoppable historical force trampling everything in its path. The contemporary Marxian understanding of dialectics, especially as creatively molded in the relevant writings of Georg Lukács and Karel Kosík,(13) stresses its usefulness as a method for uncovering the hidden, but real, aspects of social life, aspects lying beyond empirical verification but providing the context within which we empirically experience society.

Marxist dialectics is best approached through the interrelated concepts of 'totality' and 'mediation.' A valid understanding of society depends on our recognizing first its inclusive, totalizing movement which provides the framework for all particular social occurrences. The category of totality implies the determining domination of the whole over the parts, the inseparability of social facts from the total whole they express. As Lukács himself puts it:(14)

> Thus, only when the theoretical primacy of the 'facts' has been broken, only when every phenomenon is recognized to be a process, will it be understood that what we are wont to call 'facts' consist of processes. Only then will it be understood that the facts are nothing but the parts, the aspects of the total processes that have been broken off, artificially isolated and ossified.

In this sense, the totality is the essentially true category of social reality. The totalizing social whole exists in and through partial totalities, manifold mediations, which are dynamically linked to each other and to the whole in constantly shifting patterns. In society there is incessant diversity within a total unity; each level of mediation is relative to its inclusive higher level and its subordinate lower level, while interacting with both, and the highest level - the concrete totality - is determining in respect to all its partial conflicting expressions. The significance of all social achievements is measured in relation to a dialectical grasp of the complex mediations constituting the structure of totality. Dialectics thus allows us to get beyond the factually given to see the elaborate network of social mediations shaping each material condition or social phenomenon we investigate. It brings into vivid focus the realization that empirical phenomena outwardly corresponding to different levels of social interaction (e.g. individual, family, class or nation), or different historical periods (e.g. past, present, future), are in reality 'internally related and connected amongst themselves and with the whole.'(15) In existential phenomenological terminology, dialectical method reveals the spatial and temporal multi-dimensionality of social life, the interconnectedness of all social phenomena and each temporal mode. Additionally, it facilitates our uncovering the essential quality of the world we are open to, that ultimate social truth that is determining with respect to each factual cluster of phenomena. Dialectics is a necessary and irreplaceable method of social inquiry for both phenomenologists and Marxists.(16)

In sum, then, there is an undeniably close connection between methodological implications of existential phenomenology and central tenets of enlightened Marxism. Existential phenomenology, in this sense, offers a radical methodological alternative and a radical ideological vision. Yet the attempt to philosophically include one in the other, to be at once a consistent existential phenomenologist and a committed Marxist, is doomed from the beginning, from whichever end we try. For the existential phenomenologist there is no 'truth,' there is no 'objective' reality, existing apart from being. The fundamental starting point of all philosophical inquiry is ontology, and here we merely interpret evidence gathered in an orthodox phenomenological procedure. Existential ontology, to repeat a point made earlier, in no way imposes itself on or against human existence; it is the necessary structure allowing each of us to experience free existence in the first place. In contrast, even the most sympathetic reading of Karl Marx, one forcibly extracting assertions even vaguely tinged with a concern for the sanctity of human subjects, fails miserably in making him a phenomenologist. The Marxist materialistic dialectic, it is claimed, creates and structures itself through an authentic historical subject, so the idea of revolution without proletarian self-consciousness is rejected. Lukács declares, 'History is at its least automatic when it is the consciousness of the proletariat that is at issue . . . [the proletariat] can be transformed and liberated only by its own actions . . .. Any transformation [of society] can only come about as the product of the - free - action of the proletariat itself.'(17) But subjectivity and freedom are defined as merely moments of the whole, participating elements in a broader, inclusive material force, the concrete totality. Despite an explicit assumption by Marxist theoreticians that subjective creativity will grow and express itself from within the dialectical whole, the crucial point is this would be a coincidence, not a theoretical necessity, because the materialist totality comprises an absolute truth that includes and determines subjectivity. The difficulties encountered by Lukács and Marcuse in their Sisyphean attempts at making Marxism subjectively relevant were focused on precisely this issue.(18) Neither could effectively assimilate a free, self-conscious subject into the materialist, objective quality of the Marxian dialectic, and both noticeably strained the imagination - their own and the readers - in attempting to do so. The lesson was well learned: contemporary Marxists sympathetic to their original goals, people like Kosík, Labriola and Gramsci, carefully form their arguments within a reflective but orthodox materialist perspective, consciously fleeing the trap of simultaneously defending subjectivity and objectivity.(19) For Marxists, phenomenological criteria of validity, based on the supremacy of subjective perspectives, are reversed, the preponderant epistemological role falling to the intersubjective totality. The materialist dialectical whole includes the subject, but is prior to it. The foundation of phenomenological dialectic, on the other hand, is the subject's existence; since this is only subjectively experienced, the social and historical dialectic is always expressed in and through the reflective self-consciousness of aware subjects. The 'concreteness' of the totality is measured by phenomenological criteria of validation.

In spite of the organic, mutually exclusive qualities of these two different approaches to reality and knowledge, their ideological similarities have been simply too powerful to ignore. Consequently, the temptation towards synthesis, the feeling that a valid phenomenological-Marxism that remains true to subjectivity while encompassing an objective, teleological understanding of history promising the liberation of all humanity, has prompted some contemporary scholars to walk this perilous, endless path. In effect, these people are entrusting themselves to performing a monumental project of synthesizing phenomenology to a non-phenomenological, Marxist perspective. The comparison to Alfred Schutz is direct and obvious: what Schutz attempted with respect to empirical social science, these intellectual radicals now hope to do with Marxism. The dual vision which blinded Schutz and his followers to the philosophical realities of their plight is reproduced in the perspectives of this group of phenomenologically-oriented neo-Marxists.

The enormity of this task has, in certain instances, had self-correcting effects. Marcuse, Lukács, and Tran Duc Thao have all explicitly renounced their early efforts at synthesis as too ill-conceived and ambiguous from a Marxist point of view. Others, primarily thinkers building on a phenomenological perspective towards a neo-Marxist synthesis, have not yet abandoned their ambitious goals, but are left defending scholarly theories that are blatantly vague at just those moments in the argument when clarity is imperative. In general, writers broaching the grand synthesis of phenomenology and Marxism can be separated into three categories: there are, first, Marxists who sense the pervasiveness of the materialist dialectic and attempt to evolve, from within, a systematic concern for subjectivity that might brake the slide towards a Stalin-like dictatorship; second, there are Husserlian phenomenologists whose radical leanings push them into blazing a new path to the materialist dialectic running directly through the transcendental reduction; and finally there is Jean-Paul Sartre, an existential phenomenologist whose ontology has melted into Marxism, producing a very curious mixture indeed. Since we have already outlined the limitations of the first group of Marxists, we will now briefly survey representative phenomenological radicals from the second and third categories to illustrate the difficulties encountered and to draw some conclusions concerning the methodological implications of phenomenological social inquiry.(20)

Enzo Paci's 'The Functions of the Sciences and the Meaning of Man,'(21) undoubtedly the single most important work produced by the so-called 'Milan School' of radical social philosophy, hopes to evolve a systematic Marxist social critique from within established principles of Husserl's transcendental phenomenology. Though complex and at times extremely difficult to keep up with, Paci's presentation can be summarily boiled down to a residue of three or four fundamental assertions that provide a theoretical skeleton for the entire movement.

The Husserlian reduction to pure or transcendental subjectivity, for Paci, is the necessary first step in any search for valid social knowledge. Although, superficially, the pure ego appears to be experienced in an ideal or metaphysical reality removed from our everyday social involvements, a closer inspection shows this to be false, a naive assumption not fulfilling the rigorous standards of phenomenological verification. The transcendental subject, phenomenologically understood, is consciousness open to temporality and indelibly stained by 'temporal irreversibility': as pure subjects irreversibly living and perceiving in the present, people experience reality as the past reverting into the future. The essential quality of man, as a pure subject, is his 'becoming,' and this is lived from within his internal consciousness of time. Transcendental subjectivity is therefore seen as intentional consciousness in time. But it is only in time that the experienced world - including its intermonadic, sensible, perceptual, corporeal and spiritual aspects - constitutes itself and is active. The pure subject, therefore, corresponds to the authentic, reflective experience of this world, not an ideal metaphysical reality. In spite of Husserl's explicit argument in section forty-nine of the 'Ideas' that the pure ego is emptied of the world, Paci now suggests 'subjectivity without the world contains it.'(22) As Paci sees it, this world we, as pure subjects, are thrown back into, is the 'Lebenswelt.' It must be distinguished from the 'mundane world' of everyday, naive existence, which covers and occludes our authentic consciousness of concrete life, i.e. the 'Lebenswelt.' Only by our instituting the epoché and experiencing the series of phenomenological reductions leading us to the level of pure subjective awareness, only through systematic reflective self-consciousness, do we break our alienation and experience the 'Lebenswelt.' Consequently, there is and can be no conflict between subjectivity, defined phenomenologically, and the experienced life-world of reflective, authentic social actions: pure subjectivity and pure objectivity correspond.

Assuming, for now, the validity of this analysis, the Marxian synthesis occurs quite easily. The mundane, alienating, fetishized world is our existence within capitalist society. Only through systematic reflection can we disocclude the 'Lebenswelt' and live full, authentic lives. The 'Lebenswelt' is a world of intersubjective co-operation and human understanding, in which we remain consciously 'open' to time - and thus to all aspects of social life, including our fellow man - never alienating our authentic selves in material goods, competitiveness, and a stagnant present. In brief: the 'Lebenswelt' is a truly communist society. Marx's materialist historical dialectic is expressed in each authentic subject's inclination to 'become,' to experience reality now as the past reverting into the future. Man's 'telos' (i.e. his subjective orientation towards his future experience of the 'Lebenswelt') and history's 'telos' (i.e. the concrete totalization of the objective materialist dialectic) correspond and will be expressed in the praxis of authentically free subjects (i.e. the proletariat). Authentic class consciousness requires we commit ourselves to 'science,' flee the mundane into intersubjective, historical truth. Phenomenology is thus synonymous with a proletariat commitment to revolutionary, authenticating praxis, it is 'the revelation of the capitalist occlusion of the subject and truth.'(23)

Paci's argument, in spite of its ingenuity and resourcefulness, is tenable only from an idealistic, metaphysical perspective, negating his original intentions. As we have seen, an argument from subjectivity leads only to subjective conclusions unless it is grounded in intersubjective criteria of validity. From Husserl's position, these are transcendental criteria, purified of subjective contingency in a reality to which anyone can accede, but still remaining ideally objective in a sense no spontaneous perception can be. Paci claims to be arguing from within Husserl's system. If he convinces at all, it is because he implicitly adopts these ideal criteria. Disclaimers notwithstanding, this does seem to be the case.

Paci proceeds in his phenomenological analysis of transcendental subjectivity as if the results are in some sense objective, intersubjectively valid. Yet the temporal openness of consciousness, as described by Paci, signifies only Paci's consciousness of the temporal openness of consciousness unless he has actually experienced an ideal mode of perceiving somehow transcending, governing each reflective activity. By throwing the transcendental subject back into society, Paci only clouds things by shifting the focus: there must now either be an ideal, metaphysical quality defining the 'Lebenswelt' or Paci's statements lack objectivity. Paci is rapidly abandoning his phenomenological commitment in favor of neo-Hegelianism. When he admits his analysis of the 'Lebenswelt' is 'an interpretation or, maybe, a correction . . . but [one] required by the coherent development of Husserlian phenomenology,'(24) he surely underestimates and confuses Husserl's intentions. Husserl's transcendental subject is necessarily purified of this world, providing his phenomenology criteria of apodicticity that are subjectively relevant and readily attainable through the reductions. It is almost inconceivable he felt criteria of objectivity were discoverable within society. This violates Husserl's life-long pursuit of 'things themselves' as subjectively perceived, in favor of mere social representations of things. Finally, there would be no reason to undertake a phenomenology of the 'Lebenswelt,' as Husserl offers in the 'Krisis' lectures, if objectively verifiable knowledge defines social life.

A pervasive air of transcendentalism thus haunts the Milan School of social theory, despite its Marxian rhetoric.(25) In Paci's writings the reader is never certain of its precise locus, but the work of people like Rovatti and Piccone is perhaps more transparently derived from Husserl's version of transcendentalism. It is only from within this latter perspective that the work is systematic and acceptable. It does not include or synthesize Marxism but rather fits as much of Marx as possible into an explicitly non-Marxist philosophical system. From our phenomenological point of view, the work doesn't really take us much beyond Husserl's transcendental presentation: we must decide whether an abstract idealism defining our subjectivity and determining the limits of free praxis is the best and most socially useful expression of a phenomenological commitment to authentic subjectivity and freedom.

Sartre, placing too much value on free human praxis to accept Paci's metaphysical limitations, is more concerned with developing an enlightened dialectical materialism that remains true to self-creating subjectivity. In the first volume of 'Critique de la raison dialectique,'(26) he asserts the dialectical aspect of man's relationship to the world, the reciprocally interrelated, interpenetrating processes of individual and social development. Beginning with the basic human quality of need, Sartre builds an argument based on the reciprocal openness of man and world, the dialectical relationship between internal and external. By successively treating notions such as scarcity, the practico-inert, seriality, group action and institutionalization, Sartre aspires to:(27)

> begin from the immediate, in particular, from the individual in his abstract 'praxis,' to rediscover through increasingly profound conditionings the

> totality of his practical relations with others, and by like means, the structures of the diverse practical multiplicities, and, through the contradictions and struggles of these multiplicities, to come to the absolutely concrete: historical man.

The proposed, but never completed, second volume would have to illustrate the historical expression of these dialectical processes, the applicability of his structures to an intelligible understanding of history.

Sartre's weakness, from our viewpoint, is his own past: his constant stress on individual praxis reflects an earlier existential ontology which outlined essential structures of free existence. Sartre desperately attempts to preserve this focus on self-defining action while replacing his ontology with a revitalized dialectical materialism. This, ultimately, satisfies from neither a phenomenological nor a Marxist persepctive. If 'the only practical and dialectical reality, the motive force of all, is individual action,'(28) then Sartre is implicitly adopting ontological conclusions from 'Being and Nothingness' as the foundation of his dialectical system.(29) The alternative is pure subjectivism, devoid of essentiality or objectivity. If the dialectic is founded in objective material conditions, as Sartre occasionally suggests in Stalinist terminology, then the stress on free praxis is self-defeating and the institutionalized party is, and should be, omnipotent.(30) The two trends constantly pull at each other throughout Sartre's later writings, a type of intellectual schizophrenia which dis-orients as it confuses. These issues are chrystallized in Sartre's introduction to the 'Critique,' now issued separately as 'Search For a Method,'(31) where the goals for the proposed two-volume work are set forth. At one point Sartre heatedly declares that historical dialectic must avoid a 'dogmatic metaphysics' and seek instead support 'in the comprehension of the living man,'(32) after previously admitting that without its 'a priori' character the dialectic 'promptly disappears,' for the dialectic 'is a reality . . . in which nobody can completely recognize himself; in short a human work without an author.'(33) Sartre here distorts fundamental principles. From a phenomenological view, material aspects of life do condition our projects, for, being part of the world we are open to, they constitute our own selves. But we do choose our projects from within the material environment and maintain the potentiality of rejecting (not avoiding) or accepting its implications. If this potential surpassing of our material environments is also part of an objective historical dialectic, then the notion of an existential project becomes a confusing illusion: we have the freedom to choose only what we must do anyway; we could not do other than what we chose. If the subject is actually a necessary moment in an inclusive object, then all Sartre's deliberations, his entire progressive-regressive method, are like so much intellectual foreplay preceding the inevitable, predictable culmination - and what could be more bourgeois than this? Who will or should stop a prospective 'totalizing third' (i.e. the human catalyst for authenticating group action) from forcing his citizenry into performing the objectively prescribed social behavior that alone is seen as subjectively meaningful and truly 'free'? Ironically, this is the danger that prompted Sartre to re-evaluate Marxism in the first place. Sartre's predicament evolves from his own ambition, for the desire to concretely totalize a multifarious net of subjectively defined and determined social actions cannot be brought to satisfactory completion.

The difficulties inherent in the work of Paci and Sartre are not superficial. The immense problems involved in synthesizing two such diverse approaches to reality as phenomenology and Marxism are too complex for the philosophical tools, at present, available. Consequently, a phenomenological understanding of the methodology of social inquiry must unequivocally bathe itself in the evidences of critical, self-consciously aware perceptions. The provocative overlapping of phenomenology and Marxism can now be soberly examined, the feverish excitement of the grand synthesis giving way to a more restrained attitude that may well be more fruitful.

Surely the most fundamental methodological similarity between Marxism and phenomenology is the emphasis both place on dialectics. The effort to get behind the empirically given in search of the concrete levels of social mediations that define, and in turn are influenced by, the original phenomenon, is characteristic of both approaches to methodology. Yet even this hypothesized similarity must be understood dialectically: theoretical mediations defining the dialectical quality of Marxism are entirely different from those defining dialectical phenomenology, as are the implications and consequences of dialectics within each system. The foundation of dialectical phenomenology is the free, reflective self-consciousness of beings who are essentially open to their spatial and temporal worlds;

the Marxian dialectic is based on a totalizing materialism that includes subjectivity as one moment within a determining objective historical movement. The former perspective sees historical progress deriving from the free praxis of creative social actors, acting from within, but never determined by, their dialectically defined environments. The 'telos' of history exists as potential, awaiting the authenticating social consequences of our own liberating reflection. The Marxist equates historical and individual 'telos,' simultaneously asserting the necessity of free praxis and the inevitability of its historical appearance. The outward convergence of both theories in a common dialectical perspective hides more than some care to admit.

Only now does the heuristic usefulness of Marxist explanatory categories command our attention. Radical Marxist ideology reveals itself as particularly suited to our existential phenomenological requirements, indeed better suited than other explanatory systems because of its dynamic, multi-dimensional, historical design. By synthetically isolating one social phenomenon - capital - we initiate a probe of an entire dynamic social totality by imparting one possible meaning to current social institutions and processes in the light of the past and future, and in terms of an interaction with all other (non-'economic') social phenomena. We are, from both Marxist and phenomenological ideological perspectives, historically conditioned by concrete material relationships that are dialectically expressed in social institutions, 'normal' behavioral patterns, values and ideas. To the extent we are, in our values and behavior, estranged from our own human qualities, our potentials as self-realizing, free social actors, we are oppressed by these material conditions. Liberation, living to our human potentials, is dialectically related to our altering these material conditions in the interests of humanity, putting them to work in creating an authenticating social environment. Both Marxism and phenomenology understand and evaluate life in modern society similarly; as ideologies they coincide. But Marxism must constantly be seen as heuristically useful, not objectively true. Because it is not an objective or scientific explanation, it cannot be blindly applied to all societies as a convenient, at-hand explaining tool. It is adequately defended only if its analytical categories survive a rigorous in-depth analysis of the particular society in question, including a detailed examination of unique, self-consciously aware historical subjects creatively surpassing their material surroundings - in brief, only to the extent it is heuristically useful in our dialectical social expedition. Implicit are two reminders: first, Marxist analytical categories (as distinct from its dialectical method) offer one possible explanatory framework - though it may, based on our present knowledge, be an invaluable propadeutic to social inquiry, it is an historical usefulness that may, in time, be surpassed; and second, the exegetical potency of these categories may fluctuate when applied to different societies, depending on the particular content of each multi-dimensional, dialectically interrelated system.

The validity of dialectical social inquiry, based on principles of existential phenomenology, is determined not by its objective truth, but by the extent to which aware citizens really did, do now, and will perceive their social worlds in the manner described. These non-empirical criteria are never absolutely confirmed, leaving our creative intellects to flirt with what is, finally, a profoundly human mystery. Yet far from relegating scholars to insignificance in the face of an essentially ambiguous human condition, an alternative phenomenological method has the opposite effect: in their social roles as educators they are charged with 'awakening' citizens to the reality of their social environments, cultivating their own theories through the self-conscious perceptions of an informed public. Here, thought and action merge. Creative scholars are no longer removed from society to insure objectivity in compiling data. Each can prove a theory only by getting involved in the common social quest, prompting those naively functioning in their material environments to self-consciously perceive their own dispirited conditions, ultimately, sculpting the future through the ideas and actions of liberated men and women. The role of theorist is important in a practical sense, unleashing forces of knowledge in the only place they have any real material social effect: the reflective perceptions of those functioning within existing material conditions. The promise of revolutionary, liberating change will remain a hypothetical possibility until it is engrained in the reflective perceptions of the oppressed. Material conditions, dialectically expressed in our social experiences, will follow suit. The orthodox Marxist alternative, regrettably, only substitutes one form of oppression for another.

The issue here is not, as some Marxists would have us believe, between a value-free materialist description of reality as it is, and a bourgeois-idealist attempt at substituting an ego-centered sentimentalism. Both Marxism and phenomenology present coherent, systematic arguments concerning the criteria of valid knowledge and the quality of true or essential reality. Similarly, both present cogent methodologies, and facilitate our examining and explaining social phenomena. Neither, however, convinces from outside its own theoretical parameters. Which perspective we adopt depends on the willful choice each of us makes, and this is determined by our perceiving and evaluating the quality of each presentation. The argument from phenomenology, as outlined, elevates free, subjectively-determined praxis over both materialist objectivism and transcendentalism, while simultaneously escaping sentimentalism. Its methodological and ideological implications make it relevant, vital, to the seemingly endless search for social justice. It infuses the stale, self-contained reality of academe with a vibrant determination, rooted in the 'telos' of self-conscious awareness and nurtured on the commitment to liberating social change.

Appendix

Selected propositions from empirical case studies based on, or influenced by, Snyder's decision-making model.

1 Richard C. Snyder and Glenn D. Paige, The United States Decision to Resist Aggression in Korea, 'Administrative Science Quarterly,' vol. III, no. 3 (December, 1958), pp. 341-78.

Decision-makers authorized to act, motivated to act, and prepared to act were present.

Direct military intervention, having the specific objective of restoring the status quo, was commensurate with the basic values threatened.

The objective could probably be achieved by a limited military commitment and without incurring total war or total national mobilization.

The risks and costs of this course of action were acceptable in terms of the values at stake; the consequences of the loss of South Korea were intolerable.

The means (air, sea and ground units), were immediately available to implement the course of action decided upon.

2 Glenn D. Paige, 'The Korean Decision' (New York: Free Press, 1968), pp. 281-322.

Organizational variables

Crisis decisions tend to be reached by ad hoc decisional units.

Crisis decisions tend to be made by decisional units that vary within rather narrow limits of size and composition.

The more need for immediate, costly action, the smaller the decisional unit.

The more technical the problems of decision implementation, the greater the role of the appropriate specialists in the decisional unit.

The greater the crisis, the greater the felt need for face-to-face proximity among decision-makers.

The greater the crisis, the greater the accentuation of positive affect relationships among decision-makers.

The greater the crisis, the greater the acceptance of responsibility for action by the leader and the more the follower expectation and acceptance of the leaders responsibility.

The greater the crisis, and the greater the past record of non-avoidant response to crisis by the leader, the greater the propensity to make a positive response.

The greater the crisis, the more the leader's solicitation of advice.

The greater the crisis, the greater the interdepartmental collaboration.

Informational variables

The greater the crisis, the greater the felt need for information.

The more limited the information, the greater the emphasis placed upon the reliability of its source.

The more varied the organizational sources and channels of communication of similar information, the greater the confidence in its validity.

The more prolonged the crisis, the greater the sense of adequacy of the information about it.

The greater the crisis, the greater the tendency for primary messages to be elevated to the top of the organizational hierarchy.

The greater the crisis, the greater the reliance upon the central themes in previously existing information.

The greater the confidence in existing information, the greater the amount of contrary evidence and the greater the authority of the sources required to bring about a change in interpretation.

The greater the crisis, the greater the propensity for decision-makers to supplement information about the objective state of affairs with information drawn from their own past experience.

Values

Crisis tends to evoke a dominant goal-means value complex that persists as an explicit or implicit guide to subsequent responses.

The goal-means value complex evoked by the crisis tends to be broad in its scope of applicability.

Crisis tends to evoke a goal-means value complex that is strongly conditioned emotionally.

Crisis tends to evoke the gradual proliferation of associated values around a dominant value core.

The wider the range of values seem to be served, the greater the willingness to accept the risk of costly commitment.

The greater the willingness to accept the risks of commitment to protect a dominant core value, the wider the range of additional values for which protection will be sought.

The greater the sense of urgency, the less the effectiveness of negative values as inhibitors of positive response.

Costly responses to crisis tend to be followed by decline in the salience of the values associated with them.

Internal and external setting variables

The greater the crisis, the greater the environmental demands for information about the probable responses that political leaders may make to it.

The greater the crisis, the more the attempts by political leaders to limit response-relevant information transmitted to the internal setting.

The greater the crisis, the greater the efforts of decision-makers to diminish popular anxieties.

The greater the crisis, the greater the reliance upon the political leader's estimate of the domestic acceptability of a response.

The greater the crisis, the greater the avoidance of response-inhibiting involvements.

The greater the crisis, the greater the avoidance of legitimacy challenging involvements.

The greater the crisis thrust upon the decision-makers from the external environment, the greater the propensity for them to receive positive reinforcing responses to their actions from individuals and groups within the internal setting.

The greater the crisis, the more the preferential

communication of crisis decisions to politically sensitive elements, the support of whom is required for effective implementation.

The greater the crisis, the more directed scanning of the international environment for information.

The greater the crisis, the greater the sensitivity to external response expectations.

The greater the crisis, the greater the environmental demands for response information.

The greater the crisis, the greater the efforts to withhold details of response execution strategies from inimical external setting elements.

The greater the crisis, the less the international acceptability of information emanating from the decision-makers directly concerned.

The greater the crisis, the more frequent and the more direct the interactions with friendly leaders in the external setting.

The greater the crisis, the greater the efforts to secure international collaborative support for an appropriate response.

The wider the range of international involvements undertaken in response to crisis, the wider the range of legitimations required to gain international acceptance of them.

The greater the crisis, the greater the clarification of the values of international political objects.

The greater the crisis, the greater the efforts directed toward the provision of opportunities for autonomous threat withdrawal by the source of the threatening behavior.

The greater the crisis, the greater the efforts devoted toward minimizing the range and degree of the threat confronted.

Decisional properties and administrative execution

The less precise the specification of behaviors expected to follow a decision that has been taken, the greater the variance between actual and anticipated behavior.

The greater the degree of negative reinforcement expected to follow faulty decisional execution, the greater the precision with which expected behaviors are specified.

The less the negative reinforcement expected to follow faulty execution, the greater the delegation of command and control functions over decisional execution.

3 James A. Robinson, Decision-Making in the House Rules Committee, William J. Gore and J. W. Dyson (eds) 'The Making of Decisions' (New York: Free Press, 1964), pp. 315-24.

When the spheres of competence of a decisional unit are not explicitly or completely prescribed, individual members of the unit are required to interpret their competences for themselves.

The greater the prestige of and respect for the sender, the greater is the impact of the information on the recipient.

The less the flow of information from system sources, the more reliance will be placed on information within the decisional unit.

The shorter the period for decision, the less thorough is the search for information.

The values and objectives that guide individual decisions in organizations include organizational values and objectives.

The values and objectives that guide individual decisions in organizations include his previous life experience or social background.

4 David C. Schwartz, Decision Theories and Crisis Behavior: An Empirical Study of Nuclear Deterrence in International Political Crisis, 'Orbis' vol. II (Summer, 1967), pp. 459-90.

Despite their perception of American strategic superiority, the Soviet Union's foreign policy decision-makers have adopted or supported crisis-initiating policies.

As the United States' overall strategic superiority becomes increasingly perceptible to opposing decision-makers, Soviet perceived threat rises.

When the balance of available crisis resources is perceived by opposents increasingly to favor the United States, the Soviet decision-makers feel increased threat.

As United States' strategic and tactical readiness is perceived by the Soviets to increase, Soviet perceptions of the resolve of American decision-makers is increased.

As the Soviets sense increased United States resolve, they perceive increased threat and United States hostility.

As the Soviets become conscious of increased American resolve and hostility, and hence increased threat to themselves, the number of perceived conceivable Soviet policy alternatives decreases from the initiation to the peak of the crisis.

As the Soviets perceive increased United States resolve and hostility, and hence increased threat to themselves, their assessments of the relative merits, consequences, costs, gains and utilities of various crisis policies will undergo significant modification.

The more direct the crisis confrontation between the United States and the Soviet Union . . . the more credible is United States strategic action.

Conditions of high or increasing threat affect the receptivity of decision-makers to messages from the opponent in crisis.

As threat increases, decision-makers tend to narrow the scope of autonomy allowed to field commanders.

A perception of favorable allied response will reinforce decision-makers in the adoption of a given policy and conversely strong actions may be the way to achieve support.

A perception of low or decreased allied support will generally argue for weaker policies on issues deemed basic to national interests.

To a lesser extent, a perception of favorable neutral support will reinforce decision-makers in the adoption of a given policy.

A perception of favorable response from the citizens of their own country will reinforce decision-makers, at least in democratic nations, in the adoption of a given policy, notwithstanding the fact that in the nuclear age decision-makers enjoy considerable latitude.

A perception of a favorable tide of history will affect the adoption of a given crisis policy.

Changes in policy (especially breakdowns) will be accomplished more easily if these changes can plausibly be rationalized within statements of long-term foreign policy objectives.

References

CHAPTER 1 PHENOMENOLOGY AND METHODOLOGY OF SOCIAL SCIENCE: The origins

1 For a brief but concise summary of this debate see George Lichtheim, 'George Lukács' (New York: Viking Press, 1970), pp.1-10.

2 Aron Gurwitsch, The Common-Sense World as Social Reality - A Discourse on Alfred Schutz, 'Social Research,' XXIX (Spring, 1962), p.72. Gurwitsch feels that Schutz's work fulfills Dilthey's goal of understanding the subjective aspects of history. See also Albert Salomon, German Sociology, 'Twentieth Century Sociology,' ed. George Gurvitch and Wilbert E. Moore (New York: Philosophical Library, 1945), pp.586-614. Salomon also claims that Dilthey's ideas are more directly related to the phenomenological search for scientific truth than even Weber's. Heinemann confirms this thesis by citing Dilthey's comment to Husserl that those chapters in 'Logical Investigations' dealing with inner experiences of the subject were extremely fruitful. This so impressed Husserl that, according to Heinemann, it made his progress to the transcendental phenomenological reduction (in 'Ideas') that much more probable. See Frederick H. Heinemann, 'Existentialism and the Modern Predicament' (New York: Harper, 1958), chapter 1.

3 Wilhelm Dilthey, 'Gesammelte Schriften' (Leipzig and Berlin: B. G. Teubner, 1923-7), esp. chapter 1, entitled Einleitung in die Geisteswissenschaften. See also 'The Essence of Philosophy,' trans. Stephan A. Emergy and William T. Emergy (Chapel Hill: University of North Carolina Press, 1954), and 'Pattern and Meaning in History,' trans. H. P. Richman (New York: Harper, 1962).

4 Wilhelm Windelband, 'History of Ancient Philosophy,' trans. Herbert E. Cushman (2nd edn; New York: C. Schribner's Sons, 1899), and 'History of Philosophy,' trans. James H. Tufts (New York: Macmillan, 1901).

5 Heinrich Rickert, 'Kulturwissenschaft und Naturwissenschaft' (Tübingen: J. C. B. Mohr, 1910), and 'Die grenzen der Naturwissenschaftlichen Begriffsbildung' (Tübingen: J. C. B. Mohr, 1921).

6 Raymond Aron, 'German Sociology,' trans. Mary and Thomas Bottomore (New York: Free Press, 1967), p.68.

7 See Max Weber, 'The Methodology of the Social Sciences,' trans. and ed. Edward A. Shils and Henry A. Finch (Chicago: Free Press, 1949) for a summary of Weber's early ideas on methodology. The articles in this volume entitled 'Objectivity' in Social Science and Social Policy (pp.50-112) and Critical Studies in The Logic of The Cultural Sciences (pp.113-88) deal most explicitly with the problems being discussed here. Valuable secondary works include Dennis Wrong (ed.), 'Max Weber' (Englewood Cliffs, N.J.: Prentice-Hall, 1970), pp.8-10; Julien Freund, 'The Sociology of Max Weber' (New York: Vintage Books, 1968), esp. pp.38-40; and H. Stuart Hughes, 'Consciousness and Society' (New York: Knopff, 1958), esp. p.309.

8 See Weber, op. cit., pp.149-52 for Weber's description of 'Wertbeziehung,' and for a critique of Rickert's view on this subject.

9 Max Weber, 'The Theory of Social and Economic Organization,' trans. A. M. Henderson and Talcott Parsons (New York: Free Press, 1969). This is an English translation of Part I of the three-volume 'Economy and Society.' Weber's relevant methodological considerations are included in this edition, primarily on pp.87-157. This work shall hereafter be referred to as 'TSEO.'

10 Weber, 'TSEO,' pp.87-8 attributes his development of 'Verstehen' to certain works by Jaspers, Rickert and Simmel. As Freund points out (Freund, op. cit., p.93), Weber was probably influenced also by the writings of Dilthey, Gottl-Ottlilienfeld, Lipps and many others. For more recent elaborations of the process of 'Verstehen' which help clarify Weber's meaning see Theodore Abel, The Operation Called 'Verstehen,' 'Readings in the Philosophy of Science,' ed. Herbert Feigl and May Brodbeck (New York: Appleton-Century-Crofts, 1953), pp.677-87; and Howard Becker, Interpretive Sociology and Constructive Typology, Gurvitch and Moore, op. cit., pp.70-95.

11 Weber, 'TSEO,' pp.101-7.

12 Ibid., p.88.
13 Max Weber, 'Basic Concepts in Sociology' (New York: Citadel Press, 1964), p.29.
14 Weber, 'TSEO,' p.101. See also pp.94-6.
15 Weber, 'Basic Concepts in Sociology,' p.30. See also 'TSEO,' pp.90-1.
16 See Weber, 'TSEO,' pp.108-9 for his criticism of non-empirical psychology as a means of studying society.
17 See Weber, 'The Methodology of the Social Sciences,' pp.63-112.
18 See Wrong, op. cit., p.25, Aron, op. cit., pp.68-9, and Freund, op. cit., pp.117-18 for concurring views. The relevant argument is in Weber, 'TSEO,' pp.107-8.
19 This has led to much criticism of Weber's methodology from the more strictly positivist scientific community. For three of the most cogent of these see Talcott Parsons, 'The Structure of Social Action' (Chicago: Free Press, 1949), esp. chapters XVI-XVII; Richard Rudner, 'Philosophy of Social Science' (Englewood Cliffs: Prentice-Hall, 1966), pp.55-62; and Robert M. Lawson, On the Possibility of an Objective Social Science, 'Kinesis,' 2 (Fall, 1969), pp.3-14.
20 See Weber, 'The Methodology of the Social Sciences,' pp.164-88.
21 Weber, 'TSEO,' p.99.
22 Weber, 'The Methodology of the Social Sciences,' p.90. See also pp.42-3.
23 Weber, 'TSEO,' pp.115-17.
24 Ibid., p.92.
25 For Weber's application of the rational ideal type to the understanding of various basic structures of social, economic and political action, see ibid., pp.115-57.
26 Ibid., p.88.
27 Ibid., p.98.
28 Ibid., p.89-90.
29 Aron, op. cit., (pp.74-5) suggests Weber implicitly accepts Karl Jasper's theory of meaning, and therefore understands it as consisting of certain attributes of mental phenomena propelling an individual towards or away from specified actions. This, however, is too speculative and ambiguous to be conclusive.
30 See Karl Loewith, Weber's Interpretation of the Bourgeois-Capitalistic World in Terms of the Guiding Principle of 'Rationalization,' Wrong, op. cit., pp.101-22. In this article, Loewith analyzes Weber's concept of freedom and concludes that it is synonomous

with Marx's definition of 'alienation.'

31 Originally published in German under the title 'Der Sinnhafte Aufbau der sozialen Welt' (Vienna: Julius Springer, 1932). The English version is 'The Phenomenology of the Social World,' trans. George Walsh and Frederick Lehnert, (Evanston, Ill.: Northwestern University Press, 1967). See pp.3-44. This work shall hereafter be referred to as 'PSW.'

32 Husserl was not the first to use this term, but was the originator of what is today recognized as phenomenological philosophy. See Herbert Spiegelberg, 'The Phenomenological Movement' (2 vols; 2nd edn rev.; The Hague: Martinus Nijhoff, 1965), vol. 1, pp.7-20 for a history of the term 'phenomenology.'

33 There are numerous texts analyzing Husserlian phenomenology in detail. The best of these, in my experience, include: Paul Ricoeur, 'Husserl, An Analysis of His Phenomenology,' trans. Edward G. Ballard and Lester E. Embree (Evanston, Ill.: Northwestern University Press, 1967). This is perhaps the best analysis of Husserl's main concepts, as expressed in the 'Ideas' and 'Cartesian Meditations,' by a most knowledgeable commentator. Aron Gurwitsch, 'Studies in Phenomenology and Psychology' (Evanston, Ill.: Northwestern University Press, 1966). This compilation of articles accurately reflects the flavor of Husserl's thought, even though some of them - especially A Non-Egological Conception of Consciousness (pp.287-300) and On the Intentionality of Consciousness (pp.124-40) - slightly alter Husserl's understanding of transcendental consciousness and intentionality. Quentin Lauer, 'The Triumph of Subjectivity' (New York: Fordham University Press, 1958); Dorian Cairns, An Approach to Phenomenology, 'Philosophical Essays in Memory of Edmund Husserl,' ed. Marvin Farber (Cambridge, Mass.: Harvard University Press, 1940), pp.3-18; Marvin Farber, 'The Foundation of Phenomenology' (Cambridge, Mass.: Harvard University Press, 1943); and Paul Thévenaz, 'What is Phenomenology?' trans. James M. Edie, Charles Courtney and Paul Brockelman (Chicago: Quadrangle Books, 1962). These last four works are concise, understandable analyses of Husserl's main ideas, with the Lauer book especially noteworthy in dealing with the transcendental ego. Finally, Richard Zaner, 'The Way of Phenomenology' (New York: Pegasus, 1970), has an excellent chapter (chapter 3) analyzing Husserl's concept of consciousness.

34 Husserl first repudiated psychologism in 'Logische

Untersuchungen' (2 vols; Halle: M. Niemeyer, 1900). A second, revised edition of this work, rendering his argument in more radical terms, was published in 1913. This revised edition appears in English as 'Logical Investigations,' trans. J. N. Findlay (2 vols; London: Routledge & Kegan Paul, New York: Humanities Press, 1970). See pp.90-196 for the relevant argument. For detailed commentary on Husserl's rejection of psychologism, see John Wild, Husserl's Critique of Psychologism, 'Philosophical Essays in Memory of Edmund Husserl,' ed. Farber, pp.19-43; Roderick Chisholm (ed.), 'Realism and the Background of Phenomenology' (Chicago: Free Press, 1960), pp.13-17; Farber, op. cit., chapter 4; and Spiegelberg, op cit., pp.93-5.

35 For excellent discussions of the historical origins, beginning with Descartes, of Husserl's concept of consciousness, see Aron Gurwitsch, Husserl's Theory of the Intentionality of Consciousness in Historical Perspective, 'Phenomenology and Existentialism,' ed. Edward N. Lee and Maurice Mandelbaum (Baltimore: Johns Hopkins Press, 1967), pp.25-57; and Zaner, op. cit., pp.83-118. Interpretations of the influence William James alone had on Husserl are offered in Spiegelberg, op. cit., pp.111-17; Alfred Schutz, Multiple Realities, 'Collected Papers,' vol. I: 'The Problem of Social Reality,' ed. Maurice Natanson (The Hague: Martinus Nijhoff, 1967), pp.207-59, and William James's Concept of the Stream of Consciousness Phenomenologically Interpreted, 'Collected Papers,' vol. III: 'Studies in Phenomenological Philosophy,' ed. I. Schutz (The Hague: Martinus Nijhoff, 1966), pp.1-14; Aron Gurwitsch, William James's Theory of the 'Transitive Parts' of the Stream of Consciousness, 'Studies in Phenomenology and Psychology,' pp.301-31, and 'Field of Consciousness' (Pittsburgh: Duquesne University Press, 1964), pp.21-9, 127-31, 184-8, and 309-17; and Bruce Wilshire, 'William James and Phenomenology' (Bloomington, Ind.: Indiana University Press, 1968).

36 See Spiegelberg, op. cit., pp.27-51.

37 See Franz Brentano, The Distinction Between Mental and Physical Phenomena, Chislhom op. cit., pp.39-61, and Genuine and Fictitious Objects, ibid., pp.71-5. Brentano uses the term 'intentional inexistence' rather than 'intentionality.' Husserl evaluates the influence of Brentano in his interpretation of consciousness in 'Logical Investigations,' II, pp.552-6.

38 See Edmund Husserl, 'Ideen zu eine reinen Phänomenologie und phänomenologischen Philosophie,' first published in 1913 in vol. 1 of the 'Jahrbuch fur philosophie und phänomenologische Forschung' (PPR). The English version is 'Ideas, General Introduction to Pure Phenomenology,' trans. W. R. Boyce Gibson (New York: Humanities Press, 1931), esp. p.23.

39 This is most clearly illustrated in Husserl, 'Logical Investigations.'

40 This concept, in a theoretically inchoate form, can be found in Husserl, 'Logical Investigations,' II, pp.760-70. It is more explicitly stated in Edmund Husserl, Philosophy as Rigorous Science, 'Phenomenology and the Crisis of Philosophy,' trans. Quentin Lauer, (New York: Harper & Row, 1965), pp.71-147, esp. pp.89-94, and 'Cartesian Meditations,' trans. Dorion Cairns (The Hague: Martinus Nijhoff, 1964), pp.27-55.

41 Dorion Cairns, An Approach to Phenomenology, 'Philosophical Essays in Memory of Edmund Husserl,' ed. Farber, pp.10-1.

42 Most of Edmund Husserl's 'Erfahrung und Urteil: Untersuchungen zur Genealogie der Logik,' posthumously published in 1939, deals with the notion of typicality and with the noetic and noematic correlates of consciousness. See also Husserl, 'Ideas,' pp.137-43, and 'Cartesian Meditations,' pp.39-49.

43 Schutz, 'Collected Papers' vol. III, pp.110-15.

44 Husserl, 'Ideas,' pp.107-11.

45 Ibid., pp.112-14.

46 This and the preceding statement are both found in ibid., p.113.

47 See ibid., pp.116-46.

48 It is Husserl's goal to utilize the 'epoché' to constitute successively purer stages of subjectivity. However, in no single work does he describe the total process of reduction from the naive attitude to absolute subjectivity. Though most commentators identify the two reductions treated here as representative of Husserl's intent, some have identified the ascent to the pure Ego as consisting of a number of different levels, each corresponding to a reduction. Thus, Lauer, op. cit., pp.51-3, identifies six levels and reductions (Psychological reduction, Eidetic reduction, Phenomenological reduction, Transcendental reduction, constitution of temporality of pure subject, and final reduction to

pure consciousness), while Joseph Kockelmans, 'Phenomenology and Physical Science' (Pittsburgh: Duquesne University Press, 1966), p.37, recognizes four (Eidetic, Phenomenological, Lebenswelt, Transcendental-phenomenological).

49 Husserl, 'Ideas,' pp.51-97 and 147-84.

50 Herbert Spiegelberg, How Subjective is Phenomenology, 'Proceedings of the American Catholic Philosophical Association,' XXXIII (1959), pp.30-5. Richard Schmitt, Husserl's Transcendental Phenomenological Reduction, 'Philosophy and Phenomenological Research,' 20 (1959-60), pp.238-45, deals with this subject more analytically, but with similar results.

51 Edmund Husserl, 'Formal and Transcendental Logic,' trans. Dorion Cairns (The Hague: Martinus Nijhoff, 1969), pp.232-93. This is an English translation of 'Formale und transzendentale Logik' (Halle: 1929). The same argument is found in 'Cartesian Meditations,' pp.27-88.

52 Ibid., pp.89-151.

53 See, for example, Chauncey B. Downes, Husserl's Theory of Other Minds: A Study of the 'Cartesian Meditations' (unpublished PhD dissertation, Department of Philosophy, New York University, 1963). Although Schutz devotes many pages to criticizing Husserl's theory of intersubjectivity, it is not central to his methodology. Consequently, we omit detailed description of it and certain related theories dealing with the logic of signs and symbols. References to these ideas of Husserl will be made when and if the occasion demands.

54 Originally published as 'Die krisis der Europäischen Wissenschaften und die transzendentale Phänomenologie,' posthumously edited by Walter Biemel, and published in 1954. The English translation is by David Carr, 'The Crisis of European Sciences and Transcendental Phenomenology' (Evanston, Ill.: Northwestern University Press, 1970). These lectures were given by Husserl at Prague, in 1935-6, and are organized into three parts. The Prague lectures constitute the central essays of the 'Krisis' group. A lecture given in Vienna, and often considered as part of the 'Krisis' lectures, entitled Philosophy and the Crisis of European Man is found in Carr, op.cit., pp.269-99, and in Husserl's 'Phenomenology and the Crisis of Philosophy,' pp.149-92. There is a two-part summary of the Prague lectures by Aron Gurwitsch, The Last Work of Edmund Husserl, 'Philosophy and Phenomenological Research,' XVI (March, 1956),

pp.380-99; XVII (March, 1957), pp.370-98. This summary is reproduced in Gurwitsch, 'Studies in Phenomenology and Psychology,' pp.397-447. There is also a briefer, less detailed summary by Joseph J. Kockelmans, The Mathematization of Nature in Husserl's Last Publication, 'Phenomenology and the Natural Sciences,' ed. Joseph J. Kockelmans and Henry Kisiel (Evanston, Ill.: Northwestern University Press, 1970), pp.45-67.

55 Husserl, 'The Crisis of European Sciences and Transcendental Phenomenology,' pp.21-100.

56 Ibid., pp.23-64.

57 Ibid., pp.68-70 and 191-7.

58 Husserl's writings on the 'Lebenswelt' are primarily contained in the 'Krisis' lectures. However, for at least fifteen years prior to these lectures Husserl was aware of certain problems relating to the 'Lebenswelt.' For example, his 'Phänomenologische Psychologie,' written between 1925 and 1928, contains reflections on aspects of the 'Lebenswelt.' See Joseph J. Kockelmans (ed.), 'Phenomenology' (New York: Doubleday, 1967), p.194. Ludwig Landgrebe, The World as a Phenomenological Problem, 'Philosophy and Phenomenological Research,' I (1940-1), pp.38-58, confirms this thesis by detailing the close relationship between Husserl's concept of the 'Lebenswelt' and his concept of 'world' contained in early writings. There is a small, but significant, minority now claiming Husserl distinguishes between the 'mundane' world and the 'Lebenswelt,' the latter referring to the locus of reflective social action. They base this assertion, which negates not only the trend of Husserl's published writings but also the overwhelming majority of scholarly commentaries, on certain of Husserl's unpublished manuscripts collected by Iso Kern in the Louvain Archives. See Pier Aldo Rovatti, A Phenomenological Analysis of Marxism: The Return to the Subject and to the Dialectic of the totality, 'Telos,' 5 (Spring, 1970), pp.161-2, especially n.2.

59 Husserl, 'The Crisis of European Sciences and Transcendental Phenomenology,' pp.103-11.

60 Ibid., p.110.

61 Ibid., pp.121-35.

62 Ibid., pp.135-89. Husserl apparently is not aware that a transcendental phenomenological study of the 'Lebenswelt' involves a possible contradiction. We cannot achieve a transcendental phenomenological analysis unless we purify our subjectivity by means

of a detailed procedure of reflection. Whether, and how, knowledge gained from such a reflective procedure relates to our actions in the pre-reflective 'Lebenswelt' remains unclear.

63 This, with important modifications that will be described later, is the path chosen by Heidegger. Since Heidegger's 'Being and Time' was published prior to the 'Krisis' lectures, it is possible Husserl was indirectly influenced by Heidegger - a former pupil whom he disagreed with but respected - to include this ontological analysis. This possibility is presented and discussed by Herbert Spiegelberg, Husserl's Phenomenology and Existentialism, 'The Journal of Philosophy,' LII (1960), pp.66-7, and James M. Edie, Recent Work in Phenomenology, 'American Philosophical Quarterly,' I (1964), pp.126-7.

64 Husserl, 'The Crisis of European Sciences and Transcendental Phenomenology,' pp.235-65.

65 This concept of science, called by Husserl 'eidetic,' will be analyzed further in chapter 4.

66 Gerd Brand, Intentionality, Reduction, and Intentional Analysis in Husserl's Later Manuscripts, 'Phenomenology,' ed. Kockelmans, pp.197-217, and James M. Edie, Transcendental Phenomenology and Existentialism 'Philosophy and Phenomenological Research,' 25 (1964-5), pp.52-63. Merleau-Ponty's ambiguous position will be further probed in chapter 4.

67 Detailed confirmation of this position is offered in Landgrebe, 'Philosophy and Phenomenological Research,' p.52; Gurwitsch, 'Studies in Phenomenology and Psychology,' p.XX; Spiegelberg, 'The Phenomenological Movement,' I, pp.159-61, and Kockelmans (ed.), 'Phenomenology,' pp.194-5.

68 We will probe this topic further in chapter 5.

CHAPTER 2 PHENOMENOLOGICAL SOCIAL SCIENCE

1 The book is Alfred Schutz, 'The Phenomenology of the Social World,' trans. George Walsh and Frederick Lehnert (Evanston, Ill.: Northwestern University Press, 1967), hereafter referred to as 'PSW.' It has been uncritically summarized by Alfred Stonier and Karl Bode, A New Approach to the Methodology of the Social Sciences, 'Economica,' IV (1937), pp.406-24. 'Die Struckturen der Lebenswelt,' co-authored by Schutz and Thomas Luckmann, has been published as

'The Structure of the Life-World,' trans. Richard Zaner and Tristam Engelhardt, Jr. (Evanston, Ill.: Northwestern University Press, 1973). This book has been interpreted and summarized by Luckmann in The Foundations of Knowledge in Everyday Life, chapter 1 of Peter L. Berger and Thomas Luckmann, 'The Social Construction of Reality' (Garden City: Doubleday, 1966), pp.19-46. Some of Schutz's unpublished notes and essays have been compiled and edited by Richard M. Zaner, 'Reflections on the Problem of Relevance' (New Haven: Yale University Press, 1970), hereafter referred to as 'RPR.' His published articles are compiled in Alfred Schutz, 'Collected Papers' (3 vols; The Hague: Martinus Nijhoff; vol. I: 'The Problem of Social Reality,' ed. Maurice Natanson, 2nd edn, 1967; vol. II: 'Studies in Social Theory,' ed. Arvid Brodersen, 1964; vol. III: 'Studies in Phenomenological Philosophy,' ed. I. Schutz, 1966). These three volumes will be referred to as 'CP,' I, 'CP,' II, 'CP,' III. Robert Bierstadt, The Common-Sense World of Alfred Schutz, 'Social Research,' 26 (Winter, 1959), pp.116-20, is a brief review of 'CP,' I. There is an uncritical summary of Schutz's work in Helmut Wagner (ed.) 'Alfred Schutz - On Phenomenology and Social Relations' (Chicago: University of Chicago Press, 1970), pp.1-50.

2 'CP,' III, p.11.

3 Gurwitsch, 'The Field of Consciousness' (Pittsburgh: Duquesne University Press, 1964), p.401.

4 'PSW,' p.44.

5 Ibid., pp.82-4. In 'RPR,' p.143, Schutz distinguishes between the 'stock of knowledge *at* hand,' and the 'stock of knowledge *in* hand.' The former refers to experiential knowledge as described above. The latter to non-thematic knowledge, such as knowledge of our own bodies, necessary for increasing our stocks of knowledge at hand. This distinction is never carefully developed.

6 'CP,' I, pp.7-8. See also Maurice Natanson, Phenomenology and Typification - A Study in the Philosophy of Alfred Schutz, 'Social Research,' 37 (Spring, 1970), pp.1-22, for a generally uncritical review of this aspect of Schutz's theory.

7 For an illustration, see Schutz, The Homecomer, 'CP,' II, pp.106-19, esp. p. 109.

8 'CP,' II, p. 234.

9 Ibid., p.236.

10 'CP,' I, p.61.

11 'CP,' II, p.237.

12 Ibid., p.95, describes when social recipes break down.
13 'CP,' I, pp.238-9, and 'CP,' II, pp.101-2. Schutz's essay The Stranger, 'CP,' II, pp.91-105 illustrates this by showing how a visitor to a foreign country can only understand this country according to the 'recipes' of his native land.
14 'CP,' II, p.132.
15 Ibid., pp.253-4.
16 Ibid., p.254.
17 'CP,' I, pp.xxix-xxx and p.224.
18 See 'PSW,' pp.104-6, 'CP,' I, p.167, and 'CP,' III, pp.73-82.
19 'CP,' I, pp.177-9.
20 See 'CP,' I, p.166, n.37 and p.196, for more exact definitions of appresentation. Richard M. Zaner, Theory of Intersubjectivity: Alfred Schutz, 'Social Research,' XXVIII (Spring, 1961), pp.71-94 uncritically describes Schutz's theory of intersubjectivity, emphasizing this notion of appresentation (esp. pp.71-87). Schutz and Husserl both write about this concept, using it as a basis for theories of communication, involving language and sign and symbol systems. 'CP,' I, pp.294-305 contains Schutz's analysis of Husserl's understanding of appresentation. Schutz's own development of it as the basis of sign and symbol systems can be found in 'CP,' I, pp.306-56 and 'PSW,' pp.118-32. Since these issues are peripheral to our argument, they are not treated separately.
21 'PSW,' pp.102-7, and 'CP,' I, pp.172-3.
22 'CP,' I, p.174.
23 See especially 'PSW,' pp.139-214, 'CP,' I, pp.16-19, and 'CP,' II, pp.20-63.
24 See Berger and Luckmann, op. cit., pp.30-3. A vivid example of the pure we-relationship is found in Schutz's essay Making Music Together, 'CP,' II, pp.159-79. This essay illustrates how music is one way of 'tuning-in' to a pure we-relationship in the vivid present.
25 'CP,' II, p.44.
26 Berger and Luckmann, op. cit., p.33.
27 'PSW,' pp.57-9.
28 Ibid., p.60.
29 Ibid., p.61.
30 Ibid.
31 'CP,' I, p.212.
32 'CP,' I, pp.77-85, and 'PSW,' pp.66-9.
33 'CP,' I, p.86. Schutz's ideas concerning the

choosing of projects are influenced by, and closely resemble, Henri Bergson's thoughts on this topic. See especially Henri Bergson, 'Time and Free Will,' trans. F. L. Pogson (New York: Macmillan, 1910), chapter 30. This quote is made by Schutz in referring to Bergson; however, it is equally applicable to his own theory. A modified Schutzian theory is described by Bernard P. Dauenhauer, Making Plans and Lived Time 'Southern Journal of Philosophy,' 7 (Spring, 1969), pp.83-90, in which the resulting act is indeterminate and subject to continual change as it progresses in action.

34 'CP,' I, pp.93-4.

35 Ibid., p.95.

36 'PSW,' pp.91-6, 'CP,' II, pp.11-3, and 'CP,' I, pp.69-72.

37 'CP,' II, p.13.

38 The phenomenological understanding of 'freedom' is, generally speaking, vague. This will be discussed further in our critical analysis of Schutz, chapter 3.

39 'CP,' I, p.20. See Husserl, 'Formal and Transcendental Logic,' trans. Dorion Cairns (The Hague: Martinus Nijhoff, 1969), pp.188-9.

40 'CP,' I, pp.20-1. The theoretical foundation of the following argument is given in ibid., pp.22-34.

41 See 'RPR,' pp.68-74. In this compilation of Schutz's notes, it is suggested that action results from the reciprocal interaction of three systems of relevance: interpretational, topical, and motivational. Schutz admits that, in the natural attitude, only the last system - consisting of because and in-order-to motives - is consciously at work. The first two are significant primarily in determining the social distribution of knowledge, especially in investigating why different people perceive the same events and phenomena as relevant or irrelevant to their interests. This task is accomplished outside the natural attitude, where all things are unquestioningly accepted. Since Schutz's method is relevant only to the common-sense world, there is little point in detailing his admittedly incomplete ideas on these systems of relevance.

42 Schutz's description of the 'multiple realities' is largely dependent on William James's analysis of 'sub-universes' ('CP,' I, pp.207-8; and Gurwitsch, 'Field of Consciousness,' pp.21-56), Henri Bergson's analysis of the different planes of consciousness ('CP,' I, pp.212-16), and G. H. Mead's theory of the generalized Other ('CP,' I, pp.216-18 and Berger

and Luckmann, op. cit., pp.13-17).
43 'CP,' I, pp.208-28. Berger and Luckmann, op. cit., pp.24-6 summarizes these ideas.
44 'CP,' I, p.231.
45 Ibid., p.232.
46 Schutz includes under cognitive style a specific tension or awareness of consciousness; a specific epoché suspending doubt in the world; a specific prevalent form of spontaneity; a specific form of self-experience; a specific form of sociality; and a specific time perspective ('CP,' I, pp.230-1). His essay Don Quixote and the Problem of Reality, 'CP,' II, pp.135-58, describes Quixote's reality in these terms and contrasts it with the paramount reality of Sancho Panza.
47 'CP,' I, p.229.
48 Ibid., p.245.
49 Ibid., p.253.
50 Ibid., p.248.
51 Ibid., p.251.
52 See ibid., pp.256-9 and 329-39, and Berger and Luckmann, op. cit., pp.36-41. This issue ties in with the concept of appresentation: see n.20.
53 'CP,' I, pp.5-7, and 'PSW,' pp.241-9.
54 'CP,' I, pp.26-7 and 254-5.
55 'PSW,' pp.239-40.
56 'CP,' I, p.33, and 'CP,' II, pp.69-72. Rationalization is defined as 'the transformation of an uncontrollable and unintelligible world into an organization which we can understand and therefore master, and in the framework of which prediction becomes possible.' ('CP,' II, p.71). The quality of 'rational behavior' will therefore vary in different societies.
57 'CP,' II, pp.83-4.
58 'CP,' I, pp.40-4 and 64-6.
59 Ibid., p.42.
60 Ibid., pp.43-4, 'CP,' II, pp.18-9, and 'PSW,' pp.237-8.
61 'CP,' I, p.45. See also 'CP,' II, p.86 for a similar statement.
62 'CP,' I, p. 65. This statement refers to Schutz's phenomenological analysis of individual and social action.
63 Ibid., pp.40-2, and 'CP,' II, pp.17-8.
64 See 'CP,' I, p.57. The following quotations are found on this page.

CHAPTER 3 PHENOMENOLOGY, FREE ACTION, EMPIRICAL SOCIAL SCIENCE: Some theoretical and practical problems

1 Maurice Natanson, A Study in Philosophy and the Social Sciences, 'Social Research,' 25 (Summer, 1958), p.160.
2 We are dealing now only with those phenomenological principles Schutz and Husserl share. This does not include, as we shall see in chapter four, the transcendental phenomenological reduction and the scientific results of this reduction.
3 'CP,' I, p.35.
4 See 'PSW,' pp.229-34.
5 Ibid., pp.231-2.
6 Ibid., p.232.
7 Robert Bierstadt, The Common-Sense World of Alfred Schutz, 'Social Research,' 26 (Winter, 1959), p.120, briefly mentions this difficulty in Schutz's presentation. However, he treats it as an isolated fault, and does not carry through his criticism to the extent that seems warranted.
8 Fernando R. Molina (ed.), 'The Sources of Existentialism as Philosophy' (Englewood Cliffs, N.J.: Prentice-Hall, 1969), p.92.
9 See Gurwitsch's introduction to 'CP,' III, pp.xvi-xvii, n.8, and Maurice Natanson, Phenomenology and Typification - A Study in the Philosophy of Alfred Schutz, 'Social Research,' 37 (Spring, 1970), p.18.
10 Martin Heidegger, 'Being and Time,' trans. John Macquarrie and Edward Robinson (New York: Harper & Row, 1962). This work will hereafter be referred to as 'BT.' The complex question of the unity of Heidegger's thought, whether the notion of being ('Sein') described in his later writings is qualitatively different - more mystical and abstract - than that described in 'BT,' is far beyond the scope of this essay. The issue is fully discussed in W. B. Macomber, 'The Anatomy of Disillusion' (Evanston: Northwestern University Press, 1967), esp. p. 113.
11 'BT,' pp.150-68.
12 Ibid., pp.203-24, esp. pp.210-11.
13 Ibid., p.225.
14 Ibid., pp.220-1.
15 Ibid., pp.163-8 and 210-24.
16 Edward A. Tiryakian, 'Sociologism and Existentialism, Two Perspectives on the Individual and Society' (Englewood Cliffs, N.J.: Prentice-Hall, 1962), p.128.
17 Heidegger's analysis of inauthentic behavior is

parelleled by many similar theories tracing our loss of creative humanity. These include: Gabriel Marcel, 'The Philosophy of Existence,' trans. Manya Harari (New York: Philosophical Library, 1949), esp. pp.2-3, 'Mystery of Being,' trans. G. S. Fraser (Chicago: Regnery, 1960), pp.22-47, 'Man Against Mass Society,' trans. G. S. Fraser (Chicago: Regnery, 1952), part II; Karl Jaspers, 'Man in the Modern Age,' trans. Eden and Cedar Paul (London: Routledge & Kegan Paul, 1951), pp.34ff, esp. pp.40-1; and Jean-Paul Sartre, 'Being and Nothingness,' trans. Hazel E. Barnes (New York: Washington Square Press, 1966), pp.56-86. Heidegger's description of 'das Man' also resembles what George H. Mead calls 'the generalized Other,' the source of the social self. See George H. Mead, 'Mind, Self, and Society' (Chicago: University of Chicago Press, 1934).

18 The 'openness' of being will be discussed, in relation to methodology, in chapter 5.

19 See 'BT,' pp.304-11.

20 Stephan Strasser, 'Phenomenology and the Human Sciences,' (Pittsburgh: Duquesne University Press, 1963), p.304.

21 See ibid., pp.277-94. Other examples can be offered. Two of the most obvious are Joseph J. Kockelmans, 'Phenomenology and Physical Science' (Pittsburgh: Duquesne University Press, 1966), esp. p.13 and p.66; and Marvin Farber, 'Naturalism and Subjectivism' (Springfield, Ill.: C. C. Thomas, 1959), esp. p.15.

22 Peter Berger, who admits to having been profoundly influenced by Schutz's ideas (p.182), describes society in similar terms. In this sense, he confirms this conclusion concerning the nature of Schutz's common-sense world. See Peter Berger, 'Invitation to Sociology' (New York: Doubleday, 1963), chapters 6 (esp. pp.122-50), 7 and 8.

23 'CP,' II, pp.101-2.

24 Natanson, Phenomenology and Typification, 'Social Research,' pp.18-20. Schutz, too, uses the word 'determinants' to describe the social and natural forces an actor finds himself surrounded by. See 'CP,' I, pp.329-30.

25 Carl G. Hempel, 'Aspects of Scientific Explanation' (New York: Free Press, 1964), p.87.

26 Joseph J. Kockelmans, Husserl's Transcendental Idealism, 'Phenomenology,' ed. Kockelmans (New York: Doubleday, 1967), p.192.

27 This close relationship between empirical realism and the common-sense world has been recognized by another phenomenologist: Harmon Chapman, Realism and

Phenomenology, 'Essays in Phenomenology,' ed. Maurice Natanson (The Hague: Martinus Nijhoff, 1969), pp.79-115. This article was originally published in John Wild (ed.), 'The Return to Reason' (Chicago: Regnery Press, 1953). In trying to reconcile a naturalist empiricism with transcendental phenomenolgy, Chapman describes the common-sense world as the sphere of behavior most amenable to empirical scientific inquiry. 'Because of the inherent extraversion of the natural attitude, empiricism is preoccupied almost exclusively with the objects of awareness to the virtual oblivion of the awareness itself,' (p.100). Our unquestioning, naive attitude dictates that scientific understanding of the common-sense world focus on impersonal 'objects of awareness' rather than on 'the awareness itself.' There is, consequently, no need for a phenomenological social science when the traditional, naturalist method of inquiry is perfectly suited to investigate the impersonal forces determining our social behavior. In the context of these ideas, Schutz's method is only a superfluous addition to the methodology of the social sciences.

28 See David Braybrooke, 'Philosophical Problems of the Social Sciences' (New York: Macmillan, 1965), pp.1-18, for a discussion of the different kinds of interaction constituting society. Heidegger is noticeably vague on this topic, never systematically approaching the question of how social interaction is possible in the authentic mode. Only recently have existential phenomenologists begun to discuss this issue seriously, opening the way to the creation of a socially-relevant existential phenomenology. As innovative examples of this new work see Martin Buber, 'Schriften zur Philosophie' in 'Werke' (3 vols; Munich: Kosel-Verlag, 1962), I, esp. pp.373-4; and Jean-Paul Sartre, 'Critique de la raison dialectique' (Paris: Gallimard, 1960). We will examine the social relevance of existential phenomenology more closely in chapter 5.

29 The first example, mailing a letter, is the one most employed by Schutz throughout his writings to illustrate how his method works.

30 See Herbert A. Simon, 'Administrative Behavior: A Study of Decision-Making Processes in Administrative Organizations' (New York: Macmillan, 1957), pp.xxvii-xxix; 'Models of Man: Social and Rational' (New York: Wiley Press, 1957), pp.196-206 and 241-73; and Joseph Frankel, 'The Making of Foreign Policy'

(New York: Oxford University Press, 1963), pp.166-75. For clear statements of the issues separating the classical and modern approaches to decision-making theory see J. G. March and Herbert A. Simon, 'Organizations' (New York: Wiley Press, 1958), pp.136-71; and J. G. March, Some Recent Substantive and Methodological Developments in the Theory of Organizational Decision-Making, 'Essays on the Behavioral Study of Politics,' ed. Austin Ranney (Urbana, Ill.: University of Illinois Press, 1962), pp.191-208.

31 Richard C. Snyder, H. W. Bruck and Burton Sapin, Decision-Making as an Approach to the Study of International Politics, 'Foreign Policy Decision-Making,' ed. Richard C. Snyder, H. W. Bruck and Burton Sapin (New York: Free Press, 1962), pp.14-185. This essay was originally published in 1954. We will hereafter talk only of 'Snyder's theory,' and refer to it as Snyder, et al. A simplified version of decision-making theory, aimed at the undergraduate, is found in Richard C. Snyder and Edgar S. Furniss, Jr, 'American Foreign Policy: Formulation, Principles, and Programs' (New York: Holt Rinehart & Winston, 1954), chapter 3.

32 Snyder, Bruck and Sapin developed decision-making theory primarily to facilitate the study of international relations. However, even in the original version, they intimate their model is applicable to other branches of political science, including local and comparative politics, and political theory (Snyder, et al., p.20). Snyder amplifies on this in Richard C. Snyder, A Decision-Making Approach to the Study of Political Phenomena, 'Approaches to the Study of Politics,' ed. Roland Young (Evanston, Ill.: Northwestern University Press, 1958), pp.3-37, esp. pp.10-5. Here, Snyder broadens his earlier theory by explicitly describing how it is useful to the study of action analysis, public administration, legislative process, non-governmental social groups, class and power structures, etc. Decision-making theory, according to Snyder, is applicable in 'any area of political science where there is an interest in policy-formation or judgement of some kind' (p.10).

33 For a more detailed picture of the background of decision-making theory see James A. Robinson and Richard C. Snyder, Decision-Making in International Politics, 'International Behavior,' ed. H. Kelman (New York: Holt Rinehart & Winston, 1965), pp.437-40.

34 For example: Heinze Eulau, Samuel J. Eldersveld and Morris Janowitz (eds), 'Political Behavior: A Reader in Theory and Research' (Chicago: Free Press, 1956), pp.352-9; Stanley H. Hoffmann (ed.), 'Contemporary Theory in International Relations' (Englewood Cliffs, N.J.: Prentice-Hall, 1960), pp.150-65; James N. Rosenau (ed.), 'International Politics and Foreign Policy' (New York: Free Press, 1961), pp.186-92 and 247-53; Kelman, op. cit., pp.435-63; and Young, op. cit., pp.3-37.

35 Even a partial listing of such studies would run for pages. The most useful bibliographies include the following: James N. Rosenau, 'The Scientific Study of Foreign Policy' (New York: Free Press, 1971), pp.265-8; Robinson and Snyder, loc. cit., pp.451-6 and 443-8; and Richard C. Snyder and James Robinson, 'National and International Decision-Making' (New York: Institute for International Order, 1961). This last study, currently out of print, lists 21 other bibliographies dealing with topics related to decision-making, and lists approximately 800 separate books and articles that are based on, or deal with, the decision-making approach.

36 For example, H. McCloskey, Strategies for a Science of International Politics, 'Foreign Policy Decision-Making,' Snyder, Bruck, Sapin (eds), p.201.

37 Arnold Wolfers, The Actors in International Politics, 'Theoretical Aspects of International Relations,' ed. W. T. R. Fox (Indiana: University of Notre Dame Press, 1959), chapter 6.

38 See Margaret and Harold Sprout, 'Foundations of International Politics' (New Jersey: Van Nostrand Press, 1962), pp.167ff.; 'Ecological Perspective on Human Affairs' (Princeton, N.J.: Princeton University Press, 1965), pp.211ff.; and 'An Ecological Paradigm for the Study of International Politics' (Princeton, N.J.: Princeton University Press, 1968).

39 Especially Robert North, Ole Holsti, M. George Zaninovich and Dina Zinnes, 'Content Analysis' (Evanston, Ill.: Northwestern University Press, 1963). For empirical application of content analysis to the period immediately preceding the outbreak of World War I, see Dina Zinnes, R. C. North and H. E. Kock, Capability, Threat, and the Outbreak of War, 'International Politics and Foreign Policy,' ed. Rosenau, pp.469-82, and Dina Zinnes, Hostility in International Decision-Making, 'Journal of Conflict Resolution,' 6 (1962), pp.236-43.

40 This is not a common reaction to Snyder's model.

Those interested in pursuing a career in the social sciences won't easily undercut their professional existences by declaring scientific study impractical. Nevertheless, those who did include Ross Stagner, 'Psychological Aspects of International Conflict' (Belmont, Cal.: Brooks-Cole Publishing, 1967); and Robert Jervis, 'The Logic of Images in International Relations' (Princeton, N.J.: Princeton University Press, 1970). The quote is taken from Stagner, op. cit., p.9.

41 Frankel, op. cit., p.218. See also Joseph Frankel, 'National Interest' (New York: Praeger, 1970), pp.97-140.

42 In Snyder, et al., p.4, the authors contend that Dean G. Pruitt, 'Problem Solving in the Department of State' (Denver, Col.: University of Denver Press, 1965) is a valid example of the decision-making model being used in a case study. In fact, Pruitt himself confesses that, though possibly significant to an understanding of the decision-making process he is concerned with, personality factors - including normative values and feelings of the actors - were ignored. In other words, Pruitt's study deals only with environmental factors that may influence decision-makers. This removes the teeth from Snyder's model, which attempts to integrate these subjective factors into an objective framework. Other organizational case studies mentioned by Snyder on page four similarly ignore one of the two major elements of the model, usually concentrating, like Pruitt, on organizational variables.

43 Glenn D. Paige, 'The Korean Decision' (New York: Free Press, 1968). This book is a lengthened version of Richard C. Snyder and Glenn D. Paige, The United States Decision to Resist Aggression in Korea: The Application of an Analytical Scheme, 'Administrative Science Quarterly,' 3 (1958), pp.342-78. In Snyder and Robinson, 'National and International Decision-Making,' the authors outline fifty-six useful research projects that could yield fruitful results if studied by means of the decision-making model. Apparently none of these have, in fact, been adapted to a full-length study.

44 Snyder, et al., pp.64-5.

45 Ibid., p.101.

46 Ibid., p.100.

47 Ibid., p.64. Snyder credits primarily Schutz's essays Choosing Among Projects of Action and Common-Sense, and Scientific Interpretation of Human Affairs.

See 'CP,' I, pp.67-96 and 3-47.
48 Snyder, et al., pp.144-61.
49 Ibid., p.82. Snyder also adopts Schutz's analysis of thematization and time. See ibid., pp.75-84.
50 Ibid., p.9.
51 Ibid., p.95. For more detailed description of the characteristics of organizations see pp.88-105.
52 See pp.42ff.
53 Snyder, et al., p.84.
54 Ibid., p.67.
55 Ibid., p.73.
56 Ibid., pp.66-73, p.92 n.12.
57 Ibid., p.90.
58 Ibid., p.105.
59 Ibid.
60 Ibid., p.106.
61 Ibid., p.107 and p.113.
62 Ibid., p.107.
63 Ibid., p.113.
64 Ibid.
65 Ibid., p.125.
66 Ibid., p.128.
67 Ibid., pp.128-32.
68 Ibid., p.140.
69 Ibid., pp.144-52.
70 In ibid., pp.153-60, the six kinds of data from which the actor's motivation must be inferred are described. They include both social factors that the actor perceives and personality traits that he exhibits. Snyder and Robinson, Decision-Making in International Politics, 'International Behavior,' ed. Kelman, pp.444-8 condense them into three kinds of data: personality characteristics, social backgrounds and experiences and personal values.
71 Snyder, et al., p.63.
72 Ibid., p.177.
73 Ibid., p.3. See also Snyder and Robinson, 'National and International Decision-Making,' pp.30-1.
74 Rosenau, 'The Scientific Study of Foreign Policy,' p.263.
75 Robert Jervis, The Costs of the Quantitative Study of International Relations, 'Contending Approaches to International Politics,' eds Klaus Knorr and James N. Rosenau (Princeton, N.J.: Princeton University Press, 1969), pp.177-217, esp. pp.186-95.
76 Ibid., p.195.
77 Paige, op. cit., p.8.
78 Ibid. Snyder and Paige had described only five such categories in their earlier article.

79 Snyder, et al., p.62.
80 Ibid., p.65.
81 Ibid., p.4.
82 Rosenau, 'The Scientific Study of Foreign Policy,' p.256.
83 Ibid., p.271.
84 In James C. Charlesworth (ed.) 'The Limits of Behavioralism in Political Science' (Philadelphia: American Academy of Political and Social Science, 1962), pp.94-123.
85 In Harold Guetzkow, Chadwick F. Alger, Richard A. Brody, Robert C. Noel and Richard C. Snyder, 'Simulation in International Relations' (Englewood Cliffs, N.J.: Prentice-Hall, 1963), pp.1-23.
86 Ibid., p.6.
87 Snyder and Robinson, Decision-Making in International Politics, 'International Behavior,' ed. Kelman, p.444.
88 Dean G. Pruitt and Richard C. Snyder (eds), 'Theory and Research on the Causes of War' (Englewood Cliffs, N.J.: Prentice-Hall, 1969), p.1.
89 Paige, op. cit., p.274, n.3.
90 Rosenau, 'The Scientific Study of Foreign Policy,' pp.271-2.
91 Ira Sharkansky, 'The Routines of Politics' (New York: Van Nostrand Reinhold, 1970). Others have studied the routines which characterize the political decision-making process with similar results, though in a less extensive manner. See, for example, Charles Lindblom, 'The Intelligence of Democracy' (New York: Free Press, 1965); Aaron Wildavsky, 'The Politics of the Budgetary Process' (Boston: Little, Brown, 1964); and Thomas J. Anton, 'The Politics of State Expenditure in Illinois' (Urbana, Ill.: University of Illinois Press, 1960).
92 See Sharkansky, op. cit., pp.3-5.
93 Ibid., p.4.
94 Ibid., pp.14-29.
95 Snyder, et al., p.4.
96 Richard C. Snyder, The Korean Decision (1950) and the Analysis of Crisis Decision-Making, 'Working Group Reports, Military Operations Research Society,' 1963; and Snyder and Robinson, Decision-Making in International Politics, 'International Behavior,' ed. Kelman, pp.440-3. Snyder's work on these crisis variables closely parallels and directly influences the ideas of Charles F. Hermann, who devotes much time to the study of crisis decision-making. His many early writings on the subject culminate in Charles F. Hermann, 'Crises in Foreign Policy - A Simulation

Analysis' (New York: Bobbs-Merill, 1969).

97 Charles F. Hermann, ibid, p.203.

98 In addition to Paige's study, which is the only empirical case study based entirely on Snyder's model, I am including certain relevant data from two other works: James A. Robinson, Decision-Making in the House Rules Committee, 'The Making of Decisions,' ed. William J. Gore and J. W. Dyson (New York: Free Press, 1964), pp.315-24. This is a very short summary outline of private research done by Robinson. Despite his stated debt to Snyder (p.318), this article is too incomplete to qualify as a full-scale empirical case study. Nevertheless, the propositions he develops are revealing; David C. Schwartz, Decision Theories and Crisis Behavior: An Empirical Study of Nuclear Deterrence in International Political Crises, 'Orbis,' II (Summer, 1967), pp.459-90. The model used by Schwartz in this article is influenced by Snyder's model (pp.459-69), but not explicitly based on it. Still, his goal is to utilize certain explicit perceptual variables in understanding why decision-makers behave as they do in certain crisis situations. The results here too are revealing. The major propositional findings of all three studies are found in the Appendix.

99 Aaron V. Cicourel, 'Method and Measurement in Sociology' (New York: Free Press, 1964), pp.4-5. See also Hugh Mehan and Houston Wood, 'The Reality of Ethnomethodology' (New York: John Wiley, 1975), pp.1-7 and 207-10.

100 Harold Garfinkel, 'Studies in Ethnomethodology' (Englewood Cliffs, N.J.: Prentice-Hall, 1967), pp.1-34 and 262-83; and Henry C. Elliot, Similarities and Differences Between Science and Common Sense, 'Ethnomethodology,' ed. Roy Turner (Baltimore, Md.: Penguin Books Inc., 1974), pp.21-6.

101 Harold Garfinkel, Studies of the Routine Grounds of Everyday Activities, 'Studies in Social Interaction,' ed. David Sudnow (New York: Free Press, 1972), p.3.

102 Paige, op. cit., p.8.

103 Emmanuel A. Schegloff, The First Five Seconds: The Order of Conversational Opening, Unpublished PhD dissertation, University of California, Berkeley, 1967. This topic apparently inspired Schegloff. He analyzes the closing of telephone conversations, or, as he puts it, the ending of a 'state of talk,' in Emmanuel Schegloff and Harvey Sacks, Opening up Closings, 'Semiotica,' vol. 8 (1973), pp.289-327. The quote is on p.326.

104 Michael Moerman, Analysis of Lue Conversation: Providing Accounts, Finding Breaches, Taking Sides, Sudnow, op. cit., pp.170-228.
105 Harvey Sacks, Notes on Police Assessment of Moral Character, ibid., pp.280-93.
106 Garfinkel, 'Studies in Ethnomethodology,' pp.116-85.
107 Emmanuel A. Schegloff, Notes on a Conversational Practice: Formulating Place, Sudnow, op. cit., pp.75-117.
108 Sheldon Twer, Tactics for Determining Persons' Resources for Depicting, Contriving, and Describing Behavioral Episodes, ibid., pp.338-57.
109 David Sudnow, Temporal Parameters of Interpersonal Observation, ibid., pp.259-79.
110 A. Lincoln Ryave and James N. Schenkein, Notes on the Art of Walking, Turner, op. cit., pp.265-74.
111 A bibliography of relevant works is offered in ibid., pp.275-8.
112 Twer, loc. cit., p.357.
113 Schegloff, Notes on a Conversational Practice: Formulating Place, Sudnow, op. cit., p.115.
114 Sacks, Notes on Police Assessment of Moral Character, ibid., p.293.
115 Ryave and Schenkein, loc. cit., esp. pp.269-74.
116 Roy Turner, Words, Utterances and Activities, 'Understanding Everyday Life,' ed. Jack Douglas (Chicago, Ill.: Aldine, 1970), p.166. A list of techniques, other than computers, for 'doing' ethnomethodology is offered in Mehan and Wood, op. cit., pp.229-38.
117 Kenneth Stoddart, Pinched: Notes on the Ethnographer's Location of Argot, 'Ethnomethodology,' ed. Turner, pp.173-9.

CHAPTER 4 THE 'OBJECTIVITY' OF EMPIRICAL SOCIAL SCIENCE: A philosophical perspective

1 For example, C. Wright Mills, 'The Sociological Imagination' (New York: Oxford University Press, 1959), pp.7-8.
2 Ralph Perry's definition, quoted in Farber, 'Naturalism and Subjectivism' (Springfield, Ill.: C. C. Thomas, 1959), p.3.
3 We rely primarily on Ernest Nagel, 'The Structure of Science: Problems in the Logic of Scientific Explanation' (New York: Harcourt, Brace & World, 1961), and Carl G. Hempel, 'Aspects of Scientific

Explanation and other Essays in the Philosophy of Science' (New York: Free Press, 1965). Each contains the important ideas of the respective authors. We shall refer to Nagel's book as 'SS,' to Hempel's as 'Aspects.'

4 'SS,' p.4.

5 Ibid.

6 'Aspects,' p.146 and pp.364-76. See also Richard Rudner, 'The Philosophy of Social Science' (Englewood Cliffs, N.J.: Prentice-Hall, 1966), p.60.

7 'SS,' p.13.

8 'Aspects,' p.141. See also 'SS,' pp.10-4. Isaac Levi summarizes this point in Induction and the Aims of Inquiry, 'Philosophy, Science, and Method,' ed. Sidney Morgenbesser (New York: St Martins Press, 1969), p.192.

9 Karel Lambert and Gordon G. Brittan,Jr., 'An Introduction to the Philosophy of Science' (Englewood Cliffs, N.J.: Prentice-Hall, 1970), p.29.

10 This emphasis on deduction, the basis of naturalism, is opposed by Felix Kaufmann, 'Methodology of the Social Sciences' (New York: Oxford University Press, 1944). By denying the epistemological world-view we have just described in the Humean theory of perception, Kaufmann hopes to limit the role of deduction to formulating hypotheses, which must be inductively (i.e. empirically) validated. This work, which is complicated and ambiguous, attempts to establish a scientific base for phenomenological social science. Schutz refers to Kaufmann often while describing how his homunculii fulfill objective criteria of validation.

11 Nagel describes four possible forms scientific explanations can take ('SS,' pp.21-4): the *deductive* model has the formal structure of a deductive argument with the added requirements that at least one statement of universal law be included in the premises, which must also refer to other laws; in *probabilistic* models the premises do not formally imply the explicandum, but statistical research will have revealed that there is a high probability that, given the premise, then the explicandum will follow; the *teleological* model indicates either the function that a unit performs in maintaining a system to which it belongs, or the role a unit plays in bringing about a systemic goal; and the *genetic* model aims at explaining why a given subject has certain characteristics by describing how this subject evolved out of an earlier one. Hempel lists three forms of

valid explanation ('Aspects,' pp.380-402): the *deductive-nomological* model corresponds to Nagel's deductive model; the *deductive-statistical* model uses at least one law or theoretical principle, which itself is based only on statistical evidence, to deduce another less comprehensive statistical law; and the *inductive-statistical* model, which closely resembles Nagel's interpretation of the probabilistic model. Hempel also deals with teleological and genetic explanations, but does not accord them separate status.

12 'SS,' p.520.
13 'Aspects,' pp.417-8.
14 Ibid., p.302 and pp.407-10.
15 'SS,' p.595. See also 'Aspects,' p.351. Both Nagel ('SS,' pp.325-35) and Hempel ('Aspects,' pp.259-65) discuss and reject the notion of 'absolute chance,' i.e. the idea that there may exist phenomena for which there are no determining conditions whatsoever. Even Quantam theory cannot prove the existence of absolute chance ('SS,' ch.9). The naturalist's attitude on this issue is exemplified by Einstein's statement to Max Born: 'You believe in God playing dice and I in perfect laws in the world of things existing as real objects, which I try to grasp in a wildly speculative way.' (Paul A. Schilpp (ed.), 'Albert Einstein, Philosopher - Scientist' (Evanston, Ill.: Library of Living Philosophers, 1949), p.176.)
16 'Aspects,' pp.380-412 and p.488.
17 'SS,' p.334. Though not inherently impossible, 'there are areas of inquiry - in physics as well as in the biological and social sciences - in which the explanation of many phenomena in terms of strictly universal causal laws is not likely to be feasible practically.' ('SS,' p.77).
18 'Aspects,' p.425.
19 For example, Israel Scheffler, 'The Anatomy of Inquiry' (New York: Alfred A. Knopf, 1963), p.35.
20 'SS,' p.422. 'Aspects,' p.326, offers a concurring presentation. Nagel's extensive treatment of teleological explanations is also contained in Ernest Nagel, Teleological Explanations and Teleological Systems, 'Readings in the Philosophy of Science,' ed. Herbert Feigl and May Brodbeck (New York: Appleton-Century-Crofts, 1953), pp.537-58.
21 'SS,' p.405.
22 The fact that non-goal directed systems cannot be explained by teleological explanations does not invalidate this conclusion. It merely means that the

'surplus meaning' of teleological explanations (i.e. their ability to apparently explain goal-directed systems in a more comprehensive manner than can deductive explanations) can always be expressed in non-teleological language. ('SS,' pp.410-21.) Hempel, rather than emphasizing the positive or 'surplus' meaning of teleological explanations as Nagel does, chooses to stress its logical inadequacies, including its inability to: explain the specific item - rather than class of items - it is relevant to, facilitate prediction, or be empirically verified. ('Aspects,' pp.308-29.) Both agree on the important point that teleological explanations can be expressed deductively, though each interprets the value of teleological explanations differently. This is why Hempel does not include teleological explanations as one of his basic explanatory models.

23 I.e. 'the assertion that a condition constitutes a functional prerequisite for a state of some specified kind (such as proper functioning) is tantamount to the statement of a law to the effect that wherever condition "n" fails to be satisfied the state in question fails to occur' ('Aspects,' p.309).

24 The implications of the converse of this notion - the belief that individuals do not react to stimulii as physical objects and therefore the social sciences do logically differ from the natural sciences - in its relation to teleological explanation, are examined by the so-called 'new teleologists,' including: Charles Taylor, 'The Explanation of Behavior' (London: Routledge & Kegan Paul, 1964); R. S. Peters, 'The Concept of Motivation' (London: Routledge & Kegan Paul, 1960); A. R. Louch, 'Explanation and Human Action' (Berkeley and Los Angeles: University of California Press, 1966); and A. I. Melden, 'Free Action' (London: Routledge & Kegan Paul, 1961). The term 'new teleologists' is developed by Richard Bernstein, 'Praxis and Action' (Philadelphia: University of Pennsylvania Press, 1971), p.236. The naturalist position with regard to the relationship of teleological explanations to the social sciences is refined in Ernest Nagel, Problems of Concept and Theory Formation in the Social Sciences, 'Science, Language and Human Rights' (American Philosophical Association, Eastern Division, Philadelphia: University of Pennsylvania Press, 1952), vol. I,

pp.43-64, and Rudner, op. cit., pp.84-111.
25 'Aspects,' p.326.
26 Ibid., pp.448-9.
27 See 'SS,' pp.564-8, and 'Aspects,' pp.447-53. This presumes, of course, that valid explanations are logically structured. The thorny technical issues concerning the logic of scientific explanation take place within naturalist epistemological principles we are now developing. Often, debates among naturalists obscure this important philosophical unity. Nagel's and Hempel's views on scientific logic are outlined in 'SS,' pp.26-68 and 75-81, and 'Aspects,' pp.51, 78-83, 145, 173-222, and 247-78.

Naturalists disagree on many technical issues. For example, there is disagreement on the exact nature of universal laws (also called nomic laws, or nomological universals). Some uphold what is called the 'entailment view,' contending universal laws are explicated only by employing irreducible model notions such as 'physical necessity,' or 'physical causality.' Antecedent and consequent terms of a universal law, in this view, are related in some absolute sense. Opposed to the entailment view is the Humean contention (see David Hume, 'Enquiries Concerning Human Understanding,' ed. L. A. Selby-Bigge (London: Oxford University Press, 1902), esp. pp.25-7) that universal laws are derived from the results of empirical verification or repeated regularities, and rest only on inductive inferences based on empirical evidence. Both Nagel and Hempel accept modified versions of this latter view. The issue is critically discussed by Jude P. Dougherty, Nagel's Concept of Science, 'Philosophy Today,' 10 (Fall, 1966), pp.215-21. Controversy also surrounds the logical role of empirically non-verifiable theories in universal laws. At least two contemporary positions can be distinguished: the 'conservative' or 'descriptive' view contends theories are either 'true' or 'false,' depending on whether or not factual conclusions can be drawn from them (the 'phenomenalist' position of Ernest Mach, Karl Pearson, Bertrand Russell, Herbert Dingle and P. W. Bridgeman); and the 'instrumentalist' view states theories are merely logical instruments for organizing sensory experiences and ordering experimental laws, and may 'exist' as intellectual tools, logical constructs that, though never translated into sense-data, do bring order and meaning to a large body of empirically confirmed facts. Nagel ('SS,' p.145) and, to a lesser degree, Hempel ('Aspects,' p.117) defend the instrumentalist position, as do relatively recent works such as Patrick Romanell, 'Towards a Critical Naturalism' (New York: Macmillan, 1958); William Dennes, 'Some Dilemmas of Naturalism' (New York: Columbia University Press, 1960); and E. M. Adams, 'Ethical Naturalism and the Modern World-view' (Chapel Hill: University of North Carolina Press, 1960). This whole issue is discussed in Lambert and Brittan, op. cit., pp.88-101.

These two debates illustrate the limits of disagreement among naturalists, and, implicitly, the broad epistemological principles all naturalists accept. The arguments, and others like them, are technical discussions concerning how to best operationalize the naturalist world-view.

28 'SS,' p.602.

29 See ibid., pp.504-5 and 595-606, and 'Aspects,' pp.233-53. Arguments for and against this approach to human behavior, and its methodological implications, are discussed in Frank Cunningham, 'Objectivity in Social Science' (Toronto: University of Toronto Press, 1973).

30 'SS,' pp.450-3.

31 Ibid., p.452.

32 Examples of controlled investigation are offered in ibid., pp.457-8.

33 Ibid., p.459.

34 This thesis is adopted and developed in relation to the study of comparative politics by Adam Przeworski and Henry Teune, 'The Logic of Comparative Social Inquiry' (New York: John Wiley, 1970).

35 See 'SS,' pp.466-71.

36 'SS,' p.546. The relevant arguments are presented on pp.475, 540-6, chapter 11 - which deals with the rules of reduction - and 'Aspects,' pp.163-4.

37 'Aspects,' p.473.

38 Carl G. Hempel, Symposium: Problem of Concept and Theory Formation in the Social Sciences, 'Science, Language, and Human Rights,' I, pp.65-86. Hempel analyzes the scientific criteria for valid ideal types further in 'Aspects,' pp.472-81. A similar presentation is offered in Rudner, op. cit., pp.54-67.

39 'SS,' p.484.

40 This point is adequately discussed in K. W. Spence, The Postulates and Methods of Behaviorism, Feigl and Brodbeck, op. cit., pp.571-84.

'Behavioralism' is a contemporary 'softening' of psychological behaviorism by naturalist-oriented social scientists interested in operationalizing empirical scientific procedure. It is easily assimilated into the naturalist framework if we admit, as naturalists have, that what people say they think (i.e. their feelings, attitudes and beliefs) is also part of their behavior. Though these expressed feelings, attitudes and beliefs can themselves be explained as determined consequences of preceding, impersonal variables, they also add to our scientific understanding of external social behavior without deviating from a naturalist epistemology. The differences between the psychological theory of behaviorism and the broader approach to social science called behavioralism are based on convenience, not principle. Though one, behavioralism, is more open to expressions of subjective states of mind, both accept naturalist principles of empirical verification and therefore see these expressions as parts of impersonal systems of determined relationships. They are both appendages to the naturalist approach to scientific knowledge. The issues are discussed, from within the naturalist perspective, in Arnold Brecht, 'Political Theory: The Foundations of Twentieth-Century Political Thought' (New Jersey: Princeton University Press, 1959), pp.117-35 and 504ff; Robert A. Dahl, The Behavioral Approach, 'American Political Science Review,' 55 (1961), pp.763-72; David Easton, The Current Meaning of 'Behavioralism,' 'Contemporary Political Analysis,' ed. James C. Charlesworth (New York: Free Press, 1967), pp.11-31; Albert Somit and Joseph Tannenhaus, 'The Development of American Political Science: From Burgess to Behavioralism' (Boston: Allyn & Bacon, 1967), chapter 12; and Alan C. Isaak, 'Scope and Methods of Political Science' (revised edition; Illinois: Dorsey Press, 1975), pp.36ff.

41 See Nagel, Problems of Concept and Theory Formation in the Social Sciences, 'Science, Language, and Human Rights,' I, pp.56-60, and 'Aspects,' p.254.

42 See 'SS,' pp.485-90, and Brecht, op. cit., pp.117-35.

43 Husserl, 'Ideas, General Introduction to Pure Phenomenology,' trans. W. R. Boyce Gibson (New York: Humanities Press, 1931), pp.158-63; and 'Phenomenology and the Crisis of Philosophy,' trans. and ed. Quentin Lauer (New York: Harper & Row, 1965),

pp.79-85.
44 Ibid., p.189.
45 Ibid., p.1.
46 This argument is based on Husserl, 'Ideas,' sections 67-71 and 75.
47 Ibid., p.201.
48 See especially ibid., pp.64-6, 207-8, 395-6, and Jacob Klein, Phenomenology and the History of Science, 'Philosophical Essays in Memory of Edmund Husserl,' ed. Marvin Farber (Cambridge, Mass.: Harvard University Press, 1940), pp.153-6.
49 See Fernando R. Molina (ed.), 'The Source of Existentialism as Philosophy,' (Englewood Cliffs, N.J.: Prentice-Hall, 1969), p.90; and Fernando R. Molina, The Husserlian Ideal of a Pure Phenomenology, 'An Invitation to Phenomenology,' ed. James M. Edie (Chicago: Quadrangle Books, 1965), pp.161-79. Husserl's idealism is explicitly confirmed by most of his students, including, among the well known, Gaston Berger, Ludwig Landgrebe, Alphonse DeWaelhens, Paul Ricoeur, Pierre Thévanaz, Aron Gurwitsch, Roman Ingarden, Quentin Lauer and Martin Heidegger. For a listing of those less influential students who interpret their mentor as a realist see H. Boelaars, De intentionaliteit der Kennis bij Edmund Husserl, 'Bijdragen,' 3 (1940), pp.112-21, and n.58 in chapter one. Those occupying a compromise or mean position, wanting to play down the idealistic bent of Husserl's philosophy without ignoring it, are forced to admit the crucial Husserlian point that an 'essence' exists *independent of* an empirical 'fact.' Examples of this approach include: Emmanuel Levinas, Intuition of Essences, 'Phenomenology,' ed. Joseph Kockelmans (New York: Doubleday, 1967), p.90; J. N. Findlay, Essential Probabilities, 'Phenomenology in America,' ed. James M. Edie (Chicago: Quadrangle Books, 1967), pp.96-108; Thomas Langan, Formal Insight into Material Nature, ibid., pp.109-24; and James M. Edie, Phenomenology as Rigorous Science, 'International Philosophical Quarterly,' 7 (March, 1967), pp.20-30, esp. pp.28-9.

Merleau-Ponty is extremely ambiguous in his treatment of Husserl's concept of essences, just as he is in his own attempt at reconciling science and philosophy. He claims Husserl was always aware of the concrete, non-idealistic character of essences, even though he also recognized that these essences revealed absolute, unimpeachable knowledge.

(Maurice Merleau-Ponty, 'The Primacy of Perception,' ed. and trans. James M. Edie (Evanston, Ill.: Northwestern University Press, 1964), pp.53-5 and 67-8, and Philosopher and Sociology, 'Signs,' trans. Richard C. McCleary (Evanston, Ill.: Northwestern University Press, 1964), pp.108-9.) After writing the 'Krisis' lectures, says Merleau-Ponty, Husserl continually de-emphasized, and eventually abandoned, his idealistic interpretation of truth. (Merleau-Ponty, 'The Primacy of Perception,' pp.73-5, 90-1, 107-8 and 'Phenomenology of Perception,' trans. Colin Smith (New York: Humanities Press, 1962), p.xvi.) Little detailed evidence is offered to support these charges, or the surprising implication that Husserl would abandon his whole lifetime's work in one series of lectures. When confronted with evidence illustrating the logical consistency of Husserl's transcendental phenomenology, Merleau-Ponty admits his interpretation of Husserl is meant to be 'optimistic,' what Husserl must have *meant* rather than what he wrote. (Quoted in Kockelmans, op. cit., p.354.) This aspect of Merleau-Ponty's philosophy is effectively presented in Albert Rabil, Jr., 'Merleau-Ponty, Existentialist of the Social World' (New York: Columbia University Press, 1967), pp.164-73. Merleau-Ponty was probably unsure himself of the validity of his interpretation of Husserl. Originally, he based his beliefs on a letter Husserl wrote to Levy-Bruhl on March 11, 1935, which stressed his recognition of the importance of the empirical life-world in constituting knowledge (Philosopher and Sociology, 'Signs,' p.108, n.7). Yet Merleau-Ponty also states that Husserl 'up until the end . . . always thought of the return to living history and the spoken word - the return to the "Lebenswelt" - as a preparatory step which should be followed by the properly philosophical task of universal constitution.' (Ibid., p.111.)

50 Herbert Spiegelberg, How Subjective is Phenomenology? 'Proceedings of the American Catholic Philosophical Association,' XXXIII (1959), p.35.

51 F. J. J. Buytendijk, The Phenomenological Approach to the Problem of Feelings and Emotions, 'Feeling and Emotions,' ed. Martin L. Reymert (New York: McGraw-Hill, 1950), p.141.

52 Theodore Abel, 'Systematic Sociology in Germany' (New York: Columbia University Press, 1929), pp.69-70.

53 A notable exception is Joseph Kockelmans,

'Phenomenology and Physical Science' (Pittsburgh: Duquesne University Press, 1966).

54 Mario Bunge, Phenomenological Theories, 'The Critical Approach to Science and Philosophy,' ed. Mario Bunge (New York: Free Press, 1964), p.236.

55 One such dialogue has occurred, between Nagel and C. J. Ducasse in 'Philosophy and Phenomenological Research' V (1944-5). The result, predictable from the outset, was stalemate: each asserting his own premises and denying the validity of his opponent's.

56 Worthwhile examples of this approach include Alphonse DeWaelhens, 'Existence et signification' (Louvain: Publications universitaires, 1958), Patrick A. Heelan, 'Quantam Mechanics and Objectivity' (The Hague: Martinus Nijhoff, 1965) and Horizon, Objectivity and Reality in the Physical Sciences, 'International Philosophical Quarterly,' 7 (September 1967), pp.375-412, and Kockelmans, 'Phenomenology and Physical Science.' More technical attempts to integrate phenomenology with specialized branches of natural science and mathematics, written by scientists rather than philosophers, are included in Kockelmans and Henry Kisiel (eds), 'Phenomenology and the Natural Sciences,' (Evanston, Ill.: Northwestern University Press, 1970), as is a bibliography of these scientists' complete works (pp.501-8). Anna-Teresa Tymieniecka, 'Phenomenology and Science in Contemporary European Thought' (New York: Farrar, Straus, and Cudahy, 1962), esp. pp.3-61, surveys this material from the author's own didactic point of view.

57 This is what Thelma Z. Lavine, a disenchanted naturalist, claims in Note to Naturalists on the Human Spirit, 'Journal of Philosophy,' I (26 February 1953), pp.145-54.

58 Ernest Nagel, On the Method of 'Verstehen' as the Sole Method of Philosophy, 'Journal of Philosophy,' I (26 February 1953), pp.154-7. This short article is in response to Lavine's assertions.

59 Some important methodologists and their relevant works in this category include: Alfred Vierkandt, 'Gesellschafteslehre: Hauptprobleme der Philosophischen Soziologie' (Stuttgart: F. Enke, 1923), re-issued as 'Kleine Gesellschaftslehre' (Stuttgart: F. Enke, 1949). Other less significant works of Vierkandt include 'Naturvolker und Kilturvoker' (Leipzig: Duncher & Humblot, 1896), and

'Die Stetigkeit im Kilturwandal' (1908); Stephan Strasser, 'Phenomenology and the Human Sciences' (Pittsburgh, Pa.: Duquesne University Press, 1963); and, though in a more imprecise sense, Maurice Natanson. Though Natanson is very familiar with Schutz's ideas, and openly praises them, there is also convincing evidence he believes empirical social science is a derivative study that assumes - and is based upon - the existence of subjectively constituted apodictic knowledge: Maurice Natanson, A Study in Philosophy and the Social Sciences, 'Social Research,' 25 (Summer, 1958), pp.171-2; Alfred Schutz on Social Reality and Social Science, 'Social Research,' 35 (Summer, 1968), pp.217-44; Alienation and Social Role, 'Phenomenology in America,' ed. Edie, pp.255-68, which is a case study detailing the role of empirical social science in validating apodictic truths; and 'The Journeying Self: A Study in Philosophy and Social Role' (Reading, Mass.: Addison-Wesley Publishing, 1970). Consequently, Natanson's concept of empirical 'science' is not what Schutz's is (see Natanson, 'Literature, Philosophy and the Social Sciences' (The Hague: Martinus Nijhoff, 1962), pp.205-8). In any case, Natanson's prolific scholarly output is primarily of an eclectic nature, critically analyzing the relationships between naturalism, phenomenology and social science - all from a phenomenological (scientific) viewpoint.

60 This is the view of Marvin Farber, a philosopher whose work is directly related to the methodology of the social sciences. For cogent statements of this position see Farber's 'Naturalism and Subjectivism' and 'Phenomenology and Existence: Towards a Philosophy Within Nature' (New York: Harper & Row, 1967). Other examples of this type of phenomenological approach to social science include: Burkart Holzner, Phenomenology and Formalization in the Human Sciences, 'Review of Existential Psychology and Psychiatry,' III (Fall, 1963), pp.263-70. This article focuses on the problem of formulating scientific theories and laws from phenomenological data; Leon J. Goldstein, The Phenomenological and Naturalistic Approaches to the Social, 'Methodos,' XIII (1961), pp.225-38. In very broad, ambiguous language Goldstein declares the supplementary relationship existing between phenomenology and naturalism, under the epistemological aegis of the latter; and Paul

Hochstim, 'Alfred Vierkandt: A Sociological Critique' (New York: Exposition Press, 1966). Hochstim's critique of Vierkandt is based on his acceptance of this heuristic role for phenomenology. T. W. Wann (ed.), 'Behaviorism and Phenomenology' (Chicago: University of Chicago Press, 1964) probably belongs in this category. This book, especially articles by Michael Scriven, Carl R. Rogers and R. B. MacLeod, mindlessly asserts the complementarity of phenomenology and behaviorism as methods of psychological research. Only B. F. Skinner explicitly defends a consistent methodological point of view, one favoring behaviorism. Presumably, the other contributors share this bias, and attempt to utilize phenomenology as an appendage to a naturalist epistemology.

61 Schutz is the most important methodologist in this category. Others attempting similar, but less detailed and teleological-oriented analyses include Taylor, op. cit.; and Margaret and Harold Sprout, 'Man-Milieu Relationship Hypotheses in the Context of International Politics' (Princeton, N.J.: Princeton University Press, 1956), 'Foundations of International Politics' (New Jersey: Van Nostrand Press, 1962), 'Ecological Perspective on Human Affairs' (Princeton, N.J.: Princeton University Press, 1965), and 'An Ecological Pardigm for the Study of International Politics' (Princeton, N.J.: Princeton University Press, 1968). A good case can be made for including Merleau-Ponty in this group. Though never developing an explicit sociological method, Merleau-Ponty did call for an empirical science of society based on ideal type motivational patterns (The Philosopher and Sociology, 'Signs,' pp.98-113, esp. pp.112-3). The weaknesses of Merleau-Ponty's notion of empirical social science, which parallel those we will now describe in Schutz, are briefly hinted at by Strasser, op. cit., pp.218-23; Gurwitsch, 'Studies in Phenomenology and Psychology' (Evanston, Ill.: Northwestern University Press, 1966), p.xix; Rabil, Jr, op. cit., pp.247-8; Thomas Langan, 'Merleau-Ponty's Critique of Reason' (New Haven: Yale University Press, 1966), the thesis of which stresses the tension between Merleau-Ponty's notions of objectivity and subjectivity; and Frederick A. Olafson, A Central Theme of Merleau-Ponty's Philosophy, 'Phenomenology and Existentialism,' ed. Edward N. Lee and Maurice

H. Mandelbaum (Baltimore: Johns Hopkins Press, 1967), pp.194-5.
62 Ervin Laszlo, 'Beyond Skepticism and Realism' (The Hague: Martinus Nijhoff, 1966), p.107.
63 'PSW,' pp.97-102.
64 'CP,' III, pp.51-84.
65 Ibid., pp.92-115.
66 This thesis of Schutz is adopted by David Michael Levin, Induction and Husserl's Theory of Eidetic Variation, 'Philosophy and Phenomenological Research,' 29 (Spring, 1968), pp.1-15, and, though in a less explicit way, by H. P. Neisser, The Phenomenological Approach in Social Science, 'Philosophy and Phenomenological Research,' 20 (1959), p.269.
67 Jitendranath Mohanty, Individual Fact and Essence in Edmund Husserl's Philosophy, 'Philosophy and Phenomenological Research,' 20 (1959), pp.222-30, summarizes this aspect of Husserl's science and refutes those who would reject the notion that this is what Husserl means.
68 'CP,' III, pp.112-14.
69 This aspect of Schutz's methodology is criticized, from an Husserlian transcendental point of view, in N. Patrick Peritore, Some Problems in Alfred Schutz's Phenomenological Methodology, 'American Political Science Review,' LXIX, 1 (March 1975), pp.132-40.
70 Laszlo, op. cit., p.110.
71 Henry Winthrop, Phenomenological Method from the Standpoint of the Empiricistic Bias, 'Journal of Philosophy,' 46 (3 February 1949), pp.57-74, defends the thesis that if Husserl's eidetic truths really are inherent to the empirical world - as he claims - then naturalism provides the only non-solipsistic method for scientifically validating them. See especially pp.65-70.

CHAPTER 5 EPILOGUE: An alternative phenomenological approach to social inquiry

1 I do not include here a knowledgeable rehash of Schutz's descriptive phenomenology of the social world, such as Hwa Yol Jung gives us in The Political Relevance of Existential Phenomenology, 'Review of Politics,' 33 (October 1971), pp.538-63, and 'Existential Phenomenology and Political Theory: A Reader' (Chicago: Henry Regnery, 1972), pp.xvii-lv.

Rather, I mean an attempt to utilize phenomenology methodologically, creating a consistent method which, when applied in specific instances by observers, helps explain aspects of society.

2 The relationship between phenomenology and radicalism is now unclear. Marvin Surkin, for example, feels a 'radical' approach to politics should be based on the phenomenological analyses of intersubjectivity and praxis developed by Schutz, Sartre and Merleau-Ponty. See Marvin Surkin, Sense and Non-Sense in Politics, 'An End to Political Science,' eds Surkin and Alan Wolfe (New York: Basic Books, 1970), pp.13-33, especially pp.14-15 and 28-9. What he doesn't state, or perhaps is not aware of, is that these ideas, all faithful to principles of phenomenology and consistent with each other, are used by Sartre and Merleau-Ponty to justify a type of Marxian radicalism and by Schutz to justify an extremely bourgeois - even conservative - ethic; a business executive by day, a professor of social science at night.

3 Generalizations regarding existential phenomenology are derived from the three most seminal theoreticians of this philosophical movement: Martin Heideggar, 'Being and Time', trans. John Macquarrie and Edward Robinson (New York: Harper & Row, 1962); Jean-Paul Sartre, 'Being and Nothingness' trans. Hazel E. Barnes (New York: Washington Square Press, 1966) and Maurice Merleau-Ponty, 'Phenomenology of Perception,' trans. Colin Smith (New York: Humanities Press, Inc. 1962).

4 Aron Gurwitsch, The Problem of Existence in Constitutive Phenomenology, 'Studies in Phenomenology and Psychology' (Evanston, Ill.: Northwestern University Press, 1966), p.118. See also pp.xvii-xix.

5 This principle sharply differentiates existential phenomenology from existentialism, which are both compared and contrasted in William Earle, Ontological Autobiography, 'Phenomenology in America,' ed. James E. Edie, (Chicago: Quadrangle Books, 1965), pp.69-79; Phenomenology and Existentialism, 'The Journal of Philosophy,' LVII (1960), pp.75-84; and Alfred Stern, 'Sartre' (2nd edn; New York: Dell, 1967), pp.22-5. Many social theorists confuse the two, mistakenly believing existential phenomenologists 'are left with no solid base on which to stand.' This confusion is blatantly exhibited in Eugene F. Miller, Positivism, Historicism, and Political Inquiry, 'American Political Science Review,' LXVI (September 1972), pp.796-826. The quote is on p.814.

6 This thesis is defended in Gurwitsch, Husserl's Theory of the Intentionality of Consciousness in Historical Perspective, 'Phenomenology and Existentialism,' ed. Edward N. Lee and Maurice Mandelbaum (Baltimore: Johns Hopkins Press, 1967), pp.25-57; and F. J. J. Buytendijk, The Phenomenological Approach to the Problem of Feelings and Emotions, 'Feelings and Emotions,' ed. Martin L. Reymert (New York: McGraw-Hill, 1950), p.127. The major tenets of Cartesian philosophy, at least as related to the phenomenological modification, are found in 'The Philosophical Works of Descartes,' trans. and ed. Elizabeth Haldane and G. R. T. Ross (New York: Macmillan, 1955), part I, art.xxxii, p.346, and art.xxiv, pp.260-82. Also part I, art.xxxiv, p.347, and part III, arts ccxi-ccxii, pp.425-7. Roy Lawrence, 'Motive and Intention - An Essay in the Appreciation of Action' (Evanston, Ill.: Northwestern University Press, 1972) presents an in-depth analysis of the pervasive influence of Descartes' thought.

7 Including a focus on governmental institutions, power, public groups, decision-making processes and systems analysis.

Most textbooks on American government utilize the first approach to politics. Excellent examples include Charles Hyneman, 'The Study of Politics' (Urbana, Ill.: University of Illinois Press, 1959), especially pp.25-6; and Roy C. Macridis, Comparative Politics and the Study of Government, 'Comparative Politics,' I (October 1968), pp.79-96.

The first contemporary political scientist to use power as a criteria of the 'political' is George E. G. Catlin, 'The Science and Method of Politics' (New York: Knopf, 1927), especially p.205, and 'Systematic Politics' (Canada: University of Toronto Press, 1962). Others of note include Harold Lasswell, 'Politics: Who Gets What, When, and How' (New York: World Publishing, 1958); Lasswell and Abraham Kaplan, 'Power and Society' (New Haven: Yale University Press, 1950); and Hans Morganthau, 'In Defense of the National Interest' (New York: Knopf, 1951), and 'Politics Among Nations' (New York: Knopf, 1968).

Those interpreting politics as conflict and compromise between organized groups in the public arena include Martin Myerson and Edward Banfield, 'Politics, Planning, and the Public Interest' (Chicago: Free Press, 1955), especially pp.304-5;

Vernon Van Dyke, 'Political Science: A Philosophical Analysis' (California: Stanford University Press, 1960), especially p.134; and William Bluhm, 'Theories of the Political System' (Englewood Cliffs, N.J.: Prentice-Hall, 1965), especially p.5.

Early examples of the 'politics as decision-making' approach include Pendleton Herring, 'Group Representation Before Congress' (New York: McGraw-Hill, 1929), Elmer Schattschneider, 'Politics, Pressures, and the Tariff' (Englewood Cliffs, N.J.: Prentice-Hall, 1937), and Peter Odegard, 'Pressure Politics - The Story of the Anti-Saloon League' (New York: Columbia University Press, 1928). Of late, decision-making theorists carry on this tradition.

The final interpretation of 'political' is exemplified by David Easton, 'The Political System' (New York: Knopf, 1953), 'A Framework for Political Analysis' (Englewood Cliffs, N.J.: Prentice-Hall, 1965), 'A Systems Analysis of Political Life' (New York: John Wiley, 1965), and An Approach to the Analysis of Political Systems, 'World Politics' (April 1957), pp.383-412: Karl Deutsch, 'The Nerves of Government' (New York: Free Press, 1966); Gabriel Almond and James Coleman (eds), 'The Politics of the Developing Areas' (Princeton, N.J.: Princeton University Press, 1960); Almond and G. Bingham Powell, 'Comparative Politics: A Developmental Approach' (Boston: Little, Brown, 1966); and Morton Kaplan, 'Systems and Process in International Politics' (New York: John Wiley, 1964). Easton and Deutsch derive their systems from socio-communication theory. The others (excepting Kaplan) use separation of powers theory as a conceptual basis.

8 Cf. David Easton's declaration that, 'Only by analysis, by chopping the world into manageable units of inquiry, by precision achieved through measurement wherever possible, can political science meet the continuing need of a complex, post-industrial society for more reliable knowledge.' See The New Revolution in Political Science, 'American Political Science Review,' LXIII (December 1969), p.1054. Robert Merton, Now the Case *for* Sociology, 'New York Times Magazine,' 16 July 1961, pp.19-20, expresses similar sentiments, stressing the need to analytically 'chop-up' society into past and present, with only the latter of concern to social scientists.

9 This is a very important point. Some phenomenologically-oriented methodologists avoid this conclusion and thus firmly establish themselves

as supporters of an empirical scientific approach to studying society, despite (in contradiction to) their existential phenomenological jargon. This is most vividly exhibited in George Gurvitch, 'La vocation actuelle de la sociologie' (Paris: Presses Universitaires de France, 1957), vol. I, 'Traite de sociologie' (Paris: Presses Universitaires de France, 1960), and 'Essais de sociologie' (Paris: Recueil Sirey, 1938). Phillip Bosserman, 'Dialectical Sociology - An Analysis of the Sociology of Georges Gurvitch' (Boston: Porter Sargent Publishers, 1968), is a useful English introduction to Gurvitch's work. The neo-empiricistic basis of Gurvitch's 'dialectical' sociology is stressed in Paul Piccone, Dialectical Logic Today 'Telos' 2 (Fall, 1968), pp.65-6; and Jean-Paul Sartre, 'Critique de la raison dialectique' (Paris: Gallimard, 1960), p.117. Friedrich Baerwald, A Sociological View of Depersonalization, 'Thought,' XXXI (Spring, 1956), pp.55-78, and Society as a Process, 'American Catholic Sociological Review' (December 1944), pp.12-28, also pays lip-service to existential phenomenology in his analyses of society, only to draw back under a methodological shield of empiricism primarily to justify his basically extra-societal, spiritual point of view. In the skilled hands of Aron Gurwitsch, Gestalt theory is integrated with Husserlian phenomenology, especially Husserl's noematic structure of perception, in an attempt to rid the Gestalt approach of its traditionally positivistic bias (which is outlined in Merleau-Ponty, The Primacy of Perception and Its Philosophical Consequences, 'The Primacy of Perception,' ed. and trans. James M. Edie (Evanston, Ill.: Northwestern University Press, 1964), p.24). See Gurwitsch, 'Field of Consciousness' (Pittsburgh: Duquesne University Press, 1964), especially pp.85-154, 'Studies in Phenomenology and Psychology,' especially chapters 1 and 10, and The Phenomenology of Perception: Perceptual Implications, 'An Invitation to Phenomenology,' ed. James M. Edie (Chicago: Quadrangle Books, 1965), pp.17-29. Gurwitsch himself admits, however, that, though his field theory of consciousness (defined in 'Field of Consciousness,' pp.155-98) is 'developed by the aid of Gestalt theoretical concepts,' these 'must lend themselves to an interpretation along [Husserlian] phenomenological lines.' (Ibid., p.7.) Thus, for Gurwitsch, the gestalt-like character of social phenomena is not the ontological expression of our existences, but the contingent result of our perceptions, understood transcendentally. Social knowledge is scientifically verified, as Vierkandt, Strasser and Natanson have outlined, by correlating empirical fact to absolute transcendental knowledge.

10 Jean-Paul Sartre, 'Search For a Method,' trans. Hazel E. Barnes (New York: Knopf, 1963), pp.174-5.

11 Karl Marx, 'Early Writings,' trans. and ed. T. B. Bottomore (New York: McGraw-Hill, 1964), p.5. The distinction between 'left' and 'right' phenomenologists is originally drawn by Pier Aldo Rovatti, A Phenomenological Analysis of Marxism: The Return to the Subject and to the Dialectic of the Totality, 'Telos,' 5 (Spring, 1970), pp.160-73.

12 Though Georg Lukács, in 'History and Class Consciousness,' trans. Rodney Livingstone (Cambridge, Mass.: MIT Press, 1973), esp. pp.1-24, pioneered in stressing the complexity and importance of mediations, a most interesting contemporary Marxian study is Bertell Ollman, 'Alienation: Marx's Concept of Man in Capitalist Society' (London: Cambridge University Press, 1971). This author's analysis of social reality - especially the reciprocally interrelated quality of all social 'levels' - resembles that presented here. However, Professor Ollman also contends that Marxism is closely related to a 'philosophy of internal relations' in which individuals are defined as relations of all other phenomena, *products* of environment, defined *entirely* by phenomena existing apart from control or alteration, *independent* of human will (see especially ibid., pp.27-42). This theory is in no sense phenomenological. Empirical social science can meaningfully explain social interaction, provided its data is somehow re-inserted into the dynamic structure of society which is described and accepted prior to existence.

13 Lukács, op. cit., Karel Kosík, Dialectic of the Concrete Totality, 'Telos,' 2 (Fall, 1968), pp.21-37, and The Concrete Totality, 'Telos,' 4 (Fall, 1969), pp.35-54. See also Dick Howard, Existentialism and Marxism, 'Towards a New Marxism,' ed. Bart Grahl and Paul Piccone (St. Louis, Mo.: Telos Press, 1973), p.101; and Piccone, Dialectic Logic Today, 'Telos,' 2 (Fall, 1968), pp.38-83.

14 Lukács, op. cit., p.184.

15 Kosík, The Concrete Totality, 'Telos,' 4, p.43. See Lukács, op. cit., p.8 for a similar point of view.

16 There are generally sympathetic arguments on this

point in: Étienne Gilson and Thomas Langan, 'Modern Philosophy' (New York: Random House, 1963), vol. III, chapter III, and Eugen Fink, L'Analyse intentionelle et le problème de la pensée speculative, 'Problèmes actuels de la Phénoménologie,' ed. H. C. Von Brada (Bruxelles, 1951), pp.83ff. This argument is explicitly rejected in Franco Voltaggio, 'Fondamenti della logica di Husserl' (Milan: 1965), and Suzanne Bachelard, 'La Logique de Husserl' (Paris: 1957).

17 Lukács, op. cit., pp.28-9.

18 Lukács's 'History and Class Consciousness' is the work that best illustrates this problem, occurring as it did mid-way between his early stress on subjective idealism and his later turn towards a more orthodox material necessity. This path is traced in István Mészáros, Lukács' Concept of Dialectic, 'George Lukácz - the man, his works, and his ideas,' ed. G. H. R. Parkinson (New York: Vintage Books, 1970), pp.34-85; and Andre Arato, Lukács's Path to Marxism (1910-1923), 'Telos,' 7 (Spring, 1971), pp.128-36. Herbert Marcuse's early flirtation with phenomenology is found in Beiträge zu einer Phänomenologie des historischen Materialismus, 'Philosophische Hefte,' I, 1 (1928), pp.45-68. The English translation is Contributions To A Phenomenology of Historical Materialism, 'Telos,' 4 (Summer, 1970), pp.3-34. Tran Duc Thao's evolution towards a more orthodox Marxism is similar to Marcuse's. In Marxisme et phénoménologie, 'Revue Internationale,' no. 2 (1946), he asserts the close theoretical relationship of these two philosophies, only to draw back after criticism and assert that the internal contradictions of phenomenology necessitate its becoming dialectical materialism. See 'Phénoménologie et matérialisme dialectique' (Paris: 1957). Relevant background information is offered by Silvia Federici, Viet Cong Philosophy: Tran Duc Thao, 'Telos,' 6 (Fall, 1970), pp.104-17. Karl Korsch's brand of Marxism, at least as expressed in his 'Marxism and Philosophy,' trans. Fred Halliday (London, 1970), is vulnerable in its stress on the identity of Marxist theory and empirical consciousness. It has been critically evaluated, from a more orthodox Marxian perspective, by Leonardo Ceppa, Korsch's Marxism, 'Telos,' 26 (Winter, 1975-6), pp.94-119, esp. pp.105ff. A complete listing and analysis of Marxist critics of phenomenology is found in Guido G. Neri, 'Prassi e conoscènza' (Milan: Feltrinelli, 1966), pp.128-208.

19 Relevant works include: Karel Kosík, Dialectic of the

Concrete Totality, 'Telos,' 2, pp.21-37, and The Concrete Totality, 'Telos,' 4 (Fall, 1969), pp.35-54. These are English translations of selections from 'Die Dialektik des Konkreten,' published in 1963; Antonio Labriola, 'Essays on the Materialist Conception of History,' trans. Charles H. Kerr (New York: Monthly Review Press, 1966); Antonio Gramsci, 'Il Materialismo storico e la filosofia de Benedetto Croce' (Turin: G. Einaudi, 1948), and 'The Modern Prince and Other Writings' (New York: International Publishers, 1967); and Ollman, op. cit. The Frankfurt School of Critical Theory spurns philosophical anthropology altogether, avoiding this dilemma but also becoming philosophically vulnerable, lacking any clear objective criteria for their critical perspective. Martin Jay, 'The Dialectical Imagination' (Boston: Little, Brown, 1973) judiciously surveys this material.

20 There are several articles detailing more precisely the historical chronology of this synthetic movement. These include: Fred R. Dallmayr, Phenomenology and Marxism: A Salute to Enzo Paci, 'Phenomenological Sociology: Issues and Applications,' ed. George Psathas (New York: John Wiley, 1973), pp.305-56; Paul Piccone, Phenomenological Marxism, 'Towards a New Marxism,' ed. Grahl and Piccone, pp.133-58; and, on a more theoretical level, Maurice Merleau-Ponty, Western Marxism, 'Telos,' 6 (Fall, 1970), pp.140-61.

21 Enzo Paci, 'The Function of the Sciences and the Meaning of Man,' trans. Paul Piccone and James E. Hansen (Evanston, Ill.: Northwestern University Press, 1972).

22 Ibid., p.35. This whole argument is contained in part I (pp.3-40). See also pp.93-4, 118-20, and Sul problema della interosoggettivita, 'Il Pensiero,' 3 (1960), pp.291-325. Supporting arguments are offered in Piccone, Dialectical Logic Today, 'Telos,' 2 (Fall, 1968), esp. p.61, n.66, Rovatti, loc. cit., pp.161-2, and Gilson and Langan, op. cit..

23 Paci, 'Functions,' p.323. This argument is derived primarily from part III, pp.289-450, though Paci's analysis of the nature and function of the sciences is offered on pp.41-288.

24 Ibid., p.37.

25 Dallmayr, loc. cit., esp. pp.328-30, offers a concurring opinion. Numerous quotations could be offered here as evidence. See, for example, Paci, op. cit., pp.88, 96, 98, 100, 122, 130-6, 354, 383, 442, 445, Rovatti, loc. cit., p.171, and Piccone,

Dialectical Logic Today, 'Telos,' 2 (Fall, 1968), pp.65-6.

26 Jean-Paul Sartre, 'Critique de la raison dialectique.' English summaries are provided in Dick Howard, loc. cit., pp.107-23, and Raymond Aron, 'Marxism and the Existentialists' (New York: Simon and Schuster, 1970), pp.164-76.

27 Sartre, 'Critique de la raison dialectique,' p.143.

28 Ibid., p.361. See also Sartre, Existentialism is a Humanism, 'Existentialism Versus Marxism,' ed. George Novack (New York: Dell, 1966), p.82, and Materialism and Revolution, ibid., pp.105ff.

29 This is Aron's position. See Aron, op. cit., p.168.

30 At one point in the 'Critique' (p.455) Sartre, affirming the necessary roles of fraternal oaths, terror, and periodic purges in institutionalizing authentic groups, suggests that duty may well force a group to eliminate certain unco-operative individuals, in which case there exists 'a practical relation of love among the lynchers.'

31 Trans. Hazel E. Barnes (New York: Knopf, 1963).

32 Ibid., p.181.

33 Ibid., p.100, n.5.

Bibliography

BOOKS

ABEL, T. (1929), 'Systematic Sciology in Germany,' Columbia University Press, New York.
ADAMS, E. M. (1960), 'Ethical Naturalism and the Modern World-View,' University of North Carolina Press, Chapel Hill.
ALMOND, G. and COLEMAN, J. (1960), (eds), 'The Politics of the Developing Areas,' Princeton University Press, N.J.
ALMOND, G. and POWELL, G. B. (1966), 'Comparative Politics: A Developmental Approach,' Little, Brown, Boston.
AMERICAN PHILOSOPHICAL ASSOCIATION, EASTERN DIVISION (1952), 'Science, Language, and Human Rights,' University of Pennsylvania Press, Philadelphia.
ANTON, T. J. (1960), 'The Politics of State Expenditure in Illinois,' University of Illinois Press, Urbana, Ill.
ARON, R. (1967), 'German Sociology,' translated by Mary and Thomas Bottomore, Free Press, New York.
ARON, R. (1970), 'Marxism and The Existentialists,' Simon and Schuster, New York.
BERGER, P. L. (1963), 'Invitation to Sociology,' Doubleday, Garden City, New York.
BERGER, P. L. and LUCKMANN, T. (1966), 'The Social Construction of Reality,' Doubleday, Garden City, New York.
BERGSON, H. (1910), 'Time and Free Will,' translated by F. L. Pogson, Macmillan, New York.
BERNSTEIN, R. (1971), 'Praxis and Action,' University of Pennsylvania Press, Philadelphia.
BLUHM, W. (1965), 'Theories of the Political System,' Prentice-Hall, Englewood Cliffs, N.J.

BOSSERMAN, P. (1968), 'Dialectical Sociology,' Porter Sargent, Boston.

BRAYBROOKE, D. (1965), 'Philosophical Problems of the Social Sciences,' Macmillan, New York.

BRECHT, A. (1959), 'Political Theory: The Foundations of Twentieth-Century Political Thought,' Princeton University Press, New Jersey.

BUBER, M. (1962), 'Werke,' 3 vols, Kosel-Verlag, Munich.

BUNGE, M. (1964), (ed.), 'The Critical Approach to Science and Philosophy,' Free Press, New York.

CATLIN, G. E. G. (1927), 'The Science and Method of Politics,' Alfred Knopf, New York.

CATLIN, G. E. G. (1962), 'Systematic Politics,' University of Toronto Press, Canada.

CHARLESWORTH, J. C. (1962), (ed.), 'The Limits of Behavioralism in Political Science,' American Academy of Political and Social Science, Philadelphia.

CHARLESWORTH, J. C. (1967), (ed.), 'Contemporary Political Analysis,' Free Press, New York.

CHISHOLM, R. (1960), (ed.), 'Realism and the Background of Phenomenology,' Free Press, Chicago.

CICOUREL, A. V. (1964), 'Method and Measurement in Sociology,' Free Press, New York.

CUNNINGHAM, F. (1973), 'Objectivity in Social Science,' University of Toronto Press, Toronto.

DENNES, W. (1960), 'Some Dilemmas of Naturalism,' Columbia University Press, New York.

DESCARTES, R. (1955), 'The Philosophical Works of Descartes,' translated and edited by Elizabeth Haldane and G. R. T. Ross, Macmillan, New York.

DEUTSCH, K. (1966), 'The Nerves of Government,' Free Press, New York.

DEWAELHENS, A. (1958), 'Existence et signification,' Publications universitaires, Louvain.

DILTHEY, W. (1923-7), 'Gesammelte schriften,' B. G. Teubner, Leipzig und Berlin.

DILTHEY, W. (1954), 'The Essence of Philosophy,' translated by Stephan A. Emery and William T. Emery, University of North Carolina Press, Chapel Hill.

DILTHEY, W. (1962), 'Pattern and Meaning in History,' translated by H. P. Rickman, Harper & Row, New York.

DOUGLAS, J. (1970), (ed.), 'Understanding Everyday Life,' Aldine, Chicago.

EASTON, D. (1953), 'The Political System,' Alfred Knopf, New York.

EASTON, D. (1965a), 'A Framework for Political Analysis,' Prentice-Hall, Englewood Cliffs, N.J.

EASTON, D. (1965b), 'A Systems Analysis of Political Life,' John Wiley, New York.

EDIE, J. M. (1965), (ed.), 'An Invitation to Phenomenology,' Quadrangle Books, Chicago.
EDIE, J. M. (1967), (ed.), 'Phenomenology in America,' Quadrangle Books, Chicago.
EULAU, H. (1956), et al. (eds), 'Political Behavior: A Reader in Theory and Research,' Free Press, Chicago.
FARBER, M. (1940), (ed.), 'Philosophical Essays in Memory of Edmund Husserl,' Harvard University Press, Cambridge, Mass.
FARBER, M. (1943), 'The Foundation of Phenomenology,' Harvard University Press, Cambridge, Mass.
FARBER, M. (1959), 'Naturalism and Subjectivism,' C. C. Thomas, Springfield, Ill.
FARBER, M. (1967), 'Phenomenology and Existence: Towards a Philosophy Within Nature,' Harper & Row, New York.
FEIGL, H. and BRODBECK, M. (1953), (eds), 'Readings in the Philosophy of Science,' Appleton-Century-Crofts, New York.
FOX, W. T. R. (1959), (ed.), 'Theoretical Aspects of International Relations,' University of Notre Dame Press, Indiana.
FRANKEL, J. (1963), 'The Making of Foreign Policy,' Oxford University Press, New York.
FRANKEL, J. (1970), 'National Interest,' Praeger Publishers, New York.
FREUND, J. (1968), 'The Sociology of Max Weber,' Vintage Books, New York.
FROMM, E. (1966), 'Marx's Concept of Man,' Ungar Publishing, New York.
GARFINKEL, H. (1967), 'Studies in Ethnomethodology,' Prentice-Hall, Englewood Cliffs, N.J.
GILSON, E. and LANGAN, T. (1963), 'Modern Philosophy,' Random House, New York.
GORE, W. J. and DYSON, J. W. (1964), (eds), 'The Making of Decisions,' Free Press, New York.
GRAHL, B. and PICCONE, P. (1973), (eds), 'Towards a New Marxism,' Telos Press, St Louis, Mo.
GRAMSCI, A. (1948), 'Il Materialismo storico e la filosofia de Benedetto Croce,' G. Einaudi, Turin.
GRAMSCI, A. (1967), 'The Modern Prince and Other Writings,' International Publishers, New York.
GUETZKOW, H. (1963), et al., 'Simulation in International Relations,' Prentice-Hall, Englewood Cliffs, N.J.
GURVITCH, G. (1938), 'Essais de sociologie,' Recueil Sirey, Paris.
GURVITCH, G. (1957), 'La vocation actuelle de la sociologie,' Presses Universitaires de France, Paris.
GURVITCH, G. (1960), 'Traite de sociologie,' Presses Universitaires de France, Paris.

GURVITCH, G. and MOORE, W. E. (1945), 'Twentieth Century Sociology,' Philosophical Library, New York.
GURWITSCH, A. (1964), 'Field of Consciousness,' Duquesne University Press, Pittsburgh.
GURWITSCH, A. (1966), 'Studies in Phenomenology and Psychology,' Northwestern University Press, Evanston, Ill.
HALDANE, E. and ROSS, G. R. T. (1955), 'The Philosophical Works of Descartes,' Macmillan, New York.
HEELAN, P. A. (1965), 'Quantam Mechanics and Objectivity,' Martinus Nijhoff, The Hague.
HEIDEGGER, M. (1962), 'Being and Time,' translated by John Macquarrie and Edward Robinson, Harper & Row, New York.
HEINEMANN, F. H. (1958), 'Existentialism and the Modern Predicament,' Harper & Row, New York.
HEMPEL, C. F. (1965), 'Aspects of Scientific Explanation and Other Essays in the Philosophy of Science,' Free Press, New York.
HERMANN, C. F. (1969), 'Crises in Foreign Policy - A Simulation Analysis,' Bobbs-Merill, New York.
HERRING, P. (1929), 'Group Representation Before Congress,' McGraw-Hill, New York.
HOCHSTIM, P. (1966), 'Alfred Vierkandt: A Sociological Critique,' Exposition Press, New York.
HOFFMAN, S. T. (1960), (ed.), 'Contemporary Theory in International Relations,' Prentice-Hall, Englewood Cliffs, N.J.
HUGHES, H. S. (1958), 'Consciousness and Society,' Knopff, New York.
HUME, D. (1902), 'Enquiries Concerning Human Understanding,' edited by L. A. Selby-Bigge, 2nd edn, Oxford University Press, London.
HUSSERL, E. (1931), 'Ideas, General Introduction to Pure Phenomenology,' translated by W. R. Boyce Gibson, Humanities Press, New York.
HUSSERL, E. (1964), 'Cartesian Meditations,' translated by Dorion Cairns, Martinus Nijhoff, The Hague.
HUSSERL, E. (1965), 'Phenomenology and the Crisis of Philosophy,' translated and edited by Quentin Lauer, Harper & Row, New York.
HUSSERL, E. (1969), 'Formal and Transcendental Logic,' translated by Dorion Cairns, Martinus Nijhoff, The Hague.
HUSSERL, E. (1970a), 'Logical Investigations,' translated by J. N. Findlay, Humanities Press, New York.
HUSSERL, E. (1970b), 'The Crisis of European Sciences and Transcendental Phenomenology,' translated by David Carr, Northwestern University Press, Evanston, Ill.

HYNEMAN, C. (1959), 'The Study of Politics,' University of Illinois Press, Urbana, Ill.

ISAAK, A. C. (1975), 'Scope and Methods of Political Science,' revised edn, Dorsey Press, Illinois.

JASPERS, K. (1951), 'Man in the Modern Age,' translated by Eden and Cedar Paul, Routledge & Kegan Paul, London.

JAY, M. (1973), 'The Dialectical Imagination,' Little, Brown, Boston.

JERVIS, R. (1970), 'The Logic of Images in International Relations,' Princeton University Press, N.J.

JUNG, H. Y. (1972), (ed.), 'Existential Phenomenology and Political Theory: A Reader,' Regnery, Chicago.

KAPLAN, M. (1964), 'Systems and Process in International Politics,' John Wiley, New York.

KAUFMANN, F. (1944), 'Methodology of the Social Sciences,' Oxford University Press, New York.

KELMAN, H. (1965), (ed.), 'International Behavior,' Holt Rinehart & Winston, New York.

KNORR, K. and ROSENAU, J. N. (1969), (eds), 'Contending Approaches to International Politics,' Princeton University Press, N.J.

KOCKELMANS, J. J. (1966), 'Phenomenology and Physical Science,' Duquesne University Press, Pittsburgh.

KOCKELMANS, J. J. (1967), (ed.), 'Phenomenology,' Doubleday, New York.

KOCKELMANS, J. J. and KISIEL, H. (1970), (eds), 'Phenomenology and the Natural Sciences,' Northwestern University Press, Evanston, Ill.

LABRIOLA, A. (1966), 'Essays on the Materialist Conception of History,' translated by Charles H. Kerr, Monthly Review Press, New York.

LAMBERT, K. and BRITTAN, G. G. (1970), 'An Introduction to the Philosophy of Science,' Prentice-Hall, Englewood Cliffs, N.J.

LANGAN, T. (1966), 'Merleau-Ponty's Critique of Reason,' Yale University Press, New Haven.

LASSWELL, H. (1958), 'Politics: Who Gets What, When, and How,' World Publishing, New York.

LASSWELL, H. and KAPLAN, A. (1950), 'Power and Society,' Yale University Press, New Haven.

LASZLO, E. (1966), 'Beyond Skepticism and Realism,' Martinus Nijhoff, The Hague.

LAUER, Q. (1958), 'The Triumph of Subjectivity,' Fordham University Press, New York.

LAWRENCE, R. (1972), 'Motive and Intention,' Northwestern University Press, Evanston, Ill.

LEE, E. N. and MANDELBAUM, M. (1967), (eds), 'Phenomenology and Existentialism,' Johns Hopkins Press, Baltimore.

LICHTHEIM, G. (1970), 'George Lukács,' Viking Press, New York.
LINDBLOM, C. (1965), 'The Intelligence of Democracy,' Free Press, New York.
LOUCH, A. R. (1966), 'Explanation and Human Action,' University of California Press, Berkeley and Los Angeles.
LUKÁCS, G. (1973), 'History and Class Consciousness,' translated by Rodney Livingstone, MIT Press, Cambridge, Mass.
MACOMBER, W. B. (1967), 'The Anatomy of Disillusion,' Northwestern University Press, Evanston, Ill.
MARCEL, G. (1949), 'The Philosophy of Existence,' translated by Manya Harari, Philosophical Library, New York.
MARCEL, G. (1952), 'Man Against Mass Society,' translated by G. S. Fraser, Regnery, Chicago.
MARCEL, G. (1960), 'The Mystery of Being,' translated by G. S. Fraser, Regnery, Chicago.
MARCH, J. G. and SIMON, H. A. (1958), 'Organizations,' Wiley Press, New York.
MARX, K. (1964), 'Early Writings,' translated and edited by T. B. Bottomore, McGraw-Hill, New York.
MARX, K. and ENGLES, F. (1959), 'Basic Writings on Politics and Philosophy,' edited by Lewis S. Feuer, Doubleday, New York.
MEAD, G. E. (1934), 'Mind, Self, and Society,' University of Chicago Press, Chicago.
MEHAN, H. and WOOD, H. (1975), 'The Reality of Ethnomethodology,' John Wiley, New York.
MELDEN, A. I. (1961), 'Free Action,' Routledge & Kegan Paul, London.
MERLEAU-PONTY, M. (1962), 'Phenomenology of Perception,' translated by Colin Smith, Humanities Press, New York.
MERLEAU-PONTY, M. (1964a), 'The Primacy of Perception,' translated and edited by James M. Edie, Northwestern University Press, Evanston, Ill.
MERLEAU-PONTY, M. (1964b), 'Signs,' translated by Richard C. McCleary, Northwestern University Press, Evanston, Ill.
MILLS, C. W. (1959), 'The Sociological Imagination,' Oxford University Press, New York.
MOLINA, F. R. (1969), (ed.), 'The Sources of Existentialism as Philosophy,' Prentice-Hall, Englewood Cliffs, N.J.
MORGANTHAU, H. (1951), 'In Defense of the National Interest,' Alfred Knopf, New York.
MORGANTHAU, H. (1968), 'Politics Among Nations,' Alfred Knopf, New York.
MORGENBESSER, S. (1969), (ed.), 'Philosophy, Science, and Method,' St Martins Press, New York.

MYERSON, M. and BANFIELD, E. (1955), 'Politics, Planning and the Public Interest,' Free Press, Chicago.
NAGEL, E. (1961), 'The Structure of Science: Problems in the Logic of Scientific Explanation,' Harcourt, Brace, & World, New York.
NATANSON, M. (1962), 'Literature Philosophy, and the Social Sciences,' Martinus Nijhoff, The Hague.
NATANSON, M. (1969), (ed.), 'Essays in Phenomenology,' Martinus Nijhoff, The Hague.
NATANSON, M. (1970), 'The Journeying Self; A Study in Philosophy and Social Role,' Addison-Wesley, Reading, Mass.
NERI, G. G. (1966), 'Prassi e conoscenza,' Feltrinelli, Milan.
NORTH, R. (1963), et al., 'Content Analysis,' Northwestern University Press, Evanston, Ill.
NOVACK, G. (1966), (ed.), 'Existentialism Versus Marxism,' Dell, New York.
ODEGARD, P. (1928), 'Pressure Politics - The Story of the Anti-Saloon League,' Columbia University Press, New York.
OLLMAN, B. (1971), 'Alienation: Marx's Concept of Man in Capitalist Society,' Cambridge University Press, London.
PACI, E. (1972), 'The Function of the Sciences and Meaning of Man,' translated by Paul Piccone and James E. Hansen, Northwestern University Press, Evanston, Ill.
PAIGE, G. D. (1968), 'The Korean Decision,' Free Press, New York.
PARKINSON, G. H. R. (1970), (ed.), 'George Lukácz - the man, his works, and his ideas,' Vintage Books, New York.
PARSONS, T. (1949), 'The Structure of Social Action,' Free Press, Chicago.
PETERS, R. S. (1960), 'The Concept of Motivation,' Routledge & Kegan Paul, London.
PRUITT, D. G. (1965), 'Problem Solving in the Department of State,' University of Denver Press, Denver, Colo.
PRUITT, D. G. and SNYDER, R. C. (1969), (eds), 'Theory and Research on the Causes of War,' Prentice-Hall, Englewood Cliffs, N.J.
PRZEWORSKI, A. and TEUNE, H. (1970), 'The Logic of Comparative Social Inquiry,' John Wiley, New York.
PSATHAS, G. (1973), (ed.), 'Phenomenological Sociology: Issues and Applications,' John Wiley, New York.
RABIL, A. (1967), 'Merleau-Ponty, Existentialist of the Social World,' Columbia University Press, New York.
RANNEY, A. (1962), (ed.), 'Essays on the Behavioral Study of Politics,' University of Illinois Press, Urbana, Ill.
REYMERT, M. L. (1950), (ed.), 'Feelings and Emotions,' McGraw-Hill, New York.

RICKERT, H. (1910), 'Kulturwissenschaft und naturwissenschaft,' J. C. B. Mohr, Tübingen.
RICKERT, H. (1921), 'Die grenzen der naturwissenschaftlichen begriffsbildung,' J. C. B. Mohr, Tübingen.
RICOEUR, P. (1967), 'Husserl, An Analysis of His Phenomenology,' translated by Edward G. Ballard and Lester E. Embree, Northwestern University Press, Evanston, Ill.
ROMANELL, P. (1958), 'Towards a Critical Naturalism,' Macmillan, New York.
ROSENAU, J. N. (1961), (ed.), 'International Politics and Foreign Policy,' Free Press, New York.
ROSENAU, J. N. (1971), 'The Scientific Study of Foreign Policy,' Free Press, New York.
RUDNER, R. (1966), 'Philosophy of Social Science,' Prentice-Hall, Englewood Cliffs, N.J.
SARTRE, J. P. (1960), 'Critique de la raison dialectique,' Gallimard, Paris.
SARTRE, J. P. (1963), 'Search for a Method,' translated by Hazel E. Barnes, Knopff, New York.
SARTRE, J. P. (1966), 'Being and Nothingness,' translated by Hazel E. Barnes, Washington Square Press, New York.
SCHAFF, A. (1970), 'Marxism and the Human Individual,' McGraw-Hill, New York.
SCHATTSCHNEIDER, E. (1937), 'Politics, Pressures, and the Tariff,' Prentice-Hall, Englewood Cliffs, N.J.
SCHEFFLER, I. (1963), 'The Anatomy of Inquiry,' Knopff, New York.
SCHILPP, P.A. (1949), (ed.), 'Albert Einstein, Philosopher-Scientist,' Library of Living Philosophers, Evanston, Ill.
SCHUTZ, A. (1967a), 'The Phenomenology of the Social World,' translated by George Walsh and Frederick Lehnert, Northwestern University Press, Evanston, Ill.
SCHUTZ, A., Collected Papers, 3 vols: vol. I, 'The Problem of Social Reality,' edited by Maurice Natanson, 2nd edn, 1967b; vol. II, 'Studies in Social Theory,' edited by Arvid Brodersen, 1964; vol. III, 'Studies in Phenomenological Philosophy,' edited by I. Schutz, 1966. Martinus Nijhoff, The Hague.
SCHUTZ, A. (1970), 'Reflections on the Problem of Relevance,' edited by Richard M. Zaner, Yale University Press, New Haven.
SCHUTZ, A. and LUCKMANN, T. (1973), 'The Structure of the Life-World,' translated by Richard Zaner and Tristam Engelhardt, Jr, Northwestern University Press, Evanston, Ill.

SHARKANSKY, IRA (1970), 'The Routines of Politics,' Van Nostrand Reinhold, New York.
SIMON, H. A. (1957a), 'Administrative Behavior: A Study of Decision-Making Processes in Administrative Organizations,' MacMillan, New York.
SIMON, H. A. (1957b), 'Models of Man: Social and Rational,' Wiley Press, New York.
SNYDER, R. C., BRUCK, H. W. and SAPIN, B. (1962), (eds), 'Foreign Policy Decision-Making,' Free Press, New York.
SNYDER, R. C. and FURNISS, E. S. Jr, (1954), 'American Foreign Policy: Formulation, Principles, and Programs,' Holt Rinehart & Winston, New York.
SNYDER, R. C. and ROBINSON, J. (1961), 'National and International Decision-Making,' Institute for International Order, New York.
SOMIT, A. and TANNENHAUS, J. (1967), 'The Development of American Political Science: From Burgess to Behavioralism,' Allyn & Bacon, Boston.
SPIEGELBERG, H. (1965), 'The Phenomenological Movement,' 2 vols, 2nd edn revised, Martinus Nijhoff, The Hague.
SPROUT, M. and H. (1956), 'Man-Milieu Relationship Hypotheses in the Context of International Politics,' Princeton University Press, N.J.
SPROUT, M. and H. (1962), 'Foundations of International Politics,' Van Nostrand Press, N.J.
SPROUT, M. and H. (1965), 'Ecological Perspective on Human Affairs,' Princeton University Press, N.J.
SPROUT, M. and H. (1968), 'An Ecological Pardigm for the Study of International Politics,' Princeton University Press, N.J.
STAGNER, R. (1967), 'Psychological Aspects of International Conflict,' Brooks-Cole, Belmond, Cal.
STERN, A. (1967), 'Sartre,' 2nd edn, Dell, New York.
STRASSER, S. (1963), 'Phenomenology and the Human Sciences,' Duquesne University Press, Pittsburgh, Pa.
SUDNOW, D. (1972), (ed.), 'Studies in Social Interaction,' Free Press, New York.
SURKIN, M. and WOLFE, A. (1970), (eds), 'An End to Political Science,' Basic Books, New York.
TAYLOR, C. (1964), 'The Explanation of Behavior,' Routledge & Kegan Paul, London.
THĒVENAZ, P. (1962), 'What is Phenomenology?,' translated by James M. Edie, Charles Courtney and Paul Brockelman, Quadrangle Books, Chicago.
TIRYAKIAN, E. A. (1962), 'Sociolgism and Existentialism, Two Perspectives on the Individual and Society,' Prentice-Hall, Englewood Cliffs, N.J.
TRAN DUC THAO, (1951), 'Phénoménolgie et matérialisme dialectique,' Minh-Tan, Paris.

TURNER R. (1974), (ed.), 'Ethnomethodology,' Penguin Books, Baltimore, Md.
TYMIENIECKA, A. T. (1962), 'Phenomenology and Science in Contemporary European Thought,' Farrar, Straus and Cudahy, New York.
VAN DYKE, V. (1960), 'Political Science: A Philosophical Analysis,' Stanford University Press, California.
VIERKANDT, A. (1949), 'Kleine Gesellschaftslehre,' F. Enke, Stuttgart.
WAGNER, H. (1970), (ed.), 'Alfred Schutz - On Phenomenology and Social Relations,' University of Chicago Press, Chicago.
WANN, T. W. (1964), (ed.), 'Behaviorism and Phenomenology,' University of Chicago Press, Chicago.
WEBER, M. (1949), 'The Methodology of the Social Sciences,' translated and edited by Edward A. Shils and Henry A. Finch, Free Press, New York.
WEBER, M. (1964), 'Basic Concepts in Sociology,' Citadel Press, New York.
WEBER, M. (1969), 'The Theory of Social and Economic Organization,' translated by A. M. Henderson and Talcott Parsons, Free Press, New York.
WILD, J. (1953), (ed.), 'The Return to Reason,' Regnery, Chicago.
WILDAVSKY, A. (1964), 'The Politics of the Budgetary Process,' Little, Brown, Boston.
WILSHIRE, B. (1968), 'William James and Phenomenology,' Indiana University Press, Bloomington.
WINDELBAND, W. (1899), 'History of Ancient Philosophy,' translated by Herbert E. Cushman, 2nd edn, C. Scribner's Sons, New York.
WINDELBAND, W. (1901), 'History of Philosophy,' translated by James H. Tufts, Macmillan, New York.
WRONG, D. (1970), (ed.), 'Max Weber,' Prentice-Hall, Englewood Cliffs, N.J.
YOUNG, R. (1958), (ed.), 'Approaches to the Study of Politics,' Northwestern University Press, Evanston, Ill.
ZANER, R. M. (1970), 'The Way of Phenomenology,' Pegasus, New York.

ARTICLES

BAERWALD, F. (December 1944), Society as a Process, 'American Catholic Sociological Review,' pp.12-28.
BAERWALD, F. (Spring, 1956), A Sociological View of Depersonalization, 'Thought,' XXXI, pp.55-78.
BIERSTADT, R. (Winter, 1959), The Common-Sense World of Alfred Schutz, 'Social Research,' 26, pp.116-20.

BOELAARS, H. (1940), De intentionaliteit der Kennis bij Edmund Husserl, 'Bijdragen,' 3, pp.112-21.
DAHL, R. A. (1961), The Behavioral Approach, 'American Political Science Review,' 55, pp.763-72.
DAUENHAUER, B. P. (Spring, 1969), Making Plans and Lived Time, 'Southern Journal of Philosophy,' 7, pp.83-90.
DOUGHERTY, J. P. (Fall, 1966), Nagel's Concept of Science, 'Philosophy Today,' 10, pp.215-21.
EARLE, W. (1960), Phenomenology and Existentialism, 'The Journal of Philosophy,' LVII, pp.75-84.
EASTON, D. (April 1957), An Approach to the Analysis of Political Systems, 'World Politics,' pp.383-412.
EASTON, D. (December 1969), The New Revolution in Political Science, 'American Political Science Review,' LXIII, pp.1046-59.
EDIE, J. M. (1964), Recent Work in Phenomenology, 'American Philosophical Quarterly,' 1, pp.115-28.
EDIE, J. M. (1964-5), Transcendental Phenomenology and Existentialism, 'Philosophy and Phenomenological Research,' 25, pp.52-63.
EDIE, J. M. (March 1967), Phenomenology as Rigorous Science, 'International Philosophical Quarterly,' 7, pp.20-30.
FEDERICI, S. (Fall, 1970), Viet Cong Philosophy: Tran Duc Thao, 'Telos,' 6, pp.104-17.
GOLDSTEIN, L. J. (1961), The Phenomenological and Naturalistic Approaches to the Social, 'Methodos,' XIII, pp.225-38.
GORMAN, R. A. (December 1970), On the Inadequacies of Non-Philosophical Political Science: A Critical Analysis of Decision-Making Theory, 'International Studies Quarterly,' XIV, pp.395-411.
GORMAN, R. A. (March 1975), Alfred Schutz - An Exposition and Critique, 'British Journal of Sociology,' XXVI, 1, pp.1-19.
GORMAN, R. A. (December 1975), The Phenomenological 'Humanization' of Social Science: A Critique, 'British Journal of Sociology,' XXVI, 4, pp.389-405.
GURWITSCH, A. (March 1956), The Last Work of Edmund Husserl, 'Philosophy and Phenomenological Research,' XVI, pp.380-99, and (March 1957), XVII, pp.370-98.
GURWITSCH, A. (Spring, 1962), The Common-Sense World as Social Reality - A Discourse on Alfred Schutz, 'Social Research,' XXIX, pp.50-72.
HEELAN, P. A. (September 1967), Horizon, Objectivity and Reality in the Physical Sciences, 'International Philosophical Quarterly,' 7, pp.375-412.

HOLZNER, B. (Fall, 1963), Phenomenology and Formalization in the Human Sciences, 'Review of Existential Psychology and Psychiatry,' III, pp.263-70.
JUNG, H. Y. (October 1971), The Political Relevance of Existential Phenomenology, 'Review of Politics,' 33, pp.538-63.
KOSIK, K. (Fall, 1968), Dialectic of the Concrete Totality, 'Telos,' 2, pp.21-37.
KOSIK, K. (Fall, 1969), The Concrete Totality, 'Telos,' 4, pp.35-54.
LANDGREBE, L. (1940-1), The World as a Phenomenological Problem, 'Philosophy and Phenomenological Research,' I, pp.38-58.
LAVINE, T. Z. (26 February 1953), Note to Naturalists on the Human Spirit, 'The Journal of Philosophy,' L, pp.145-54.
LAWSON, R. M. (Fall, 1969), On the Possibility of an Objective Social Science, 'Kinesis,' 2, pp.3-14.
LEVIN, D. M. (Spring, 1968), Induction and Husserl's Theory of Eidetic Variation, 'Philosophy and Phenomenological Research,' 29, pp.1-15.
MACRIDIS, R. C. (October 1968), Comparative Politics and the Study of Government, 'Comparative Politics,' I, pp.79-96.
MARCUSE, H. (Summer, 1970), Contributions to a Phenomenology of Historical Materialism, 'Telos,' 4, pp.3-34.
MERLEAU-PONTY, M. (Fall, 1970), Western Marxism, 'Telos,' 6, pp.140-61.
MERTON, R. (16 July 1961), Now the Case for Sociology, 'New York Times Magazine,' pp.19-20.
MILLER, E. F. (September 1972), Positivism, Historicism, and Political Inquiry, 'American Political Science Review,' LXVI, pp.796-826.
MOHANTY, J. (1959), Individual Fact and Essence in Edmund Husserl's Philosophy, 'Philosophy and Phenomenological Research,' 20, pp.222-30.
NAGEL, E. (26 February 1953), On the Method of 'Verstehen' as the Sole Method of Philosophy, 'The Journal of Philosophy,' L, pp.154-57.
NATANSON, M. (Summer, 1958), A Study in Philosophy and the Social Sciences, 'Social Research,' 25, pp.158-72.
NATANSON, M. (Summer, 1968), Alfred Schutz on Social Reality and Social Science, 'Social Research,' 35, pp.217-44.
NATANSON, M. (Spring, 1970), Phenomenology and Typification - A Study in the Philosophy of Alfred Schutz, 'Social Research,' 37, pp.1-22.

NEISSER, H. P. (1959), The Phenomenological Approach in Social Science, 'Philosophy and Phenomenological Research,' 20, pp.198-212.
PACI, E. (1960), Sul problema della interosoggettivita, 'Il Pensiero,' 3, pp.291-325.
PERITORE, N. P. (March 1975), Some Problems in Alfred Schutz's Phenomenological Methodology, 'American Political Science Review,' LXIX, 1, pp.132-40.
PICCONE, P. (Fall, 1968), Dialectical Logic Today, 'Telos,' 2, pp.38-83.
ROVATTI , P. A. (Spring, 1970), A Phenomenological Analysis of Marxism: The Return to the Subject and to the Dialectic of the Totality, 'Telos,' 5, pp.160-73.
SCHEGLOFF, E. and SACKS, H. (1973), Opening Up Closings, 'Semiotica,' 8, pp.289-327.
SCHMITT, R. (1959), Husserl's Transcendental Phenomenological Reduction, 'Philosophy and Phenomenological Research,' 20, pp.238-45.
SCHWARTZ, D. C. (Summer, 1967), Decision Theories and Crisis Behavior: An Empirical Study of Nuclear Deterrence in International Political Crises, 'Orbis,' 11, pp.459-90.
SNYDER, R. C. (1963), The Korean Decision (1950) and the Analysis of Crisis Decision-Making, 'Working Group Reports, Military Operations Research Society.'
SNYDER, R. C. and PAIGE, G. D. (1958), The United States Decision to Resist Aggression in Korea: The Application of an Analytical Scheme, 'Administrative Science Quarterly,' 3, pp.342-78.
SPIEGELBERG, H. (1959), How Subjective is Phenomenology, 'Proceedings of the American Catholic Philosophical Association,' XXXIII, pp.30-5.
SPIEGELBERG, H. (1960), Husserl's Phenomenology and Existentialism, 'Journal of Philosophy,' 57, pp.62-74.
STONIER, A. and BODE, K. (1937), A New Approach to the Methodology of the Social Sciences, 'Economica,' IV, pp.406-24.
WINTHROP, H. (3 February 1949), Phenomenological Method from the Standpoint of the Empiricistic Bias, 'Journal of Philosophy,' 46, pp.57-74.
ZANER, R. M. (Spring, 1961), Theory of Intersubjectivity: Alfred Schutz, 'Social Research,' 28, pp.71-94.
ZINNES, D. (1962), Hostility in International Decision-Making, 'Journal of Conflict Resolution,' 6, pp.236-43.

UNPUBLISHED MATERIAL

DOWNES, C. B. (1963), Husserl's Theory of Other Minds: A Study of the 'Cartesian Meditations,' unpublished PhD dissertation, New York University.

SCANLON, J. D. (1967), Husserl's Conception of Philosophy as a Rigorous Science, unpublished PhD dissertation, Tulane University.

SCHEGLOFF, E. A. (1967), The First Five Seconds: The Order of Conversational Opening, unpublished PhD dissertation, University of California, Berkeley.

WILSHIRE, B. W. (1966), Natural Science and Phenomenology: William James, 'Principles of Psychology,' as a Search for Reconciliation, unpublished PhD dissertation, New York University.

Index

Routledge Social Science Series

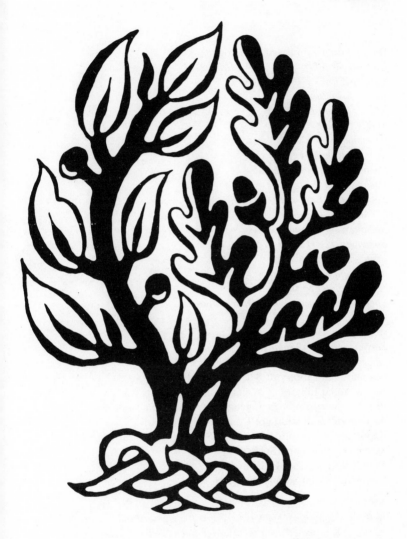

Routledge & Kegan Paul London and Boston
68–74 Carter Lane London EC4V 5EL
9 Park Street Boston Mass 02108

Contents

Authors wishing to submit manuscripts for any series in this catalogue should send them to the Social Science Editor, Routledge & Kegan Paul Ltd, 68–74 Carter Lane, London EC4V 5EL

● *Books so marked are available in paperback*
All books are in Metric Demy 8vo format (216 × 138mm approx.)

International Library of Sociology

General Editor John Rex

GENERAL SOCIOLOGY

Barnsley, J. H. The Social Reality of Ethics. *464 pp.*
Belshaw, Cyril. The Conditions of Social Performance. *An Exploratory Theory. 144 pp.*
Brown, Robert. Explanation in Social Science. *208 pp.*
● Rules and Laws in Sociology. *192 pp.*
Bruford, W. H. Chekhov and His Russia. *A Sociological Study. 244 pp.*
Cain, Maureen E. Society and the Policeman's Role. *326 pp.*
Gibson, Quentin. The Logic of Social Enquiry. *240 pp.*
Glucksmann, M. Structuralist Analysis in Contemporary Social Thought. *212 pp.*
Gurvitch, Georges. Sociology of Law. *Preface by Roscoe Pound. 264 pp.*
Hodge, H. A. Wilhelm Dilthey. *An Introduction. 184 pp.*
Homans, George C. Sentiments and Activities. *336 pp.*
Johnson, Harry M. Sociology: *a Systematic Introduction. Foreword by Robert K. Merton. 710 pp.*
Mannheim, Karl. Essays on Sociology and Social Psychology. *Edited by Paul Keckskemeti. With Editorial Note by Adolph Lowe. 344 pp.*
Systematic Sociology: *An Introduction to the Study of Society. Edited by J. S. Erös and Professor W. A. C. Stewart. 220 pp.*
Martindale, Don. The Nature and Types of Sociological Theory. *292 pp.*
●**Maus, Heinz.** A Short History of Sociology. *234 pp.*
Mey, Harald. Field-Theory. *A Study of its Application in the Social Sciences. 352 pp.*
Myrdal, Gunnar. Value in Social Theory: *A Collection of Essays on Methodology. Edited by Paul Streeten. 332 pp.*
Ogburn, William F., and **Nimkoff, Meyer F.** A Handbook of Sociology. *Preface by Karl Mannheim. 656 pp. 46 figures. 35 tables.*
Parsons, Talcott, and **Smelser, Neil J.** Economy and Society: *A Study in the Integration of Economic and Social Theory. 362 pp.*
●**Rex, John.** Key Problems of Sociological Theory. *220 pp.*
Discovering Sociology. *278 pp.*
Sociology and the Demystification of the Modern World. *282 pp.*
●**Rex, John** (Ed.) Approaches to Sociology. *Contributions by Peter Abell, Frank Bechhofer, Basil Bernstein, Ronald Fletcher, David Frisby, Miriam Glucksmann, Peter Lassman, Herminio Martins, John Rex, Roland Robertson, John Westergaard and Jock Young. 302 pp.*
Rigby, A. Alternative Realities. *352 pp.*
Roche, M. Phenomenology, Language and the Social Sciences. *374 pp.*
Sahay, A. Sociological Analysis. *220 pp.*
Urry, John. Reference Groups and the Theory of Revolution. *244 pp.*
Weinberg, E. Development of Sociology in the Soviet Union. *173 pp.*

FOREIGN CLASSICS OF SOCIOLOGY

●**Durkheim, Emile.** Suicide. *A Study in Sociology. Edited and with an Introduction by George Simpson. 404 pp.*

Professional Ethics and Civic Morals. *Translated by Cornelia Brookfield. 288 pp.*

●**Gerth, H. H.,** and **Mills, C. Wright.** From Max Weber: *Essays in Sociology. 502 pp.*

●**Tönnies, Ferdinand.** Community and Association. (*Gemeinschaft und Gesellschaft.*) *Translated and Supplemented by Charles P. Loomis. Foreword by Pitirim A. Sorokin. 334 pp.*

SOCIAL STRUCTURE

Andreski, Stanislav. Military Organization and Society. *Foreword by Professor A. R. Radcliffe-Brown. 226 pp. 1 folder.*

Coontz, Sydney H. Population Theories and the Economic Interpretation. *202 pp.*

Coser, Lewis. The Functions of Social Conflict. *204 pp.*

Dickie-Clark, H. F. Marginal Situation: *A Sociological Study of a Coloured Group. 240 pp. 11 tables.*

Glaser, Barney, and **Strauss, Anselm L.** Status Passage. *A Formal Theory. 208 pp.*

Glass, D. V. (Ed.) Social Mobility in Britain. *Contributions by J. Berent, T. Bottomore, R. C. Chambers, J. Floud, D. V. Glass, J. R. Hall, H. T. Himmelweit, R. K. Kelsall, F. M. Martin, C. A. Moser, R. Mukherjee, and W. Ziegel. 420 pp.*

Jones, Garth N. Planned Organizational Change: *An Exploratory Study Using an Empirical Approach. 268 pp.*

Kelsall, R. K. Higher Civil Servants in Britain: *From 1870 to the Present Day. 268 pp. 31 tables.*

König, René. The Community. *232 pp. Illustrated.*

●**Lawton, Denis.** Social Class, Language and Education. *192 pp.*

McLeish, John. The Theory of Social Change: *Four Views Considered. 128 pp.*

Marsh, David C. The Changing Social Structure of England and Wales, 1871-1961. *288 pp.*

Mouzelis, Nicos. Organization and Bureaucracy. *An Analysis of Modern Theories. 240 pp.*

Mulkay, M. J. Functionalism, Exchange and Theoretical Strategy. *272 pp.*

Ossowski, Stanislaw. Class Structure in the Social Consciousness. *210 pp.*

Podgórecki, Adam. Law and Society. *About 300 pp.*

SOCIOLOGY AND POLITICS

Acton, T. A. Gypsy Politics and Social Change. *316 pp.*

Hechter, Michael. Internal Colonialism. *The Celtic Fringe in British National Development, 1536–1966. About 350 pp.*

Hertz, Frederick. Nationality in History and Politics: *A Psychology and Sociology of National Sentiment and Nationalism. 432 pp.*

Kornhauser, William. The Politics of Mass Society. *272 pp. 20 tables.*
Laidler, Harry W. History of Socialism. *Social-Economic Movements: An Historical and Comparative Survey of Socialism, Communism, Co-operation, Utopianism; and other Systems of Reform and Reconstruction. 992 pp.*
Lasswell, H. D. Analysis of Political Behaviour. *324 pp.*
Mannheim, Karl. Freedom, Power and Democratic Planning. *Edited by Hans Gerth and Ernest K. Bramstedt. 424 pp.*
Mansur, Fatma. Process of Independence. *Foreword by A. H. Hanson. 208 pp.*
Martin, David A. Pacifism: *an Historical and Sociological Study. 262 pp.*
Myrdal, Gunnar. The Political Element in the Development of Economic Theory. *Translated from the German by Paul Streeten. 282 pp.*
Wootton, Graham. Workers, Unions and the State. *188 pp.*

FOREIGN AFFAIRS: THEIR SOCIAL, POLITICAL AND ECONOMIC FOUNDATIONS

Mayer, J. P. Political Thought in France from the Revolution to the Fifth Republic. *164 pp.*

CRIMINOLOGY

Ancel, Marc. Social Defence: *A Modern Approach to Criminal Problems. Foreword by Leon Radzinowicz. 240 pp.*
Cain, Maureen E. Society and the Policeman's Role. *326 pp.*
Cloward, Richard A., and **Ohlin, Lloyd E.** Delinquency and Opportunity: *A Theory of Delinquent Gangs. 248 pp.*
Downes, David M. The Delinquent Solution. *A Study in Subcultural Theory. 296 pp.*
Dunlop, A. B., and **McCabe, S.** Young Men in Detention Centres. *192 pp.*
Friedlander, Kate. The Psycho-Analytical Approach to Juvenile Delinquency: *Theory, Case Studies, Treatment. 320 pp.*
Glueck, Sheldon, and **Eleanor.** Family Environment and Delinquency. *With the statistical assistance of Rose W. Kneznek. 340 pp.*
Lopez-Rey, Manuel. Crime. *An Analytical Appraisal. 288 pp.*
Mannheim, Hermann. Comparative Criminology: *a Text Book. Two volumes. 442 pp. and 380 pp.*
Morris, Terence. The Criminal Area: *A Study in Social Ecology. Foreword by Hermann Mannheim. 232 pp. 25 tables. 4 maps.*
Rock, Paul. Making People Pay. *338 pp.*
● **Taylor, Ian, Walton, Paul,** and **Young, Jock.** The New Criminology. *For a Social Theory of Deviance. 325 pp.*

SOCIAL PSYCHOLOGY

Bagley, Christopher. The Social Psychology of the Epileptic Child. *320 pp.*
Barbu, Zevedei. Problems of Historical Psychology. *248 pp.*
Blackburn, Julian. Psychology and the Social Pattern. *184 pp.*

● **Brittan, Arthur.** Meanings and Situations. *224 pp.*

Carroll, J. Break-Out from the Crystal Palace. *200 pp.*

● **Fleming, C. M.** Adolescence: Its Social Psychology. *With an Introduction to recent findings from the fields of Anthropology, Physiology, Medicine, Psychometrics and Sociometry. 288 pp.*

● The Social Psychology of Education: *An Introduction and Guide to Its Study. 136 pp.*

Homans, George C. The Human Group. *Foreword by Bernard DeVoto. Introduction by Robert K. Merton. 526 pp.*

● Social Behaviour: *its Elementary Forms. 416 pp.*

● **Klein, Josephine.** The Study of Groups. *226 pp. 31 figures. 5 tables.*

Linton, Ralph. The Cultural Background of Personality. *132 pp.*

● **Mayo, Elton.** The Social Problems of an Industrial Civilization. *With an appendix on the Political Problem. 180 pp.*

Ottaway, A. K. C. Learning Through Group Experience. *176 pp.*

Ridder, J. C. de. The Personality of the Urban African in South Africa. *A Thermatic Apperception Test Study. 196 pp. 12 plates.*

● **Rose, Arnold M.** (Ed.) Human Behaviour and Social Processes: *an Interactionist Approach. Contributions by Arnold M. Rose, Ralph H. Turner, Anselm Strauss, Everett C. Hughes, E. Franklin Frazier, Howard S. Becker, et al. 696 pp.*

Smelser, Neil J. Theory of Collective Behaviour. *448 pp.*

Stephenson, Geoffrey M. The Development of Conscience. *128 pp.*

Young, Kimball. Handbook of Social Psychology. *658 pp. 16 figures. 10 tables.*

SOCIOLOGY OF THE FAMILY

Banks, J. A. Prosperity and Parenthood: *A Study of Family Planning among The Victorian Middle Classes. 262 pp.*

Bell, Colin R. Middle Class Families: *Social and Geographical Mobility. 224 pp.*

Burton, Lindy. Vulnerable Children. *272 pp.*

Gavron, Hannah. The Captive Wife: *Conflicts of Household Mothers. 190 pp.*

George, Victor, and **Wilding, Paul.** Motherless Families. *220 pp.*

Klein, Josephine. Samples from English Cultures.

1. Three Preliminary Studies and Aspects of Adult Life in England. *447 pp.*
2. Child-Rearing Practices and Index. *247 pp.*

Klein, Viola. Britain's Married Women Workers. *180 pp.*

The Feminine Character. *History of an Ideology. 244 pp.*

McWhinnie, Alexina M. Adopted Children. *How They Grow Up. 304 pp.*

● **Myrdal, Alva,** and **Klein, Viola.** Women's Two Roles: *Home and Work. 238 pp. 27 tables.*

Parsons, Talcott, and **Bales, Robert F.** Family: Socialization and Interaction Process. *In collaboration with James Olds, Morris Zelditch and Philip E. Slater. 456 pp. 50 figures and tables.*

SOCIAL SERVICES

Bastide, Roger. The Sociology of Mental Disorder. *Translated from the French by Jean McNeil. 260 pp.*

Carlebach, Julius. Caring For Children in Trouble. *266 pp.*

Forder, R. A. (Ed.) Penelope Hall's Social Services of England and Wales. *352 pp.*

George, Victor. Foster Care. *Theory and Practice. 234 pp.*

Social Security: *Beveridge and After. 258 pp.*

George, V., and **Wilding, P.** Motherless Families. *248 pp.*

● **Goetschius, George W.** Working with Community Groups. *256 pp.*

Goetschius, George W., and **Tash, Joan.** Working with Unattached Youth. *416 pp.*

Hall, M. P., and **Howes, I. V.** The Church in Social Work. *A Study of Moral Welfare Work undertaken by the Church of England. 320 pp.*

Heywood, Jean S. Children in Care: *the Development of the Service for the Deprived Child. 264 pp.*

Hoenig, J., and **Hamilton, Marian W.** The De-Segregation of the Mentally Ill. *284 pp.*

Jones, Kathleen. Mental Health and Social Policy, 1845-1959. *264 pp.*

King, Roy D., Raynes, Norma V., and **Tizard, Jack.** Patterns of Residential Care. *356 pp.*

Leigh, John. Young People and Leisure. *256 pp.*

Morris, Mary. Voluntary Work and the Welfare State. *300 pp.*

Morris, Pauline. Put Away: *A Sociological Study of Institutions for the Mentally Retarded. 364 pp.*

Nokes, P. L. The Professional Task in Welfare Practice. *152 pp.*

Timms, Noel. Psychiatric Social Work in Great Britain (1939-1962). *280 pp.*

● Social Casework: *Principles and Practice. 256 pp.*

Young, A. F. Social Services in British Industry. *272 pp.*

Young, A. F., and **Ashton, E. T.** British Social Work in the Nineteenth Century. *288 pp.*

SOCIOLOGY OF EDUCATION

Banks, Olive. Parity and Prestige in English Secondary Education: a Study in Educational Sociology. *272 pp.*

Bentwich, Joseph. Education in Israel. *224 pp. 8 pp. plates.*

● **Blyth, W. A. L.** English Primary Education. *A Sociological Description.*

1. Schools. *232 pp.*
2. Background. *168 pp.*

Collier, K. G. The Social Purposes of Education: *Personal and Social Values in Education. 268 pp.*

Dale, R. R., and **Griffith, S.** Down Stream: *Failure in the Grammar School. 108 pp.*

Dore, R. P. Education in Tokugawa Japan. *356 pp. 9 pp. plates.*

Evans, K. M. Sociometry and Education. *158 pp.*

● **Ford, Julienne.** Social Class and the Comprehensive School. *192 pp.*

Foster, P. J. Education and Social Change in Ghana. *336 pp. 3 maps.*

Fraser, W. R. Education and Society in Modern France. *150 pp.*

Grace, Gerald R. Role Conflict and the Teacher. *About 200 pp.*

Hans, Nicholas. New Trends in Education in the Eighteenth Century. *278 pp. 19 tables.*

● Comparative Education: *A Study of Educational Factors and Traditions. 360 pp.*

Hargreaves, David. Interpersonal Relations and Education. *432 pp.*

● Social Relations in a Secondary School. *240 pp.*

Holmes, Brian. Problems in Education. *A Comparative Approach. 336 pp.*

King, Ronald. Values and Involvement in a Grammar School. *164 pp.*

School Organization and Pupil Involvement. *A Study of Secondary Schools.*

● **Mannheim, Karl,** and **Stewart, W. A. C.** An Introduction to the Sociology of Education. *206 pp.*

Morris, Raymond N. The Sixth Form and College Entrance. *231 pp.*

● **Musgrove, F.** Youth and the Social Order. *176 pp.*

● **Ottaway, A. K. C.** Education and Society: An Introduction to the Sociology of Education. *With an Introduction by W. O. Lester Smith. 212 pp.*

Peers, Robert. Adult Education: *A Comparative Study. 398 pp.*

Pritchard, D. G. Education and the Handicapped: *1760 to 1960. 258 pp.*

Richardson, Helen. Adolescent Girls in Approved Schools. *308 pp.*

Stratta, Erica. The Education of Borstal Boys. *A Study of their Educational Experiences prior to, and during, Borstal Training. 256 pp.*

Taylor, P. H., Reid, W. A., and **Holley, B. J.** The English Sixth Form. *A Case Study in Curriculum Research. 200 pp.*

SOCIOLOGY OF CULTURE

Eppel, E. M., and **M.** Adolescents and Morality: *A Study of some Moral Values and Dilemmas of Working Adolescents in the Context of a changing Climate of Opinion. Foreword by W. J. H. Sprott. 268 pp. 39 tables.*

● **Fromm, Erich.** The Fear of Freedom. *286 pp.*

● The Sane Society. *400 pp.*

Mannheim, Karl. Essays on the Sociology of Culture. *Edited by Ernst Mannheim in co-operation with Paul Kecskemeti. Editorial Note by Adolph Lowe. 280 pp.*

Weber, Alfred. Farewell to European History: *or The Conquest of Nihilism. Translated from the German by R. F. C. Hull. 224 pp.*

SOCIOLOGY OF RELIGION

Argyle, Michael and **Beit-Hallahmi, Benjamin.** The Social Psychology of Religion. *About 256 pp.*
Nelson, G. K. Spiritualism and Society. *313 pp.*
Stark, Werner. The Sociology of Religion. *A Study of Christendom.*
Volume I. *Established Religion. 248 pp.*
Volume II. *Sectarian Religion. 368 pp.*
Volume III. *The Universal Church. 464 pp.*
Volume IV. *Types of Religious Man. 352 pp.*
Volume V. *Types of Religious Culture. 464 pp.*
Turner, B. S. Weber and Islam. *216 pp.*
Watt, W. Montgomery. Islam and the Integration of Society. *320 pp.*

SOCIOLOGY OF ART AND LITERATURE

Jarvie, Ian C. Towards a Sociology of the Cinema. *A Comparative Essay on the Structure and Functioning of a Major Entertainment Industry. 405 pp.*
Rust, Frances S. Dance in Society. *An Analysis of the Relationships between the Social Dance and Society in England from the Middle Ages to the Present Day. 256 pp. 8 pp. of plates.*
Schücking, L. L. The Sociology of Literary Taste. *112 pp.*
Wolff, Janet. Hermeneutic Philosophy and the Sociology of Art. *About 200 pp.*

SOCIOLOGY OF KNOWLEDGE

Diesing, P. Patterns of Discovery in the Social Sciences. *262 pp.*
● **Douglas, J. D.** (Ed.) Understanding Everyday Life. *370 pp.*
● **Hamilton, P.** Knowledge and Social Structure. *174 pp.*
Jarvie, I. C. Concepts and Society. *232 pp.*
Mannheim, Karl. Essays on the Sociology of Knowledge. *Edited by Paul Kecskemeti. Editorial Note by Adolph Lowe. 353 pp.*
Remmling, Gunter W. (Ed.) Towards the Sociology of Knowledge. *Origin and Development of a Sociological Thought Style. 463 pp.*
Stark, Werner. The Sociology of Knowledge: *An Essay in Aid of a Deeper Understanding of the History of Ideas. 384 pp.*

URBAN SOCIOLOGY

Ashworth, William. The Genesis of Modern British Town Planning: *A Study in Economic and Social History of the Nineteenth and Twentieth Centuries. 288 pp.*
Cullingworth, J. B. Housing Needs and Planning Policy: *A Restatement of the Problems of Housing Need and 'Overspill' in England and Wales. 232 pp. 44 tables. 8 maps.*

Dickinson, Robert E. City and Region: *A Geographical Interpretation 608 pp. 125 figures.*

The West European City: *A Geographical Interpretation. 600 pp. 129 maps. 29 plates.*

● The City Region in Western Europe. *320 pp. Maps.*

Humphreys, Alexander J. New Dubliners: *Urbanization and the Irish Family. Foreword by George C. Homans. 304 pp.*

Jackson, Brian. Working Class Community: *Some General Notions raised by a Series of Studies in Northern England. 192 pp.*

Jennings, Hilda. Societies in the Making: *a Study of Development and Redevelopment within a County Borough. Foreword by D. A. Clark. 286 pp.*

● **Mann, P. H.** An Approach to Urban Sociology. *240 pp.*

Morris, R. N., and **Mogey, J.** The Sociology of Housing. *Studies at Berinsfield. 232 pp. 4 pp. plates.*

Rosser, C., and **Harris, C.** The Family and Social Change. *A Study of Family and Kinship in a South Wales Town. 352 pp. 8 maps.*

RURAL SOCIOLOGY

Chambers, R. J. H. Settlement Schemes in Tropical Africa: *A Selective Study. 268 pp.*

Haswell, M. R. The Economics of Development in Village India. *120 pp.*

Littlejohn, James. Westrigg: *the Sociology of a Cheviot Parish. 172 pp. 5 figures.*

Mayer, Adrian C. Peasants in the Pacific. *A Study of Fiji Indian Rural Society. 248 pp. 20 plates.*

Williams, W. M. The Sociology of an English Village: *Gosforth. 272 pp. 12 figures. 13 tables.*

SOCIOLOGY OF INDUSTRY AND DISTRIBUTION

Anderson, Nels. Work and Leisure. *280 pp.*

● **Blau, Peter M.,** and **Scott, W. Richard.** Formal Organizations: *a Comparative approach. Introduction and Additional Bibliography by J. H. Smith. 326 pp.*

Eldridge, J. E. T. Industrial Disputes. *Essays in the Sociology of Industrial Relations. 288 pp.*

Hetzler, Stanley. Applied Measures for Promoting Technological Growth. *352 pp.*

Technological Growth and Social Change. *Achieving Modernization. 269 pp.*

Hollowell, Peter G. The Lorry Driver. *272 pp.*

Jefferys, Margot, *with the assistance of Winifred Moss.* Mobility in the Labour Market: *Employment Changes in Battersea and Dagenham. Preface by Barbara Wootton. 186 pp. 51 tables.*

Millerson, Geoffrey. The Qualifying Associations: *a Study in Professionalization. 320 pp.*

Smelser, Neil J. Social Change in the Industrial Revolution: *An Application of Theory to the Lancashire Cotton Industry, 1770-1840. 468 pp. 12 figures. 14 tables.*

Williams, Gertrude. Recruitment to Skilled Trades. *240 pp.*

Young, A. F. Industrial Injuries Insurance: *an Examination of British Policy. 192 pp.*

DOCUMENTARY

Schlesinger, Rudolf (Ed.) Changing Attitudes in Soviet Russia.

2. The Nationalities Problem and Soviet Administration. *Selected Readings on the Development of Soviet Nationalities Policies. Introduced by the editor. Translated by W. W. Gottlieb. 324 pp.*

ANTHROPOLOGY

Ammar, Hamed. Growing up in an Egyptian Village: *Silwa, Province of Aswan. 336 pp.*

Brandel-Syrier, Mia. Reeftown Elite. *A Study of Social Mobility in a Modern African Community on the Reef. 376 pp.*

Crook, David, and **Isabel.** Revolution in a Chinese Village: *Ten Mile Inn. 230 pp. 8 plates. 1 map.*

Dickie-Clark, H. F. The Marginal Situation. *A Sociological Study of a Coloured Group. 236 pp.*

Dube, S. C. Indian Village. *Foreword by Morris Edward Opler. 276 pp. 4 plates.*

India's Changing Villages: *Human Factors in Community Development. 260 pp. 8 plates. 1 map.*

Firth, Raymond. Malay Fishermen. *Their Peasant Economy. 420 pp. 17 pp. plates.*

Firth, R., Hubert, J., and **Forge, A.** Families and their Relatives. *Kinship in a Middle-Class Sector of London: An Anthropological Study. 456 pp.*

Gulliver, P. H. Social Control in an African Society: a Study of the Arusha, Agricultural Masai of Northern Tanganyika. *320 pp. 8 plates. 10 figures.*

Family Herds. *288 pp.*

Ishwaran, K. Shivapur. *A South Indian Village. 216 pp.*

Tradition and Economy in Village India: *An Interactionist Approach. Foreword by Conrad Arensburg. 176 pp.*

Jarvie, Ian C. The Revolution in Anthropology. *268 pp.*

Jarvie, Ian C., and **Agassi, Joseph.** Hong Kong. *A Society in Transition. 396 pp. Illustrated with plates and maps.*

Little, Kenneth L. Mende of Sierra Leone. *308 pp. and folder.*

Negroes in Britain. *With a New Introduction and Contemporary Study by Leonard Bloom. 320 pp.*

Lowie, Robert H. Social Organization. *494 pp.*

Mayer, Adrian C. Caste and Kinship in Central India: *A Village and its Region. 328 pp. 16 plates. 15 figures. 16 tables.*

Peasants in the Pacific. *A Study of Fiji Indian Rural Society. 248 pp.*

Smith, Raymond T. The Negro Family in British Guiana: *Family Structure and Social Status in the Villages. With a Foreword by Meyer Fortes. 314 pp. 8 plates. 1 figure. 4 maps.*

SOCIOLOGY AND PHILOSOPHY

Barnsley, John H. The Social Reality of Ethics. *A Comparative Analysis of Moral Codes. 448 pp.*

Diesing, Paul. Patterns of Discovery in the Social Sciences. *362 pp.*

● **Douglas, Jack D.** (Ed.) Understanding Everyday Life. *Toward the Reconstruction of Sociological Knowledge. Contributions by Alan F. Blum. Aaron W. Cicourel, Norman K. Denzin, Jack D. Douglas, John Heeren, Peter McHugh, Peter K. Manning, Melvin Power, Matthew Speier, Roy Turner, D. Lawrence Wieder, Thomas P. Wilson and Don H. Zimmerman. 370 pp.*

Jarvie, Ian C. Concepts and Society. *216 pp.*

Pelz, Werner. The Scope of Understanding in Sociology. *Towards a more radical reorientation in the social humanistic sciences. 283 pp.*

Roche, Maurice. Phenomenology, Language and the Social Sciences. *371 pp.*

Sahay, Arun. Sociological Analysis. *212 pp.*

Sklair, Leslie. The Sociology of Progress. *320 pp.*

International Library of Anthropology

General Editor Adam Kuper

Brown, Paula. The Chimbu. *A Study of Change in the New Guinea Highlands. 151 pp.*

Lloyd, P. C. Power and Independence. *Urban Africans' Perception of Social Inequality. 264 pp.*

Pettigrew, Joyce. Robber Noblemen. *A Study of the Political System of the Sikh Jats. 284 pp.*

Van Den Berghe, Pierre L. Power and Privilege at an African University. *278 pp.*

International Library of Social Policy

General Editor Kathleen Jones

Bayley, M. Mental Handicap and Community Care. *426 pp.*

Butler, J. R. Family Doctors and Public Policy. *208 pp.*

Holman, Robert. Trading in Children. *A Study of Private Fostering. 355 pp.*

Jones, Kathleen. History of the Mental Health Service. *428 pp.*
Thomas, J. E. The English Prison Officer since 1850: *A Study in Conflict. 258 pp.*
Woodward, J. To Do the Sick No Harm. *A Study of the British Voluntary Hospital System to 1875. About 220 pp.*

International Library of Welfare and Philosophy

General Editors Noel Timms and David Watson

● **Plant, Raymond.** Community and Ideology. *104 pp.*

Primary Socialization, Language and Education

General Editor Basil Bernstein

Bernstein, Basil. Class, Codes and Control. *2 volumes.*
1. *Theoretical Studies Towards a Sociology of Language. 254 pp.*
2. *Applied Studies Towards a Sociology of Language. About 400 pp.*

Brandis, W., and **Bernstein, B.** Selection and Control. *176 pp.*
Brandis, Walter, and **Henderson, Dorothy.** Social Class, Language and Communication. *288 pp.*
Cook-Gumperz, Jenny. Social Control and Socialization. *A Study of Class Differences in the Language of Maternal Control. 290 pp.*
● **Gahagan, D. M.,** and **G. A.** Talk Reform. *Exploration in Language for Infant School Children. 160 pp.*
Robinson, W. P., and **Rackstraw, Susan D. A.** A Question of Answers. *2 volumes. 192 pp. and 180 pp.*
Turner, Geoffrey J., and **Mohan, Bernard A.** A Linguistic Description and Computer Programme for Children's Speech. *208 pp.*

Reports of the Institute of Community Studies

Cartwright, Ann. Human Relations and Hospital Care. *272 pp.*
● Parents and Family Planning Services. *306 pp.*
Patients and their Doctors. *A Study of General Practice. 304 pp.*
● **Jackson, Brian.** Streaming: *an Education System in Miniature. 168 pp.*
Jackson, Brian, and **Marsden, Dennis.** Education and the Working Class: *Some General Themes raised by a Study of 88 Working-class Children in a Northern Industrial City. 268 pp. 2 folders.*
Marris, Peter. The Experience of Higher Education. *232 pp. 27 tables.*
Loss and Change. *192 pp.*

Marris, Peter, and **Rein, Martin.** Dilemmas of Social Reform. *Poverty and Community Action in the United States. 256 pp.*

Marris, Peter, and **Somerset, Anthony.** African Businessmen. *A Study of Entrepreneurship and Development in Kenya. 256 pp.*

Mills, Richard. Young Outsiders: *a Study in Alternative Communities. 216 pp.*

Runciman, W. G. Relative Deprivation and Social Justice. *A Study of Attitudes to Social Inequality in Twentieth-Century England. 352 pp.*

Willmott, Peter. Adolescent Boys in East London. *230 pp.*

Willmott, Peter, and **Young, Michael.** Family and Class in a London Suburb. *202 pp. 47 tables.*

Young, Michael. Innovation and Research in Education. *192 pp.*

● **Young, Michael,** and **McGeeney, Patrick.** Learning Begins at Home. *A Study of a Junior School and its Parents. 128 pp.*

Young, Michael, and **Willmott, Peter.** Family and Kinship in East London. *Foreword by Richard M. Titmuss. 252 pp. 39 tables.*

The Symmetrical Family. *410 pp.*

Reports of the Institute for Social Studies in Medical Care

Cartwright, Ann, Hockey, Lisbeth, and **Anderson, John L.** Life Before Death. *310 pp.*

Dunnell, Karen, and **Cartwright, Ann.** Medicine Takers, Prescribers and Hoarders. *190 pp.*

Medicine, Illness and Society

General Editor W. M. Williams

Robinson, David. The Process of Becoming Ill. *142 pp.*

Stacey, Margaret, *et al.* Hospitals, Children and Their Families. *The Report of a Pilot Study. 202 pp.*

Monographs in Social Theory

General Editor Arthur Brittan

● **Barnes, B.** Scientific Knowledge and Sociological Theory. *About 200 pp.*

Bauman, Zygmunt. Culture as Praxis. *204 pp.*

● **Dixon, Keith.** Sociological Theory. *Pretence and Possibility. 142 pp.*

● **Smith, Anthony D.** The Concept of Social Change. *A Critique of the Functionalist Theory of Social Change. 208 pp.*

Routledge Social Science Journals

The British Journal of Sociology. *Edited by Terence P. Morris. Vol. 1, No. 1, March 1950 and Quarterly. Roy. 8vo. Back numbers available. An international journal with articles on all aspects of sociology.*

Economy and Society. *Vol. 1, No. 1. February 1972 and Quarterly. Metric Roy. 8vo. A journal for all social scientists covering sociology, philosophy, anthropology, economics and history. Back numbers available.*

Year Book of Social Policy in Britain, The. *Edited by Kathleen Jones. 1971. Published annually.*

Printed in Great Britain by Unwin Brothers Limited
The Gresham Press Old Woking Surrey
A member of the Staples Printing Group